MAVERICK GUIDE TO
The GREAT
BARRIER REEF

D1365074

mav • er • ick (mav'er-ik), *n* 1. an unbranded steer. Hence [colloq.] 2. a person not labeled as belonging to any one faction, group, etc., who acts independently. 3. one who moves in a different direction than the rest of the herd—often a nonconformist. 4. a person using individual judgment, even when it runs against majority opinion.

The Maverick Guide Series

MAVERICK GUIDE TO
The GREAT
BARRIER REEF

Len Rutledge

Researched by
Phensri Athisumongkol

PELICAN PUBLISHING COMPANY
Gretna 1997

ISBN: 1-56554-193-6

Information in this guidebook is based on authoritative data
available at the time of printing. Prices and hours of operation of
businesses listed are subject to change without notice. Readers are
asked to take this into account when consulting this guide.

Maps by Len Rutledge

Manufactured in the United States of America
Published by Pelican Publishing Company, Inc.
1101 Monroe Street, Gretna, Louisiana 70053

Contents

8. Cairns and the Northern Great Barrier Reef

LIST OF MAPS

ACKNOWLEDGMENTS

I continue to be amazed at the help I receive from many people while I am researching and writing these guide books. In particular I would like to acknowledge the following:

Ken Boys, Mark Williams, Margie Mcgregor, Joane Libline, James Corvan, Arthur Mosely, Kayleen Allen, Steve Noakes, John Lyneham, Andrew Steel, Paul Ewart, Paula MacDonald, Rory O'Connor, and Bill Condon.

MAVERICK GUIDE TO
The GREAT BARRIER REEF

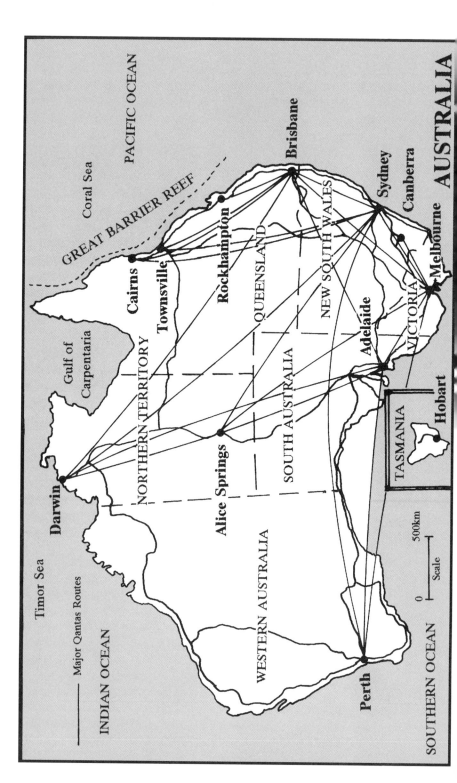

1

Why Go to the Great Barrier Reef?

Few places in the world attract as much comment and interest as the Great Barrier Reef. It is the largest coral reef system in the world and the most diverse environment known to mankind, but to many it is much more than this. Somehow it has taken on a character and mystique of its own: one that makes it something that many travelers long to experience, despite its distance from much of the world, and despite the cost involved in getting there and enjoying the uniqueness of it all.

Just how much of that mystique is associated with the country of Australia is difficult to tell, but there is little doubt that the almost universal interest that exists in that vast, strange continent certainly helps. The fact that the Great Barrier Reef is situated in Australian waters is also positive in a number of ways.

First, Australia is part of the New World, so there has been no long-term destructive civilization living close by to damage the reef or the environment. Certainly Aboriginal Australians have been here for thousands of years, but their numbers have been relatively small, and they generally have lived in sympathy with nature.

Second, Australia is a relatively wealthy country with a growing interest in, and ability to financially support, preservation of the natural environment.

Third, there is a growing interest within Australia in research to discover the mysteries of the complex inter-relationships that exist in the natural world and how mankind impinges on those relationships.

Then, there are the modern visitor facilities that exist to make it possible for people to actually see this great natural wonder in relative comfort.

All this means that the Great Barrier Reef is generally being well preserved and studied, and that facilities for visitors are of a high standard. It means that a visit to the Great Barrier Reef can be a significant educational and sightseeing experience for non-swimmers, snorkelers, divers, and researchers. Here is a chance to experience at close quarters one of the world's most unique World Heritage sites.

Tourist Great Barrier Reef in Summary

- The Great Barrier Reef stretches for more than 2,000 kilometers along the Queensland coast off northeast Australia.
- The reef is situated from 30 to around 200 kilometers off the coast, but many parts are accessible by boat, helicopter, and seaplane, and a few locations are accessible by aircraft.
- There are only three opportunities at present to stay in accommodations on a reef coral cay, but there are camping options on other coral islands, and many resorts on mainland-type islands in the region.
- The majority of reef visitors are sightseers who travel on day trips aboard fast powered catamarans from centers along the Queensland coast.
- More visitors use Cairns as their reef sightseeing base than any other center. At the height of the June to October tourist season, some 2,000 visitors leave Cairns daily for reef visits. Townsville is the scientific, research, and education center for reef-based activities.
- The reef aquarium run by the Great Barrier Reef Marine Park Authority at Reef Wonderland in Townsville contains by far the largest on-land coral reef in the world. It can be a wonderful educational introduction to this amazing complex ecosystem and is highly recommended.
- Many scuba divers consider the reef has some of the best dive sites in the world. Many are available on regular day trips or on extended trips on specially equipped live-aboard dive boats.
- While the reef is hundreds of kilometers north of Brisbane, the Gold Coast, and the Sunshine Coast, tours are now available from these centers so that visitors to these areas can visit the southern section of the reef on a day trip.

The Confessional

It is possible to get quite a deal of information about Australia from several sources. In that information there will certainly be something about the

Great Barrier Reef. Just how useful it is to you will depend on the purpose for which you need information. I have yet to find anything, however, that substitutes for this book. When writing it, I have assumed that you the reader require information on three levels: enough general information to decide if the destination is correct for you; enough detail to plan a trip; and sufficient local information and contact addresses so that you can enjoy the destination to the fullest once you are here. If you are serious about a trip to the Great Barrier Reef, you need to read and reread this book on those levels.

Unlike many other guidebooks, this one contains neither overt nor covert advertising. The opinions expressed here are entirely mine, and they are based on personal experience over a considerable length of time. You may not always agree with the opinions, but you will know that they are given openly and honestly without the need to repay favors or cover a debt.

I have had the luxury of living in the reef region for much of the past 25 years. This has given me a strong background from which to work, but since being commissioned to write this book I have revisited many areas to update myself about the latest developments. This information is reflected in the sections on accommodations, restaurants, tours, shopping, nightlife, and so forth. At the time of writing (late 1995), the information was as accurate as I could make it. I deliberately stayed in a wide range of accommodations; ate at many restaurants, fast food outlets, and pubs; experienced some guided tours; and checked out the nightlife. I traveled by plane, train, bus, car, taxi, helicopter, and boat, and visited reef pontoons, islands, sand cays, and almost 2,000 kilometers of mainland coastline.

Despite all this, it was obviously not possible for me to experience every hotel, restaurant, shop, tour, or nightspot that readers will experience. In the end I must rely on you the reader to extend the coverage of future editions. If you end up in a place that is not mentioned in this book, and it is different, friendly, interesting, or just good value, please tell me about it, so that I can visit before completing the next edition of this guide.

Travel writing has been a major part of my life for more than 25 years. The experiences that I have had, have made me a different person; one who hopefully has become more tolerant and understanding with age, while still keeping young at heart. These experiences have in the most part been different from those I would have had if I had stayed home, and I rejoice in the differences. Please bring that philosophy with you when you come to Australia. At first glance Australia is much the same as much of the Western world. The population speaks English, the hotels have familiar names, and the international fast food outlets are here. But while Australia may sound like England, and appear to have a similar culture to North America, it has the sense to be a different country in many ways. Discovering how it is different will be one of the greatest pleasures on a trip "Down Under."

Getting the Most Out of This Book

This guide is arranged in a pattern similar to that of the other Maverick guides. It is a format that commenced with *The Maverick Guide to Hawaii* in 1977, and has been well tried and tested in the years since. It is designed so that you get a good feel for the Great Barrier Reef region and the Australian people, while at the same time getting the specifics that are so necessary when you are traveling.

After this introductory chapter, there is a chapter on how to travel to and within the Great Barrier Reef region and how to minimize the potential hassles involving packing, climate, communications, money, safety, government regulations, and a whole lot more. This is followed by a chapter on the land and life of Queensland, the Australian state containing the reef and the reef waters. Chapter 4 is a background chapter on the Great Barrier Reef: the explorers, the coral, the plants and animals, and how to see, stay on, dive, and manage this extraordinary environment. The rest of the book consists of four specific area chapters covering the regions of interest to visitors.

Each of the area chapters is divided into 12 numbered sections. After you become familiar with them in one chapter, you will know where to look for these same subjects in each of the other chapters. The categories are as follows:

1. **The General Picture**
2. **Getting There**
3. **Local transportation**
4. **The Accommodations Scene**
5. **Dining and Restaurants**
6. **Sightseeing**
7. **Guided Tours**
8. **The Reef and Islands (except Southeast Queensland)**
9. **Sports**
10. **Shopping**
11. **Entertainment and Nightlife**
12. **The Contact List**

The book has been set up to be used in three ways. First, you can read through it quickly to get a general feel for the region to decide if the Great Barrier Reef is the place for your next vacation. Second, you should read it thoroughly before you finalize the plans for your trip. Decide where you would like to visit and what you would like to do when you are there. Consider the choice of islands, reef trips, and diving options; decide if there are some specific land-based hotels, restaurants, and attractions that you would like to visit; make a list of the activities in which you would like to participate and the things you would like to buy while you are away; work out how much time all this might take, then how much time you can spend in the reef region; then go talk to your travel agent.

Travel agents are well qualified to advise on airfares and some package tours, and some have access to computer information on destinations around the world, but remember that it is unrealistic to expect them to be experts on all locations. A good agent will appreciate your making informed suggestions because this makes his or her job of satisfying you much easier. I know of several agents who have used the contact names and telephone and fax numbers from Maverick guides to help with the planning and booking of a trip for their clients.

The book is also designed to be used when you are in the Great Barrier Reef region of Australia. Do not lose sight of the fact that this region is large. Most people have neither the time nor the money to explore it all, so you will end up having to make choices. You will find that the recommendations on tours, hotels, restaurants, and shopping will help in making these choices and in smoothing your travels. The information on modes of travel, sightseeing, sports, and entertainment may help broaden your horizons and encourage you to explore things that many people miss. All of the sections are geared toward helping you save time and money.

In this volume, I have included many maps that will help you orientate yourself quickly and show you where hotels, restaurants, attractions, and shops are located. There are also some regional maps that give you a wider picture and help you plan a practical itinerary. More detailed maps are readily available from motoring and tourist organizations in Australia, and I urge you to obtain these, particularly if you are planning extensive independent land travel.

Some Quick Comments

This book is a good source of information about the Great Barrier Reef region; I also hope you find it a good read. The descriptive chapters are designed to give you a good background to the reef, the islands, the adjacent mainland, and the people. If you bring this knowledge with you, you will find that it is easy to quickly build on it when you reach Australia, so that you will get far more from your visit than the average tourist.

There is quite an amount of good tourist literature available on Queensland and Australia. Much of it is prepared by the Australian Tourist Commission and the Queensland Tourist and Travel Corporation. I urge you to obtain and use this as an additional source of reliable information. Contact addresses of some of the offices where information is available are provided in the next chapter. You should also go to your library and look at some of the full-color publications on Australia that are almost certain to be there.

Once you have decided on where you are going, write to other addresses you find throughout this book and tell them of your interest and plans to visit. You will find that some will respond with the latest information from that area, and this will allow you to do further reading before you go. Appreciate that when you get there, you will probably have little time for detailed reading.

Prices quoted in this book are all in Australian dollars because this is what you will be using. Unlike people in some other countries in this region, Australians are not interested in any currency other than their own. You will have no problem changing your currency at a bank, money exchange, or many hotels, but don't expect restaurants or shops to take anything else but Australian dollars. Citizens from the United States, Canada, New Zealand, Singapore, Hong Kong, and so forth, please note that when an Australian says dollars, it always means local dollars. It is also worth noting that unlike many Asian countries, there are no local and visitor prices for anything in Australia; everyone pays the same.

I have a final plea. When you have made your trip to the Great Barrier Reef region, would you please write me (care of the publisher) and tell me about your experience? Information from readers has proved invaluable in updating other books in this series, and I anticipate that the same will apply here. Use either the enclosed letter/envelope form, or if that is not enough space, copy the address onto your own envelope and include as many pages as you like. Your reactions to both the book and the destination are earnestly solicited and will be warmly appreciated.

Good Traveling!
LEN RUTLEDGE

2

Happy Landings

How to Get There

Australia is the world's largest island and the smallest continent, so there are only two ways of reaching it: by plane or by ship. Many years ago there were many shipping companies serving Australia with passenger vessels from ports around the world. That era has finished. You can still reach Australia by ship, but now it will be on a freighter or a cruise liner. Both modes are strictly for a limited number of people.

Freighters serve several Australian ports. Some carry general cargo, others are bulk carriers, while others carry containers. Some have provision to carry a small number of passengers. I have never had the luxury of the time necessary to take one of these trips, but there is a small dedicated band of enthusiasts who insist it is a great way to travel. The standard of accommodations and the level of facilities varies somewhat, so it would be a good idea to check out the details of a particular ship before committing yourself. Some trips are nonstop between continents, so on these be prepared for many days of nothing but sea. There may be a small number of other passengers, and you will mix with some of the crew, but there will be little or no organized activities, so a trip such as this will only appeal to a small group of individuals.

Cruise liners on the other hand are chock full of activities and people.

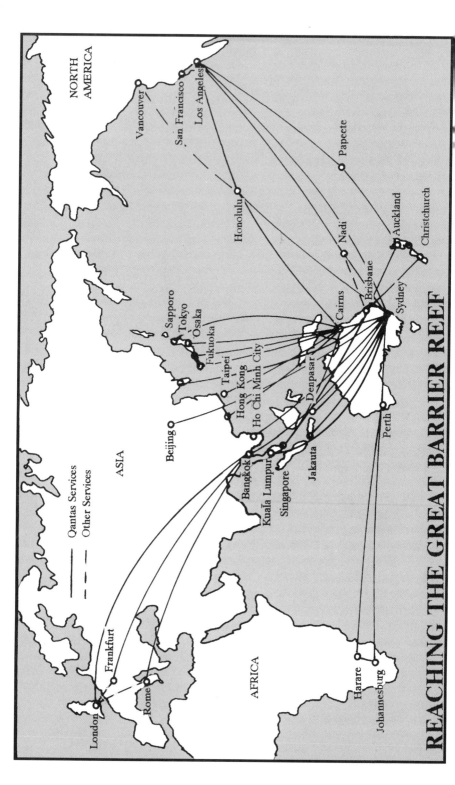

REACHING THE GREAT BARRIER REEF

NORTH AMERICA

ASIA

AFRICA

Vancouver
San Francisco
Los Angeles
Papeete
Honolulu
Nadi
Auckland
Christchurch
Brisbane
Cairns
Sydney
Sapporo
Tokyo
Osaka
Fukuoka
Taipei
Hong Kong
Ho Chi Minh City
Beijing
Denpasar
Perth
Jakauta
Bangkok
Kuala Lumpur
Singapore
Harare
Johannesburg
London
Frankfurt
Rome

—— Qantas Services
– – – Other Services

Each year there are a few vessels from Europe and America visiting Australia. Some of these are on "around the world cruises," and they tend to be expensive, conservative, and carrying mainly elderly passengers. I am not knocking these for one minute because some of the cruises are on board the best vessels afloat, and the service and facilities are absolutely top class. Clearly, though, they have limited appeal to many people. The other option is when shipping lines are repositioning vessels at the end of the season; from the northern hemisphere to the southern hemisphere in October or November, for instance. Passengers can then take a one-way cruise and return by air. Your travel agent should be able to provide details of what might be available when you wish to travel.

For the rest of us, the only option is air. While a ship can take a week to reach northern Australia from Asia, from North America it can take two weeks, and from Europe up to four weeks, by plane the times are hours rather than weeks. A large number of airlines fly to Australia from points around the globe. The majority of flights are destined for Sydney, although some call at other points before reaching there. Sydney is still a long way from the Great Barrier Reef, so you could look at flights to Brisbane, Cairns, or Townsville as possible alternatives.

Qantas Airways, the largest Australian airline, has more flights to Australia than any other operator. In the past it has been very Sydney-orientated, but now with restrictions on flights to Sydney airport it is opening up new gateways to the reef at Brisbane and Cairns. These have already become significant gateways from Asia and are likely to grow further. Qantas operates Boeing 747 and 767 aircraft on its international services. The company has an enviable reputation for safety, and it is good to see that in-cabin services are now of a high order. My philosophy is that when vacationing, it is good to use the airline of your destination if that matches the facilities of the opposition. You start your vacation some hours early, and you may pick up some useful information from the crew on the trip. On top of that, when flying Qantas you can sample Australian beer and wines (both excellent) and perhaps try some Down Under specialities such as lamb, meat pies, or Pavlova.

Qantas these days has code-sharing agreements with several other airlines; Air New Zealand and Canadian Airlines, for example. This allows an airline to offer services to additional cities without necessarily operating its own aircraft to those points. For passengers this can be confusing because some sectors may be operated by a partner airline. A good travel agent will be able to advise you on this.

Ansett Australia is the other major Australian carrier. It has only recently started overseas services and is developing these carefully. At present it is restricting itself to Asian ports. It also has high service, maintenance, and safety standards.

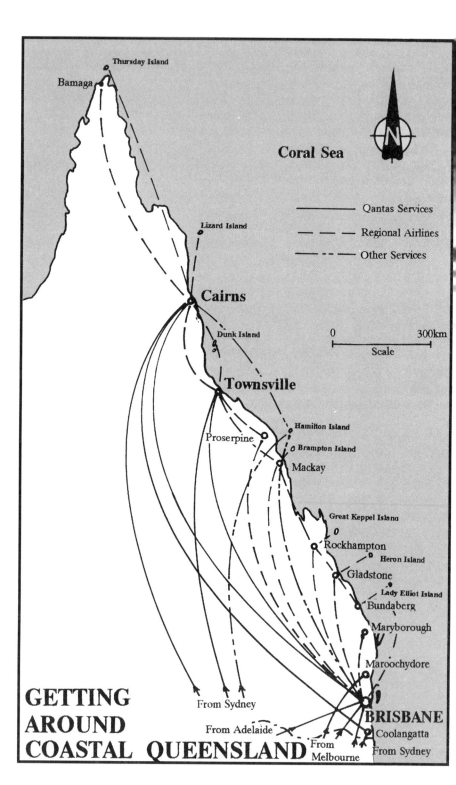

Coral Sea

Thursday Island
Bamaga

Lizard Island

——— Qantas Services
– – – Regional Airlines
–·–·– Other Services

Cairns

Dunk Island

0   300km
Scale

Townsville

Hamilton Island
Proserpine
Brampton Island
Mackay

Great Keppel Island

Rockhampton
Heron Island
Gladstone
Lady Elliot Island
Bundaberg
Maryborough

Maroochydore

GETTING
AROUND
COASTAL QUEENSLAND

From Sydney

From Adelaide

BRISBANE
Coolangatta
From Sydney
From Melbourne

Many other international airlines fly to Sydney or Great Barrier Reef region airports. Some have daily services from North America, Asia, and Europe, and there are connections from Africa and South America. Your travel agent will be able to provide details.

Transportation Within the Great Barrier Reef Region

Air. It is around 2,500 kilometers from the Gold Coast to the Torres Strait islands, so it is no surprise to find that air travel is the transport mode of first choice. Qantas and Ansett both have many jet services within this region with operations centered on Brisbane, Cairns, Townsville, and the Gold Coast (Coolangatta Airport). Regional airlines, either owned or associated with these two majors, serve these and other cities, towns, and islands. A Brisbane-Townsville direct service takes around one hour and forty minutes, while a Brisbane-Cairns flight takes just over two hours.

Several islands have airports with regular flights from a mainland center. These include Lady Elliot Island, Great Keppel Island, Brampton Island, Hamilton Island, Dunk Island, and Lizard Island. Heron Island has a helicopter service and Orpheus Island, Hinchinbrook Island, and some others have a seaplane service. Further details of these are found in the area chapters.

There is a wide range of airfares available. Some are only available to those with an international air ticket, and some are only available when booking within Australia. It is extremely difficult to advise overseas residents about the best deals. In general, it is fair to say that an international add-on is probably the best option at times of high demand—the Christmas/New Year period or during school vacations. At other times it may be possible to buy a cheaper ticket after you arrive in Australia, provided you have plenty of time and the flexibility to meet the conditions that always apply to special low-priced offers. You should ask your travel agent to look at all the possibilities.

Train. Naturally you cannot take a train to the reef or the islands, but you can use train services between centers along the coast. There is a new electric train service from Brisbane to the Gold Coast, and there are long-distance electric trains all the way north to Rockhampton. From Rockhampton to Townsville and Cairns there are airconditioned diesel-hauled trains that have both sitting and sleeping facilities. The train from Brisbane to Townsville takes around 20 hours for the trip.

Bus. Long-distance bus services are well developed, but the number of operators has dropped in recent years as the industry has consolidated.

Because of competition from air and rail, bus fares have fallen, and bus is now considered to be the budget travel method. Travel times are similar to the train.

Boat. There are no coastal passenger services, but fast powered catamarans have become the major transport mode to many of the islands from mainland centers. A few islands also have barge services so that visitors can take vehicles with them.

Cruise boats have become popular in recent years with services departing from Mackay, Townsville, and Cairns. Specially built dive boats also operate from Townsville and Cairns for extended dive trips into the Coral Sea.

Car Rental. This is an increasingly popular activity for overseas visitors. Traffic keeps to the left, and this is confusing for some, but drivers are reasonably disciplined, and once away from Brisbane and the Gold Coast traffic is light.

Camper vans (recreational vehicles) are available from several centers, and one-way rentals can be arranged. Main roads are of fair standard although freeways are few and far between. Stop-over facilities along the main north-south road (Bruce Highway) are good.

Travel Facts

Climate. The Great Barrier Reef region is mainly in the tropics, so the weather is almost always warm or hot. As this is the southern hemisphere and things are reversed from many people's usual experience, the temperature rises as you travel north. Consequently Cairns is the hottest of the major coastal centers, and the Gold Coast is the coolest. From around Mackay north there is usually a pronounced summer wet season from December through to May. It is longest and wettest in Cairns, and this should be borne in mind by visitors.

Packing. My standard advice to all travelers is to travel light. In this region you will never need large quantities of warm clothing, so leave them at home. Australian clothes and footwear are reasonably priced, and there is a wide range of styles, sizes, and colors, so you can always buy something you badly need. Most parts of coastal Queensland have a casual attitude to fashion, so aim to be comfortable. I always take some sort of jacket with me, and I recommend this particularly if you are visiting Brisbane. Shorts and t-shirts sound like tropical wear, but remember that at times you will need to cover up from the sun, so cotton trousers and some long-sleeve casual shirts are essential. Swimming trunks, hat, sneakers, and sun block are all needed for reef visits.

I recommend you take your favorite cosmetics and medicines even though you will find equivalent products readily available in Australia. If your electric appliances operate on 110 volts, leave them all at home. You can get transformers and adapters, but it is not worth the effort.

Public Holidays. Australians have more holidays than many countries, and Queenslanders follow that tradition. The whole state stops on New Years Day, Australia Day (January 26), Good Friday, Easter Sunday, Easter Monday, Anzac Day (April 25), May Day (first Monday in May), Queens Birthday (Monday in early June), Christmas Day (December 25), and Boxing Day (December 26). Most local centers have a holiday for the annual show (usually in the July to September period).

Mail and Telephone Services. Australian mail, telephone, and fax services are some of the best in the world, so you should have no problems in the reef region. All centers have one or more post offices where you can post mail and carry out other services. The postal service is operated by a government agency called Australia Post. It has become entrepreneurial in recent years, so now post offices also act as limited-service banks, collection agencies for public service providers, philatelic bureaux, and so forth. Apart from regular mail and air mail services there are next-day delivery, express, certified mail, and collect payment services. All post offices operate from 9 A.M. to 5 P.M. Monday to Friday, but some also operate for extended hours.

Local telephone and fax services are provided by Telstra, a government telecommunications agency. Local calls from both private and public telephones are charged per call, but there is no time limit imposed. Public telephone calls currently cost 40 cents. Mobile telephone services and long-distance calls are provided by both Telstra and Optus, a private company established in the early 1990s. You can chose which company to use from any telephone, but one operator will be automatically connected unless you dial a set of digits to get the other. The service from both operators is similar.

Long-distance and direct-dial overseas calls can be made from any public telephone. Some telephones take credit or charge cards, and others only accept cash. Operator-connected and collect calls (reverse charge calls) can also be made. To dial the United States, for instance, from the reef region, you would dial the Australian international access code (0011), then the country code (1 for the United States and Canada), then the three-digit area code, then the telephone number. In the reverse direction, from the United States to Townsville, for instance, dial 011, the country code (61), the area code less the first 0 (77), then the telephone number. Calls are usually connected immediately, and the prices are reasonable.

Metrics and Electrics

Metrics. The metric system of weights and measures has been used in Australia for more than 20 years, but you will still find some people who understand and prefer the "English" system. This is particularly in areas where the average person has little contact with current usage. You will find that older Australians still give their height in feet and inches, and their weight in stones and pounds. Many young people, however, know nothing about these measures. If you are not familiar with the metric system, you can quickly learn a few conversions that will help you make sense of the strange terms you will meet in the Great Barrier Reef region.

Temperature. If you want to know what tomorrow's temperature will be, you must know something about the Celsius system. The most important basics are that water boils at 100 degrees and freezes at zero degrees. From a climatic point of view, 10 degrees Celsius is cold, 20 degrees is temperate, 30 degrees is quite warm, and 40 degrees is extremely hot. In Fahrenheit, these are equivalent to 50 degrees, 68 degrees, 86 degrees, and 104 degrees respectively.

Distance. Distances throughout the Great Barrier Reef region are vast. They look even farther to visitors more used to miles, because all signs are in kilometers. To do a rough conversion to miles, remember that five kilometers is roughly three miles, and 100 kilometers is roughly 60 miles. Average travel speeds on Australian roads are quite high, so you can often legally travel 90 kilometers in an hour.

For small distances, remember that five centimeters equals two inches, 30 centimeters equals one foot, and a meter and a yard are roughly equal.

Electricity. Voltages, amperages, and cycles are a total mystery to most of us. All you need to know is that the standard Australian electric current is powered at 240 volts, more than twice the rate of United States and Canadian systems. Appliances that are designed for 110 volts will fry. In the process you may blow some other power outlets and be more inconvenienced than ever. The answer is to leave these appliances at home. Some hotels have a 110 outlet in the bathroom for an electric shaver, but don't rely on it.

The other problem is that Australia uses 50 cycles compared to the United States which uses 60 cycles. Even if you can adjust the voltage to suit, electric motors designed for 60 cycles will run slower than normal on 50 cycles so clocks, phonographs, and so forth will not operate properly. For a shaver, it doesn't matter.

Then there is the question of Australian sockets. Australia and New Zealand have their own unique system of three-pronged outlets with the prongs not set parallel to each other. It is a good system, but plugs from anywhere else in the world will not work without an adapter. If this is all sounding a bit too difficult, it is good to know that most Australian hotels have an iron, an electric razor, and a hair drier available for guests either in the room or on request.

One final point. Australian power outlets all have a switch as part of the fitting. You turn off the power by switching off the switch rather than pulling out the plug. All power outlets and light switches operate on the up is off, down is on, principle.

Money and Prices

Money. The value of the Australian dollar has fluctuated over a wide range in the past few years. As I am writing this, it is on a rising trend against the U.S. dollar and the Japanese yen, but there is no guarantee that this will continue. The trend over the past 10 years has been for the Australian dollar to fall against many of the major world currencies. At present the Australian dollar is worth around 80 U.S. cents and around 85 Japanese yen.

Australian bank notes come in different sizes and colors for different denominations. In recent years Australia has been experimenting with plastic notes and now claims that these have been perfected. They have been progressively introduced, and the A$100 note is the only paper note left, but they are not particularly popular with the public. At the same time the smaller denomination notes have been replaced with coins. The result is a strange collection of coin shapes and sizes which bear no relationship to their value. The two-dollar coin is smaller than the one-dollar coin, and both are much smaller than the 50 cent coin. There are also 20, 10, and five cent coins. One and two cent coins that previously existed are no longer used even though you will see prices quoted as 79 cents (you pay 75 cents or 80 cents if you are just buying this item). Stores, supermarkets, and many other outlets round down the total purchase price to the nearest five cents.

Many world currencies can be changed at major Australian banks, but it is worthwhile picking up some Australian currency from your bank before you leave on a trip. This lets you become familiar with the notes, and it is useful for taxis and other minor expenses when you first arrive. All airports have banks or currency exchange outlets, but you do not necessarily get the best exchange rates here. A city bank is often better. Hotel cashiers usually offer lower rates.

Credit cards are readily accepted in Australia, and it is rare to have to pay any surcharge. Visa, MasterCard, American Express, and Diners Club are the most accepted cards.

Traveler's checks are accepted at banks and by most larger hotels, but are not seen much at restaurants, small motels and hotels, or shops. Australian dollar checks are the best with U.S. dollars, sterling, and the other major currencies second choice. Banking hours vary a little from place to place, but in Queensland they are usually Monday to Thursday 9:30 A.M. to 4 P.M. and Friday 9:30 A.M. to 5 P.M.

Prices. In general your money will go far farther in the Great Barrier Reef region than it will in most European and American cities. Brisbane and the other tourist areas have hotel and restaurant rates that are certainly cheaper than their equivalent in Europe. Because you will probably travel long distances, travel costs may be higher than you anticipate; however, they are still lower than they would be for equivalent distances in Europe, Asia, or North America.

Visitors may find that by modifying their normal lifestyle to better suit the Australian "norm," they can save a considerable amount of money. And who is going to complain about eating Australian steak, shrimp, and Pavlova rather than his traditional home-style cuisine?

Tipping. I live in Australia, and I don't tip unless I receive exceptional service. Twenty years ago it was almost an insult to tip someone, but with the expansion of international tourism, tipping has crept into certain parts of the industry. Maybe I am fighting a long-lost battle, but I encourage visitors only to tip if something exceptional is offered. Bellboys, taxi drivers, restaurant waiters, and others are all being paid a reasonable wage to do their job, and they do not rely on tips to make a living. A reasonable level of service should be expected and encouraged without a tip. If ever any comment is made by anyone about wanting a tip, I urge you to immediately report the incident to the management.

Government Fiddle-Faddle

Passports and Visas. You will need a passport to enter Australia and to get back into your own country. You should ask your travel agent or the relevant government department about how to get a passport.

Additionally, unless you are a New Zealander, you will need a visa to enter Australia. This is issued by the Australian government and must be applied for by each passport holder. There is considerable debate at present about this system because it clearly has a detrimental effect on tourist numbers going to Australia, particular when nearby countries offer short-term tourist visas upon arrival at the airport. By the time you read this, Australia may have modified its system, so check with your travel agent.

Australian visas are issued by Australian consulates and embassies around the world. Your travel agent will know the location of the office nearest you, or you could contact one of the following to inquire:

Canada—50 O'Connor St., Ottawa K1P 6L2 (Tel: 236-0841)
—175 Bloor St. East, Toronto, ONT M4W 3R8 (Tel: 323-1155)
Germany—Godesberger Allee 107, 5300 Bonn (Tel: 2288-1030)
Hong Kong—25 Harbour Road, Wanchai (Tel: 2573-1881)
Japan—2-1-14 Mita, Minato-ku, Tokyo (Tel: 5232-4111)
Singapore—25 Napier Road, Singapore 10 (Tel: 737-9311)
UK—Australia House, Strand, London WC2B 4LA (Tel: 379-4334)
USA—1601 Massachusetts Ave. NW, Washington (Tel: 797-3000)
—630 Fifth Ave., New York, NY 10111 (Tel: 408-8400)

Health. Normally there are no health certificates or vaccinations required to enter Australia; however, if you are passing through or come from an area where yellow fever or similar infectious disease is prevalent, you will probably need something to show the Australian authorities.

Customs. Australia generally allows visitors to bring into the country whatever they need for a short stay. Obviously there are restrictions on such things as firearms, items made from ivory, and drugs, and Australia is very wary about animals, wooden products, plants, food, and so forth. It's best not to take anything in this category with you.

You should also be aware that your home country may have similar restrictions when you return. Many countries now issue pamphlets explaining the situation. I strongly suggest you read these.

Departure Tax. There is a hefty departure tax of A$27 imposed by the Australian government on all departing passengers. The authorities are in the process of changing the collection system from buying a tax stamp at the airport to making the airlines add it to the cost of the ticket. For some months you will need to check to see if the charge is listed on your ticket.

Traveler's Guide

Safety. Australia is one of the safer destinations in the world. Because of its relative isolation, and the non- controversial nature of its policies, the country has escaped much of the political and terrorism problems that now plague many parts of the world. Queensland has been even further removed from this problem in the past, so you should not experience any problems on a short visit.

Crime is also less of a problem than in some places. That doesn't mean that there is no crime, and you should certainly take normal precautions with your money and possessions, but few travelers have problems. Most people are amazed to learn that I lived in Townsville for 15 years without locking my door. About five years ago I decided to change my ways and bought some locks which I used religiously. Two years later the house was broken into, and I lost some of my favorite things.

All places within the Great Barrier Reef region are, in general, safe at night. There may be some small areas of a city to avoid at a particular time, however, so ask your hotel about that before you venture out.

Business Hours. Most Queensland businesses open by 8:30 A.M. then operate all day until around 5 P.M. for offices and around 6 P.M. for shops, five days a week. In addition, most towns and cities have at least one night of late-night shopping until 9 P.M., and at least Saturday until 1 P.M. In Brisbane, the Gold Coast, parts of the Sunshine Coast, Cairns, Townsville, and some other tourist centers, there are extended shopping hours which can include all day Saturday and Sunday trading and some extra late-night trading. These hours vary somewhat between centers, so check with the locals.

Tourist Information. General information about Australia, Queensland, and the Great Barrier Reef region is available from several sources. Most overseas readers will find that the offices of the Australian Tourist Commission, the Queensland Tourist and Travel Corporation, and Qantas Airways will be the most useful. The following are some of those offices:

Australian Tourist Commission

Auckland—Level 13, 44 Emily Place (Tel: 379-9594)
Frankfurt—Neue Mainzerstrasse 22, D60311 (Tel: 274-0060)
Hong Kong—Level 10, 18 Harbour Rd., Wanchai (Tel: 2802-7700)
London—Gemini House, 10 Putney Hill, SW15 1AE (Tel: 780-2227)
Los Angeles—2121 Ave of the Stars, CA 90067 (Tel: 552-1988)
New York—489 Fifth Avenue, NY 10017 (Tel: 687-6300)
Tokyo—9-13, Akasaka 1-chrome, Minato-ku 107 (Tel: 3582-2191)

Queensland Tourist and Travel Corporation

London—Queensland House, Strand, WC2R 0LZ (Tel: 836-7242)
Los Angeles—1800 Century Park East, CA 90067 (Tel: 788-0997)
Munich—Level 4, Neuhauserstrasse 27, 80331 (Tel: 260-9693)

Singapore—101 Thompson Road, Singapore 1130 (Tel: 253-2811)
Taipei—333 Keeling Rd., Section 1, 10548 (Tel: 723-3196)

Qantas Airways

Bangkok—942/145 Charn Issara Bldg, Rama IV Rd. (Tel: 236-0306)
Frankfurt—Bethmannstrasse 56 (Tel: 23-0041)
Hong Kong—Swire House, 11 Charter Rd., Central (Tel: 842-1442)
London—182 Strand, WC2 1ET (Tel: 071-497-2571)
Los Angeles—300 N. Continental Blvd., El Segundo (Tel: 535-1950)
New York—712 Fifth Avenue (Tel: 399-3450)
San Francisco—360 Post Street (Tel: 445-1400)
Singapore—300 Orchard Road (Tel: 730-9222)
Tokyo—3-2-2- Manunouchi Chiyoda-Ku (Tel: 3593-5500)
Vancouver—1111 West Georgia Street (Tel: 684-1055)

Regional Tourist Offices

Brisbane Visitors and Convention Bureau—City Hall, King George Square, Brisbane 4002 (Tel: 07-3221-8411)
Bundaberg District Tourism—Bourbong & Mulgrave Sts., Bundaberg 4670 (Tel: 071-522-333)
Capricorn Tourism Organisation—The Spire, Gladstone Rd., Rockhampton 4700 (Tel: 079-272-055)
Far North Qld. Development Bureau—Grafton and Hartley Sts., Cairns 4870 (Tel: 070-513-588)
Gladstone Area Promotion Ltd—56 Goondoon Street, Gladstone 4680 (Tel: 079-724-000)
Gold Coast Tourism Bureau—64 Ferny Ave., Surfers Paradise 4217 (Tel: 07-5592-2699)
Tourism Mackay—320 Nebo Rd., Mackay 4740 (Tel: 079-522-034)
Tourism Sunshine Coast—126 Alexandra Parade, Alexander Headland 4572 (Tel: 074-436-400)
Townsville Enterprise—6 The Strand, Townsville 4810 (Tel: 077- 713-061)
Whitsunday Visitors Bureau—The Esplanade, Airley Beach 4802 (Tel: 079-466-730)

News Media. Queensland has reasonable newspapers, a few local magazines, numerous radio stations on both the AM and FM band, and five television networks that are becoming increasingly national (Sydney-based) in content. All the mainstream media, with the exception of some programs on the SBS television network, are in English. Foreign speakers will find weekly newspapers in many European and Asian languages, and there are some foreign language programs on the community radio stations. There are no

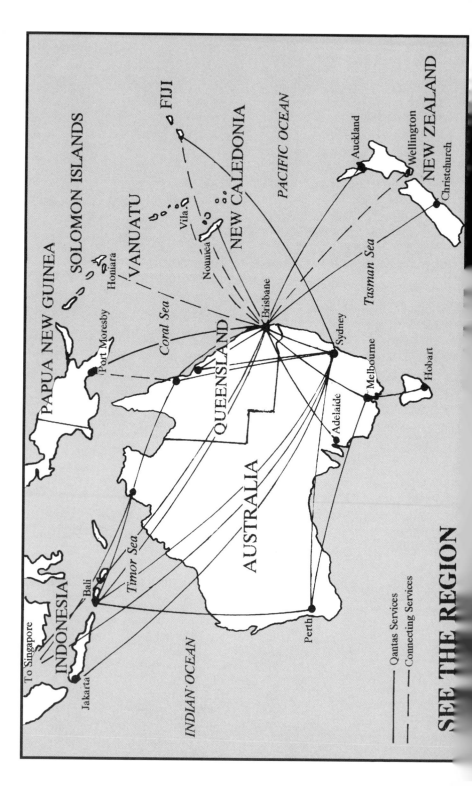

SEE THE REGION

regular foreign language news broadcasts on local radio or television, but Radio Australia broadcasts can be picked up on the short-wave band.

There is only one national daily general newspaper (*The Australian*), and one state-wide daily newspaper (*The Courier Mail*). Both are part of the Rupert Murdock-owned News Corporation. Major centers such as the Gold Coast, Rockhampton, Mackay, Townsville, and Cairns have their own local daily newspapers.

Visit the Region

The Great Barrier Reef region is well placed so that visitors can easily include other destinations in the same general area. The most obvious of these are other areas of Australia, but because of good air connections it is easy to visit other countries as well. Here are some suggestions.

Outback Australia is hard to define geographically, but its attraction is clear. This region of few people, amazing wildlife, vast distances, pioneering spirit, and harsh conditions fascinates both Australians and others from around the world. You can be in the outback, 75 kilometers inland from Townsville, but probably the best-known areas are Central Australia around Alice Springs and Ayers Rock, and the Top End of the Northern Territory around Darwin and Kakadu National Park.

South East Australia is the area which is probably most familiar to visitors. This is where you find the two largest cities in the country, Sydney and Melbourne, and also the national capital, Canberra. This is the most densely populated part of Australia, and in some ways it is the most developed. There are major attractions such as the wilderness areas of Tasmania, the penguin parade at Phillip Island in Victoria, the Great Ocean Road along the southern coast, the Australian alps with their winter snow fields, and the Blue Mountains west of Sydney.

New Zealand is about three hours flying time from Brisbane. This picturesque country has a wide diversity in a relatively small area. Visitors can be absorbed in Maori culture, walk among bubbling mud pools and geysers, and visit ski fields all in one day. The wilderness areas of the South Island with their mountain trails, fjords, and glaciers are most impressive. Auckland, Wellington, Christchurch, and Queenstown are all worthy of some time.

Papua New Guinea provides a rare opportunity to travel back in time. There are areas of the country that were visited by outsiders for the first time only 30 years ago. Today, many areas are accessible by aircraft, and hotels and lodges cater to visitors in relative luxury. It is still possible to make excursions into areas where traditional agricultural practices and lifestyles have changed little over centuries. There is spectacular mountain scenery in the highlands, vast wetlands in the valleys of the Sepic and Fly Rivers, and some great beaches on many of the islands. Everywhere there are fascinating people learning to live with the late 20th century. Unfortunately, there are law and order problems in some areas.

New Caledonia is a French territory, **Vanuatu** is a former joint British and French territory, and the **Solomon Islands** was once a British colony. All now offer opportunities to see how colonial powers have given South Sea island states an extra dimension. Each has hotels and resorts catering to visitors, but there is still life outside the tourism industry which can be fascinating to visitors. There are air connections from Brisbane to all these places.

Fiji is the South Seas island nation with the most developed tourism industry. There are numerous first-class resorts along the southern coast of the main island, and there are some hotels and smaller resorts elsewhere. Most of the major resorts are self-contained, and some visitors rarely leave the confines of the resort, but there is a whole world outside that can be extremely interesting for visitors from other cultures. You will find that most people are friendly, and there are few safety problems.

Indonesia provides the gateway between Australia and Asia. This is one of the most densely populated large nations on earth. It has an ancient civilization that has built some impressive monuments, and in places the old culture is well preserved. There are some large cities, some fine beaches, exotic resorts and hotels, and interesting souvenirs to buy.

3

The Land and Life of Queensland

Queensland is the second largest state in Australia, accounting for 22.5 percent of the total area. It is approximately twice the size of Texas. Although this book is about the Great Barrier Reef, it is useful to discuss some issues from a Queensland perspective because this is the state you will be in for the entire time of your reef visit. The following sections of this chapter are concerned with coastal and near coastal Queensland from the New South Wales border in the south to the border with Papua New Guinea in the north.

The Great Barrier Reef is off the Queensland coast in the region from Lady Elliot Island, about 300 kilometers north of Brisbane, to north of the tip of Cape York. This gives the reef a length of over 2,000 kilometers. In the Cape Flattery area, north of Cooktown, the reef and the edge of the continental shelf are only 30 to 40 kilometers from the coast, but progressing southwards, it slowly diverges away from the coast until at Rockhampton it is about 250 kilometers off the coast at the Swain Reefs formation. This massive coral structure is the only life form on earth that is visible from the moon.

Geography

The landforms of Queensland, except for the coastal regions, have probably changed little since man first roamed across its surface. Apart from

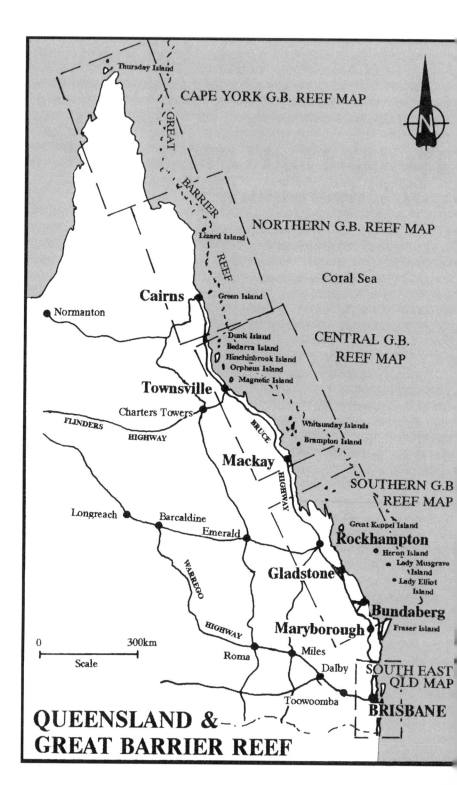

some high country in the northwest, most of Queensland consists of a seemingly flat, featureless interior of low relief, broken by the erratic, north-south sprawl of the Great Dividing Range in the east. This pattern divides the state into four main divisions: the eastern highlands, the western plains, the northwest uplands, and the coastal plains, islands, and reefs.

The coastal plains are on the Pacific Ocean side of the Great Dividing Range. The plains form a narrow coastal strip that extends the full length of the state and supports all the main coastal cities and towns which contain the bulk of the state's population. The drainage system of the ranges and coastal plains consists of either short, fast-flowing perennial streams cutting sharp tracts through the highlands, or slower tributaries of the large river systems. North of Cairns, most rivers and streams fall into the former class; however, to the south, nearly all streams are part of either the Burdekin, Fitzroy, Burnett, Mary, or Brisbane River systems.

Landforms of the coastline of Queensland have been determined largely by the effects of onshore winds and ocean swells. The exposed high-wave-energy coasts of the south consist of long sandy beaches like the Gold Coast, the Sunshine Coast, and the leeward side of the southern islands. North of Gladstone, the coast is protected by the Great Barrier Reef, so the smooth shape of the beaches is controlled by the strength, direction, and frequency of the onshore winds.

Climate

Queensland stretches from 10 degrees south to 29 degrees south, so it experiences a tropical and sub-tropical climate. The coastal north has a wet summer/dry winter climate, while the coastal south has more pronounced seasons with both summer and winter rain. Remember that Queensland is in the southern hemisphere, so summer here occurs during the northern hemisphere winter. The tropical areas from Mackay north are influenced by the monsoonal trough in summer. This often introduces persistent inflows of warm moist tropical air, and as a consequence these areas can experience heavy tropical rains which, from Mission Beach north, can last for days at a time. Cyclones are common during this season and are also responsible for widespread rain.

The major winter weather influence is the intense high pressure systems that move east across southern Australia. This brings to Queensland the trade winds that sweep in across the sea from the southeast. The highs are frequently reinforced by cold air from the Antarctic which is carried by low-pressure systems, and this causes the winter rains on the southern coastal parts.

Except for a few isolated reefs and islands in the south, the whole of the reef is in the tropics, so the reef region is almost always warm, and in summer it can be very humid. In Rockhampton, average monthly maximum temperatures range from near 30 degrees C. in December, January, and February, to just above 20 degrees C. in June and July. The July average minimum is around 10 degrees C. As you move north, the maximum and minimum winter temperatures slowly rise until in Cairns the average July maximum is 24 degrees C., and the average July minimum is 15 degrees C.

Rainfall varies considerably along the Great Barrier Reef coast, and this can have a major influence on whether you enjoy your visit. No one wants to battle with rain, high winds, or huge seas while trying to see the reef. Divers hope for clear skies and light winds so that visibility will be at its best, while sailors want small seas and consistent breezes. Records indicate that over the past 80 years, the Cairns region has had more cyclones than other areas of the coast, yet in recent years the number has been small. Cairns also has more rainy days than most other areas, and this causes problems for some short-term visitors in summer.

In my opinion, the best time to visit the reef region is May to November from Townsville south, and June to early November for the area north.

The Government

There are three tiers of government in Australia—federal, state, and local. Queensland was one of the six self-governing British colonies which in 1901 united to form the Commonwealth of Australia. Each of the colonies had adopted the British system of cabinet or responsible government where the queen or her representative performed governmental acts on the advice of ministers who were chosen from members of Parliament belonging to the party or coalition that had a majority of members.

At federation, the colonies became states, with legislative and executive powers divided between the commonwealth and state parliaments and governments. The constitution that brought about this system was drafted by conventions of Australian statesmen, and it was given legal force through enactment by the British Parliament. The federal Parliament was located in Melbourne from 1901 until 1927 when it was transferred to the new capital of Canberra.

At present, the executive power of the federal Parliament is vested in the queen and is exercisable by the governor-general as her representative. As Australia approaches celebrations for its first 100 years, there is growing debate about the need to change this system. Queensland and the other five states each have their own governor, who is the queen's representative. State legislatures are bicameral, except in Queensland where the upper house was abolished in 1922.

There had been a colonial penal settlement at Moreton Bay since 1824, but the real development of Queensland started in 1843 when the settled area of Moreton Bay became a distinct electoral division of New South Wales. In 1859, Queensland was proclaimed separate from New South Wales, and the colony of Queensland came into being. In 1901, it joined the other colonies to form Australia. Under the constitution, the governor gives royal assent to legislation passed by the Legislative Assembly.

Broadly, state governments administer such fields as finance, justice, industrial development, education, health, public works, public housing, ship, road, and rail transport, agriculture, mining, conservation, Crown lands and national parks, tourism, and community welfare. In addition, a number of authorities established by the state government have controlled activities such as electricity, gas, and the marketing of some agricultural products. Many of these are now being privatized.

In Queensland, as in all other states, local authorities are granted powers by the state legislature to do certain things on a local level. These councils are elected every three years and are responsible for such items as town planning, water supply, sewerage and drainage schemes, the supervision of building and health regulations, the construction and maintenance of local roads and streets, the maintenance of civic cleanliness, and the provision of parks, public swimming pools, libraries, and so forth. In Queensland there are three main political parties and a number of smaller organizations; however, many local authorities are controlled by people independent of the main political organizations.

The Economy

Compared to many other areas of the world, the Queensland economy is comparatively young. Development, however, has been rapid and the standard of living is high. Early economic development saw an emphasis on primary production, but in recent years there has been an emphasis on large-scale mining and industrial development. During the 1980s rapid development of the tourism industry occurred.

The Queensland population is growing rapidly due to migration from overseas and from other states, and this is causing large investment in the building and retailing sectors, and in financial institutions. The resultant economy is well mixed, although there is less manufacturing than in some states. The high technology and the service sectors are playing an increasingly important role. Queensland's share of Australia's gross national product in the early 1990s was 17 percent, which is an increase from 12.5 percent in the early 1970s and 15 percent in the early 1980s. Coal, meat, sugar, cereals, and non-ferrous metals are the major exports from Queensland.

The People

The Queensland population is around 3.2 million people, making this the third largest Australian state in population. The area within a 200-kilometer radius of Brisbane is home to 65 percent of the state's population, although there are some major centers along the coast to the north. About 80 percent of Queenslanders reside in urban centers, and 87 percent of the state's area has a population density of less than one person for every two square kilometers.

Outside of the southeast corner, the major centers are Townsville (130,000), Cairns (90,000), Rockhampton (65,000), and Mackay (55,000). All these centers are along the coast within the Great Barrier Reef region.

Today, approximately one-third of the state's population was born overseas or has one or both parents born overseas. People have come from a large number of countries with Italy, Greece, the Balkan countries, Vietnam, and the Philippines providing some of the largest ethnic groups. Aborigines and Torres Strait Islanders account for approximately two per cent of the population with about one-third of these people choosing to live in reserve communities.

Language

All Australians speak English but, at times, some visitors seem to doubt that. North Americans and others can be confronted by a sentence that makes absolutely no sense to them. (You probably think the same about some of the sentences in this book!) There are several reasons for this.

Just as there are differences between British and American speech patterns, similar differences apply to Australian speech. The first difference is the incorporation of Aboriginal words into the language. "Boomerang" and "kookaburra," for instance, are Aboriginal words for things that have no English equivalent. The second thing is that Australians love to shorten words. Mosquito becomes "Mozzie," and afternoon becomes "arvo." To complicate it further, most Australians sound A just like I, so "mate" becomes "mite" to many foreign ears. Then there are some words that have been invented by Aussies for their own purposes. All this results in what some people call the Australian "Strine"—a language that can at times be totally incomprehensible.

To help you overcome these problems, I have listed some of the words that you are most likely to come across. You will impress your Australian friends if you can use and recognize these when you are visiting "Down Under." There are very few words that are peculiar to Queensland, but you will notice throughout the state a tendency to add an "ay" near or at the end of many sentences such as: "It's bloody cold today, ay mate?" Do that, and you will become a true-blue Queenslander.

These may require some explanation:

Accommodation—Room where you are staying.

Anzac—Originally a member of the Australian and New Zealand Army Corps in World War I, but now often used to describe all Australians and New Zealanders.

Arvo—Afternoon.

Aussie—Australian.

Banana bender—Queenslander.

Barbie—Barbecue.

Big mobs—Large amount, heaps.

Bikey—One who rides bikes or motorcycles.

Billabong—A cut-off water hole in a river bed.

Billy—Tin container used for boiling water to make tea.

Biscuit—Both a cookie (sweet biscuit) or cracker (dry).

Bitumen—Asphalt or blacktop road.

Bloke—Man, used like "guy" in the United States.

Bloody—All-purpose adjective, often profane.

Bludger—Lazy person who won't work.

Bonnet—Hood of a car.

Boot—Trunk of a car.

Brissie—Brisbane.

Bulldust—Fine, powdery dust on unsealed outback roads.

Bush—Countryside outside the cities and towns.

BYO—Bring your own (wine to a restaurant, meat to a BBQ).

Casket—Queensland lottery.

Chemist—Pharmacist.

Chips—French-fried potatoes (with fish).

Chook—Chicken.

Coach—Long-distance bus.

Corroboree—Aboriginal dancing ceremony.

Counter meal—Cheap pub meal.

Damper—Bush bread cooked in a camp oven.

Didjeridoo—Aboriginal musical instrument.

Dill—Fool.

Dunny—Toilet.

Esky—Large insulated portable box for keeping food cold.
Fair dinkum—The whole truth.
Flash—Fancy or ostentatious.
Flat out—As fast as you can go.
Footpath—Sidewalk or pavement.
Fossick—To prospect or search.
Gear—Clothing or equipment.
G'day—Good day, traditional Australian greeting.
Good on ya!—Term of approval.
Grazier—Sheep or cattle rancher.
Greenies—Environmentalists.
Grog—Beer or other alcoholic drink.
Hire—To rent.
How are ja?—Greeting. Reply: "Good thanks, how are you?"
Jackaroo—An apprentice cowboy, station hand.
Joey—Baby kangaroo.
Jumbuck—Sheep (as in "Waltzing Matilda").
Lamington—Cake covered in chocolate sauce and coconut.
Lollies—Sweets or candy.
Loo—Slang for toilet.
Mate—Your best buddy (does not mean spouse).
Medibank—Australian public health plan.
Mob—A group of persons or animals.
Mozzie—Mosquito.
No worries—That's OK.
Outback—Remote part of the bush.
Paddock—Large field or meadow.
Pavlova—Dessert made from meringue, fruit, and cream.
Petrol—Gasoline.
Piss—Beer (not polite).
Pokies—Slot machines found in hotels, clubs, and casinos.
Prang—Accident, vehicle crash.
Pub—Bar, drinking establishment.
Ripper—Something particularly good.
STD—Direct long-distance telephone dialing.
Shout—Buy someone a drink.
Snag—Sausage.
Station—Large farm or ranch.
Stinger—Dangerous marine box jellyfish.
Stockman—Cowboy, station hand.
Stubby—Small bottle of beer.
Swagman—Rural tramp (as in "Waltzing Matilda").

TAB—Legal offtrack betting shop.
Take-away food—Takeout.
Telly—Television.
Two up—Traditional gambling game played with two coins.
Tucker—Food (bush term).
Up-market—Higher priced, sophisticated.
Ute—Pick-up truck.
"Waltzing Matilda"—Much loved and sung national song.
Yank—American.

Culture and Lifestyle

While the Great Barrier Reef may be your catalyst for visiting Down Under, you will probably find that the Aussies themselves become almost the greatest attraction once you get there. In this regard Australia is very different from many places in the world. Most people visiting Paris to see the Eiffel Tower and the Louvre, for instance, will not spend long periods in a pub or elsewhere enjoying conversation or fun with the locals. Likewise, while the cultures of Asia may be fascinating to see, it is difficult on a short visit to be any more than an observer. In Australia, however, you would have to be a recluse or downright antisocial to avoid meeting and mixing with Australians almost everywhere you go.

It is never easy writing about yourself, so this is the difficult part of this book. Perhaps it is sufficient to say that Australians in general are unpretentious, entertaining, casual, and accommodating. Queenslanders tend to be even more laid-back than southern Australians: No one seems to be dashing about too much, drivers don't get too excited, cars often give way to pedestrians, and when five o'clock comes, most workers head for the pub, the golf course, or the beach.

It is probably fair comment to say that Australia is one of the most egalitarian countries on earth. There is a huge middle-class and very little either end. This means that most Australians are not class conscious, and in fact they enjoy making fun of those who show any sign of snobbery. Visitors are not immune from this. In Queensland, there are very few places where "the average Queenslander," and hence most visitors, would not feel comfortable. Despite this, you will still find a few places that insist on dress rules and will not let you in unless you comply.

Australia, in common with most Western countries, has been influenced by the United States mass media in recent years. This may make it easier for North Americans to feel at home, but it has had some detrimental effect on traditional Australian values. The other major influence is the continuing migration program that allows people from around the world to settle in Australia. This has made Australia a genuine multi-racial country, and the various ethnic groups have contributed greatly to modern Australian culture. Most areas within Queensland show this multi-culturism in various ways, and the visitor benefits.

The wide, open spaces, great weather, high standard of living, and good facilities have made Australia a keen sporting nation. The country has a small population, but there are a large number of Australians who feature regularly in the top sporting events around the world. Visitors see this enthusiasm for sport throughout Queensland, and they are welcome to use the public facilities which are provided. Surfing, golf, tennis, and boating are just some of the options.

At the same time there is a growing interest in the Arts. Melbourne and Sydney are the traditional centers for opera, ballet, theater, and visual art, but several Queensland centers now feature these performances and exhibitions on a regular basis. Australian popular music has at various times burst onto the world scene, and there are many venues where you can see and hear local talent. Australian country music has its own distinct sound which some visitors will enjoy.

Accommodations

The best hotels in Australia provide a level of comfort and service similar to that found worldwide. Most of the international management groups have properties in Australia, and there are some excellent Australian managed properties as well. Within the reef region you will find Hilton, Hyatt, Sheraton, Radisson, Holiday Inn, and so forth properties at rates around A$150-A$200. Below this, there are many excellent hotels that will cost A$75-A$140. As well, there are plenty of two-to-three-star hotels, family-style motels, boutique hotels, bed and breakfast houses and inns, and so forth.

At the budget end of the market, there are older central city or country "pubs," special backpackers places, caravan parks, and a few guest houses. In general, they are all clean and well run. Some are excellent value. Fortunately, there are very few places that should be avoided. The area chapters provide details of individual properties.

Food and Drink

Australia's growing ethnic population from around the world has broadened and improved the range of Australian food, to the point that some restaurants now provide some of the world's best cuisine at prices considerably cheaper than in Europe or North America. There are fine restaurants serving the best of European and Asian cuisine, others which have successfully blended Eastern and Western dishes, and others that have developed a specific Australian cuisine.

In the reef region, the fresh beef, seafood, tropical fruits, and local vegetables form the basis for many dishes. Most of the larger centers have good restaurants offering cuisine based on these ingredients, and some are remarkably well priced. Brisbane, the Gold Coast, the Sunshine Coast, Townsville, Cairns, and Port Douglas are particularly recommended. Some of the islands also have outstanding cuisine. Hayman, Orpheus, and Bedara are particularly noteworthy.

The major international fast-food and family-food companies have outlets within the reef region. In some places, local equivalents compete on price, quality, and service. Also competing are fish and chip shops, outlets selling Australian meat pies and sausage rolls, pizza parlors, and Middle East and Asian serveries.

Australian wines have an enviable world-wide reputation. No significant wine is produced within the reef region, but the best Australian wine is readily available at hotels, restaurants, and liquor outlets. Australian beers, fruit juices, and rums are excellent and are readily available. Fresh milk and flavored milk in many varieties are widely drunk, as is tea and coffee. Tap water can be drunk everywhere.

History

Queensland is part of what is some of the oldest land on earth. Parts of the north and northwest have exposed rocks that are up to 1,800 million years old. Because the earth's crust was unstable, the rocks have been subjected to great stress and upheaval, and you can see this today in many parts. Much, much later, when the Gulf of Carpentaria was a huge marshy swamp, prehistoric animals roamed the land. The bones of many of these prehistoric creatures have been found recently in northwest Queensland, and some have been dated as up to 150 million years ago.

In Cape York, there are thousands of rock shelters with wall paintings and engravings. These have been painted by Australian Aborigines. The paintings cover a period of many thousands of years up to about 150 years ago. Kenniff Cave in southern Queensland has paintings, and shields and axes have been found here. Evidence indicates that people lived here 19,000 years ago. Dating of other remains seems to indicate that Aborigines inhabited most of the land 50,000 years ago, although little visible evidence remains. Aborigines had no need to cultivate plants, domesticate animals, or build permanent dwellings as they were a nomadic race. They did, however, form extended family groups, particularly along the coastline and adjacent to major lakes and rivers.

The Aborigines were able to live successfully in inhospitable areas by being totally familiar with, and adapting to, their environment. Aboriginal groups practiced carefully scheduled seasonal movement throughout a region. This was timed to coincide with food abundance and often included feasting, celebration, the performance of rituals, and the renewal of old friendships. Traditional skills are still practiced by some Aborigines in Queensland today. Less is known about the Torres Strait Islanders, but it is thought that they too have occupied their land for many thousands of years.

In comparison, the history of European exploration and settlement is short. The first recorded exploration of the northern coast of Australia was that of a Dutchman, William Jansz, in 1606. A few months later, two Spaniards, Prado and Torres, passed through the Torres Strait, unaware of the proximity of the Queensland coast. In 1623 Dutchman Jan Carstensz sailed into the Gulf of Carpentaria and named the Staaten River. Dutch explorer Abel Tasman, who discovered Van Dieman's Land (Tasmania) and New Zealand, in 1644 named Cape York Peninsula "Capricornia Land." Further Dutch exploration of the Australian continent was abandoned in 1645 as "unprofitable."

Interest was not renewed for another 125 years until, as a result of rivalry between Britain and France over unexplored lands in the Pacific, Capt. James Cook sailed from England in 1768. On May 16, 1770, he was off Point Danger, the start of the present border between New South Wales and Queensland. The next day he named Cape Morton (now Moreton), and the Glasshouse Mountains. Cook landed nine times in what is now Queensland. He also sighted and named numerous capes, bays, passages, and islands along the coast until his ship the *Endeavour* ran aground on a reef near Cape Tribulation. A few days later, he beached and repaired his ship on the banks of what he called the Endeavour River. Cook then sailed north, named Cape York, then landed on Possession Island and took possession in the name of King George III of the whole eastern coast of Australia from "latitude 38 degrees south to this place," naming it New South Wales. Little interest was taken in the new "South Land" for the next 15 years.

As a consequence of the American War of Independence, the British government was obliged to seek an alternative destination for convicts from its overcrowded prisons. Botany Bay was recommended as a suitable site by Sir Joseph Banks, Cook's botanist. The first fleet of 11 ships, led by Capt. Arthur Phillip, arrived at Botany Bay in 1788 after eight months at sea. Phillip found the site unsuitable and decided to move the convict settlement north to Port Jackson, landing at Sydney Cove (now the site of Sydney) on January 26, 1788.

With the establishment of a permanent settlement, further detailed exploration of the eastern coastline began. In 1799 Capt. Matthew Flinders explored and charted Moreton Bay and its environs, named Moreton Island, climbed Beerrburrum in the Glasshouse Mountains, and later explored Hervey Bay. In 1802, Flinders circumnavigated Australia. He discovered Port Curtis (the port for present-day Rockhampton), examined Shoalwater Bay, Broad Sound, and Keppel Bay farther north, and named Pera Head after Jan Carstensz's vessel. He also proved that New South Wales and New Holland were not two land masses, but one continent. The next important exploration of the Queensland coast was made by Lt. Phillip King in several voyages between 1819 and 1822. He named Mount Bellender Ker in North Queensland and Mount Cook on the south side of the Endeavour River.

By 1823, the increase in the number of influential free settlers in New South Wales made it difficult for the government to maintain the penal and reformatory character of the colony. The colonial office sought to establish convict settlements outside the Port Jackson area. Lieutenant John Oxley ventured north to find possible sites for a new settlement. It was to be a "remote area to which the worst kind of convict would be sent." In August 1824 a penal settlement was established at Redcliffe. Convicts who committed crimes after they had been transported were now sent to the new penal settlement in Moreton Bay. Six months later, the settlement was reestablished on the banks of the Brisbane River at the site which is now Queensland's capital city.

Major Edmond Lockyer carried out exploration in the Moreton region in 1823, naming Redbank where he noticed coal deposits. In 1825 he penetrated past the junction of the Brisbane and Stanley Rivers and discovered Lockyer Creek. Captain Patrick Logan in 1826 found the Coomera River and the river which now bears his name. He was later killed by convicts or Aborigines while exploring the Brisbane Valley. Alan Cunningham led an expedition to explore the western side of the Great Dividing Range and discovered large pastoral plains which he named the Darling Downs.

Until 1839, free settlers could not settle within 80 kilometers of the penal colony at Moreton Bay. In that year, transportation to Moreton Bay ended and the restrictions were lifted. In 1840, squatters began to move from the south into the Darling Downs region. This was a time of great development as free settlers moved farther westward and northward. The first coal seam was opened, the first Brisbane newspaper was established, and Brisbane was declared a port of entry and communications. In 1844, Ludwig Leichardt left the Darling Downs, named the Dawson River, crossed the Great Dividing Range, discovered the MacKenzie, Isaacs, Burdekin, Lynd, and Mitchell Rivers, skirted the Gulf of Carpentaria, and arrived at Port Essington in the Northern Territory, an overland journey of about 4,800 kilometers and, at that time, the longest trek by an explorer in Australia.

In 1845 Sir Thomas Mitchell with Edmund Kennedy discovered the upper reaches of the Barcoo, Warrego, and Belyando Rivers and their exploration led to the opening up of the rich Central Queensland pastoral areas. In 1848 Kennedy, while leading an expedition to Cape York, was killed by Aborigines near Shellbourne Bay. In 1846, Charles Gregory's expedition from northwest Australia entered Queensland near the Gulf and made its way to Brisbane. Two years later he led an unsuccessful search for Leichardt's party which had disappeared without a trace in 1848.

The people who came north as free settlers wanted to manage their own affairs and not be totally governed by people in faraway Sydney. By 1851, the people of the north had been allowed to elect one member of parliament to represent them, and by 1858 they had nine members. Eventually in 1859 the people were given what they really wanted: a separate colony of Queensland. Sir George Bowen was the first governor. In the same year, the municipality of Brisbane was proclaimed, and John Petrie was elected as the first mayor. The first meeting of the parliament of Queensland took place on May 22, 1860, with R. G. W. Herbert as the state's first premier.

4

What Is the Great Barrier Reef?

An amazing barrier, made up of more than 2,900 individual reefs and about 900 islands, exists off the northeastern coast of Australia. It stretches for more than 2,000 kilometers through the Coral Sea. It is the biggest structure on earth made by living creatures and is called the Great Barrier Reef.

The reef is home to a bewildering abundance of life forms. Something like 4,000 molluscs; thousands of different sponges, worms, crustaceans, and echinoderms; 1,500 species of fish; and 400 different types of hard and soft corals share this space with giant humpback whales, sea turtles, and grazing dugong. But that is not all. The region is one of Australia's major tourist destinations. It also supports an important fishing industry. Now it is providing scientists with a fascinating challenge to discover how all of this amazing system works.

Reefs have grown on the continental shelves of northern Queensland for as long as 18 million years, but the reef that we know today is surprisingly recent. The sea level has changed dramatically over the years, and during the last ice age, the level was 100 meters below what it is now. This exposed the old reefs as limestone hills, and drained the continental shelf so that it would have been possible to walk out to where the Great Barrier Reef now stands. The ice age ended about 20,000 years ago, and by 10,000 years ago, the limestone hills were submerged for the first time in 100,000 years. Once again the conditions were conducive to coral growth, so reefs slowly formed on the old eroded limestone platforms, growing upwards as the sea level continued to rise. Only when the sea level stabilized about 6,000 years ago was it possible for reef flats to expand and provide potential sites for the formation of cays.

Coral is built by billions of tiny marine animals, called marine polyps. The living polyps excrete lime, and when they die, this skeleton remains. New polyps grow on their dead predecessors, and in this way reef is slowly formed. Coral requires warm, clean, salty water for proper growth, and the outer edge of the central and northern Queensland continental shelf provides near perfect conditions. This is where the reef is best and the viewing most spectacular.

Coral cannot live above water, but as the plants and animals which form and live on a coral reef die, the smaller debris is swept towards the leeside of the reef. Sometimes this sand and shingle is swept into a particular part of the reef flat, and it can be the initial stage in the formation of a coral cay or island. At first, this is little more than an unstable sand bank, but if it continues to grow in size, its position on the reef becomes more stable. King tides can then build it up to levels that are only overlapped a few times a year, and seabirds are encouraged to nest on its crown. These birds bring in plant seeds, either attached to their feathers or in droppings, and so vegetation commences, helping to stabilize the sand surface. This vegetation adds organic matter to the raw sands of the cay, and this is further enriched by the phosphate guano from the nesting birds.

In time, rainwater mixes the phosphate with the sand, forming a hard material called cay sandstone. Once a cay exceeds a few hectares in area, a small natural reservoir of fresh ground water may form beneath the cay, allowing trees and other plants to establish. By now the cay is almost stable. You can see examples of such cays in both the southern and northern sections of the reef.

The reef formation itself comes in different shapes and sizes. There are basically three types of reef: fringing, patch, and ribbon. Fringing reefs grow off the sloping sides of continental-type islands or even sometimes along the mainland coast. For visitors, they can be important for their accessibility, but unfortunately many have been damaged by overuse, adjacent land-based development, and pollution. Patch reefs are usually round or oval, and they grow like platforms on the continental shelf. In many areas, these are the reefs most visited by tourist boats, and they can provide excellent coral viewing opportunities.

Ribbon reefs occur only in the northern section of the reef. They are relatively narrow reefs on the edge of the continental shelf, and they can have dramatic dropoffs on the ocean side. These reefs are not continuous, but they form a substantial barrier and have been the demise of many vessels over recent centuries. The Great Barrier Reef is generally considered to consist of the ribbon reefs and the outer patch reefs. In places this can be up to 300 kilometers from the coast, but as it moves north it runs much closer to shore.

Reef region islands come in several types. What you have to realize is that most of these islands are not actually on the Great Barrier Reef at all. Even some of the popular "reef resorts" are in fact nowhere near the true Great Barrier Reef. This is very confusing and can be extremely disappointing to visitors. The true reef islands are coral cays, and most of these are very small, have little vegetation, and generally have no water. There are also coral cays associated with some of the patch reefs. Some of these have good vegetation cover and can provide interesting visitor experiences. All of the larger islands are continental-type and are not on the reef. These are the tops of flooded mountains. They can have dense vegetation, good beaches, and rugged headlands. Most resorts are on this type of island.

Explorers of the Reef

The Great Barrier Reef was explored and used by the Australian Aborigines for thousands of years. It is thought that these people arrived in Australia about 40,000 years ago when there was a land bridge with Asia. Those living near the coast would have experienced many changes as the sea level rose and the shore line moved west. It appears likely that for periods of time, Aborigines actually lived on some of the continental-type islands that formed. Others retreated to the mainland but made forays to the islands and used the reef as a food supply. Shell middens, which are the accumulated remains of shellfish feasts, are found on many islands.

Captain Cook was the first European to gain first-hand experience of the Great Barrier Reef and to accurately record his journey. He reported seeing Aborigines on several islands and traveling in their canoes between reefs and islands in the region. Cook's journey in 1770 was a demonstration of remarkable skill and persistence by a remarkable man. Cook was sent to make astronomical observations from Tahiti. He then proceeded to what is now New Zealand. After circumnavigating both islands, he chose to sail west and eventually found land again at Point Hicks in southern Australia. Cook turned north and charted much of the east coast. He named many points along the coast and a variety of islands, and had sailed 1,000 kilometers inside the Great Barrier Reef without realizing it was there.

Cook's problems began when his ship *Endeavour* struck a reef at night not far from Cape Tribulation. After jettisoning ballast, guns, and some masts, he was able to pull the craft off the reef using the ship's longboats. After searching for four days, Cook finally edged his way into the Endeavour River where Cooktown now stands. The ship remained there for two months while repairs were carried out. After an eventful trip farther north, when he almost foundered again on the reef, Cook reached the northern tip of Australia and named it Cape York. From a small rocky island known as Possession Island, Cook then took ceremonial possession of the coast for Britain.

In 1801, Capt. Matthew Flinders and his crew sailed the *Investigator* from England to Sydney. In 1801 and 1802, at the age of only 27, Flinders circumnavigated Australia and produced some amazing maps and charts that have been used until recent times. From July to October 1802, Flinders traveled up the north coast and through part of the inner passage of the Great Barrier Reef. Like Cook before him, Flinders decided that the inner reef was too hazardous, so he carefully mapped out a safe path through the reef to open water. This today is known as Flinders' Passage. Captain Flinders' knowledge of botany and marine biology made him a reliable source for scientists, and his perceptions of the coral, building process, and marine creatures was remarkable. Flinders was the first to use the term Great Barrier Reef, and it will forever be a great reminder of a remarkable man.

Since Cook and Flinders, there have been numerous expeditions of survey and exploration. Even today, there are research teams constantly working within the Great Barrier Reef region. One of the most active organizations is the prestigious Australian Institute of Marine Science, based near Townsville. The James Cook University of North Queensland, and the Great Barrier Reef Marine Park Authority, both also based in Townsville, also carry out considerable research and record-keeping activities in this area. The Royal Australian Navy is conducting an on-going survey of the reef region to update charts and provide safer passage for all.

The pageant of early development of Australia is revealed by the remains of vessels to be found today in Great Barrier Reef waters. Wreck sites represent a priceless irreplaceable heritage. About 1,200 shipwrecks before 1900 are on record, starting from Cooks' *Endeavour* objects. Since 1900 the number of ships being wrecked has diminished, but the *Yongala,* which was wrecked off Townsville in 1911, is of significant importance and is a marvelous modern dive site. All wrecks and relics within state marine parks are protected, and several important wrecks are "declared wrecks" and have protective zones around them.

Corals and Plant Life

Coral reefs are mainly composed of limestone overlaid with a living surface. Coral reefs are named after the tiny polyps which produce a skeleton of limestone, and then divide to form new polyps, thus creating what are known as coral colonies. Coral colonies grow upwards towards the light and provide a framework for all sorts of other reef life. Reefs are destroyed by heavy seas, chemicals, and creatures of the reef. If the rate of accumulation of the dead skeletons exceeds the rate of erosion, then a reef is slowly formed.

The coral polyp has a simple structure; a soft cylinder of tissue, closed at the bottom, with a mouth at the top. Inside is a stomach cavity, and there is an external skeleton underneath. Polyps in a colony are connected with extensions of their tissues, so that if one catches food the whole colony benefits. They feed by extending their mouth tentacles to catch microscopic floating animals from the waters around them and by taking nutrients from the water that passes through them.

Algae are important in the reef-building process. An encrusting coralline algae helps to cement together the coral skeletons. It also forms a hard covering on reef crests. The other vital ingredient is the tiny single-cell plants called zooxanthellae, which live in the polyps. These harness energy from sunlight, and in doing so they use carbon dioxide produced by the coral. In return they pass some materials back to the coral, enhancing the growing rate. This symbiosis is what creates supercorals from small colonies. The zooxanthellae are most efficient at depths between 10 and 20 meters. They cannot work at depths where there is insufficient light, and they have a problem of too much ultraviolet light in shallow depths. Like humans, they use a UV sunscreen to help guard against sunburn.

Coral colonies occur in a great variety of shapes and sizes. The general appearance of the colony depends on the way individual polyps build their skeletons and how they bud off new polyps. Wave action, currents, and the exposure of the colony at high tide also have an effect. Many polyps reproduce sexually by releasing a bundle of eggs and sperm into the seawater on one or two nights each year. This can be accurately predicted, and it is an amazing sight to see. In corals which grow in sheets, new polyps are added around the edge of the colony. In dome-shaped colonies, new polyps are added within the surface of the dome, and there are annual growth layers, rather like the rings of a tree. This helps scientists gather climatic information from the past.

Seaweeds and algaes are conspicuous on some reefs. Large fleshy brown seaweeds can be seen on fringing reefs in summer, green grape seaweed on reef crests and flats, coralline green algae in deeper lagoons and reef slopes, and the important nondescript grey-green turf algae covering dead coral. Closer to the mainland, pastures of seagrass cover mudflats on sheltered inner shelf reefs, and these are foraged by turtles, dugong, and many fish.

The Reef Animals

It is said that the Great Barrier Reef has more species of fish than any other sea habitat, but that is only the start of the marine life in this amazing environment. Corals themselves belong to a large group of animals called the Coelenterata. Others in this group are jellyfish, sea anemones, sea fans, and hydroids. Another group of animals are the Crustacea. These are probably one of the most important groups in the world, and on the reef they are represented by prawns, shrimp, crabs, crayfish, and barnacles. Many plankton are also in this group. Copepods are the most common planktonic animals, and these are probably the most numerous and valuable marine food in the oceans.

Coral reef shells belong to the group called the Mollusca, which is the second largest animal group in the world. They come in many shapes, colors, and sizes, and include sea snails, sea slugs, squid, cuttlefish, and the lovely cowries. Starfish are common, but they are not molluscs. They belong to the Echinoderm family in common with sea urchins and sea cucumbers. Another common animal is the sponge. They are often confused with plants as their simple bodies can take on a huge variety of shapes and are like individual cells living in a colony rather than a single animal made of many different types of cells.

To many people, the reef fish are the most interesting of all reef inhabitants. Scientists have recorded over 1,500 types of fish on the Great Barrier Reef, and there can be several hundred on a single reef. Many of the smaller fish have striking colors and shapes, and some can change color to match their surroundings when threatened. In places their numbers can be almost overwhelming. Other fish have intimate relationships with larger creatures. Some small wrasse fish are cleaners, taking parasites from larger fish; even eels and huge manta rays visit these "cleaning stations" for service. Certain intrepid species live within the poisonous tentacles of the giant anemone in complete safety.

In some places, fish seem completely without fear and can be hand fed by divers and others. When that fish is a three-meter-long grouper weighing 350 kilograms (900 pounds), hand feeding can be a mind-blowing experience. Some fish species are plant eating, others scavenge, some bite coral and seaweed off dead corals, some feed on small invertebrates, while some are predatory. The inexperienced must be cautious about what they eat from the reef as some fish and crabs can be poisonous to humans. Ciguatera, or fish poisoning is a problem at certain times with a variety of common fish.

Three sea turtles are common in reef waters. The green turtles were once killed for food, and there were even turtle processing plants on some of the islands. Now sea turtles are protected within the Great Barrier Reef Marine Park except that Aborigines and Torres Strait Islanders may legally take them as a traditional food. Large loggerhead turtles and smaller hawksbill turtles are also common, while some rare and endangered turtles, such as the huge leathery turtle are sometimes seen in the reef area. All sea turtles must return to land to lay their eggs. Turtles nest on many sandy Great Barrier Reef islands and at a few spots along the mainland coast. On moonlight nights the large females lumber ashore and lay up to 100 eggs at a time in a shallow trench above the high tide mark. The eggs hatch 6 to 12 weeks later.

The other interesting reef creature is the dugong. These mammals, which are sometimes called sea cows, have whale-like bodies up to three meters long, and they graze on seagrass in shallow tropical waters.

The reef also has its collection of "nasties." About 15 types of sea snake occur in Great Barrier Reef waters. They are all excellent swimmers, and all have very lethal venom, but they have small fangs and are not usually aggressive. Fortunately, there have been no reports of deaths from sea snakes in the Great Barrier Reef waters. Sharks are fairly common but, fortunately, most reef species are not dangerous if left alone. Large tiger sharks and hammerheads are not common, but if encountered by divers, these should be treated very warily. It is wise to avoid swimming at dusk or when there is any blood in the water.

Many bony fish have spikes, and minor injuries are common among fishing people. Reef walkers should be wary of the well-camouflaged stonefish which has strong, sharp dorsal spines and a potent venom. They cause intense pain if stood on and can cause death. You should also never pick up a spectacular cone shell as these have a potent venom that has caused some deaths in reef waters. The crown of thorns starfish and some sea urchins can inflict a painful wound with their sharp spines, so stay well away from them.

All swimmers must be aware of the deadly box jellyfish that inhabits coastal waters from November to April. This is the most venomous marine animal known, and it has caused scores of deaths over the years. The risks are minimized by swimming in stinger-resistant netted enclosures that are found on many beaches along the coast. Fortunately, the stingers generally do not extend as far offshore as the main Great Barrier Reef.

Sea birds are another piece of the jigsaw. Cays provide an ideal home for several varieties of birds. The reef seas abound in food and the islands provide relatively safe nesting grounds. Terns are probably the most numerous of the seabirds. On some cays they are found in their thousands. Reef herons are also common, and you can see them at low tide stalking their prey on the reef flats. Gulls, shearwaters (mutton birds), and gannets are other seabirds that inhabit some cays, while some of the vegetated islands have colonies of land birds that depend on the forest rather than the sea for survival.

Managing the Great Barrier Reef

The reef region was declared a marine park in 1975. It is administered by the Great Barrier Reef Marine Park Authority (GBRMPA), P.O. Box 1379,

Townsville, Queensland 4810, Australia. The day-to-day management of the park is undertaken by the Queensland Department of Environment and Heritage through the National Parks and Wildlife Service. The concept of the marine park is based upon a balance between the conservation of the reef and its prolific animal and plant life, and reasonable use by fishermen, collectors, charter operators, tourists, scientists, and others. The GBRMPA has, with the help of the public, developed zoning plans for the whole of the reef region. These plans define the range of activities which may take place within each zone.

The Great Barrier Reef was inscribed on the World Heritage list in 1981. The International Convention for the Protection of World Culture and Natural Heritage, was adopted by UNESCO in 1972. The purpose of the convention is to ensure international co-operation for the protection and care of the world's irreplaceable heritage. The items that are protected by the convention are those that are of outstanding universal value from the point of view of history, art, science, or aesthetics. At present there are some 200 places recognized as World Heritage sites. The reef region is almost unique in that it has two heritage listings; the Great Barrier Reef and the Wet Tropics rain forest region.

In the nomination of the Great Barrier Reef for inclusion on the World Heritage list, the Australian government said:

> The Great Barrier Reef is by far the largest single collection of coral reefs in the world. Biologically the Great Barrier Reef supports the most diverse ecosystem known to man. Its enormous diversity is thought to reflect the maturity of an ecosystem which has evolved over millions of years on the northeast continental shelf of Australia.
>
> The Great Barrier Reef provides some of the most spectacular scenery on earth and is of exceptional natural beauty. The Great Barrier Reef provides major feeding grounds for large populations of the endangered species dugong dugon and contains nesting grounds of world significance for the endangered turtle species green turtle and loggerhead turtle.
>
> The area nominated also meets the condition of integrity in that it includes the area of the sea adjacent to the Reef. The areas of this nomination contain many middens and other archaeological sites of Aboriginal and Torres Strait Islander origin. There are over 30 historic shipwrecks in the area, and on the islands, many of which are Queensland national parks, there are ruins and operating lighthouses which are of cultural and historical significance.

Regulations provide the means for implementing the provisions of the zoning plans. A concerted effort in the areas of education, planning, and research and monitoring is the principal means of achieving effective management of the reef. A significant milestone in 1992 was the development of a 25-year strategic plan for the area. This plan has established directions for the reef's reasonable use and conservation into the 21st century. The ultimate responsibility, of course, lies with those who use the reef, to ensure the conservation of this important part of our world heritage, now and in the future. Please bear this in mind when you visit the reef.

Seeing the Reef

Tourism is the largest commercial activity on the reef in terms of both money and people. Over a million people visit the reef each year, and the numbers are growing. There are few resorts actually on the Great Barrier Reef, but there are around 25 on islands within the reef region. Resort guests and day visitors to the region make use of reefs and waters for recreational activities including fishing, diving, snorkeling, water sports, sightseeing, reef walking, and some collecting.

The best introduction to this region for first-time reef visitors is the marvelous Great Barrier Reef Aquarium run by the Great Barrier Reef Marine Park Authority at Reef Wonderland in Townsville. The aquarium houses several hundred varieties of reef fish and more than 1,000 coral colonies made up of around 150 hard and soft coral species. The aquarium operates as a completely closed system. Tank water is recycled, and water purification takes place using the nutrient-absorbing behavior of marine algae. The community of the reef exhibit is as self-maintaining as the natural environment on the reef. All the inhabitants find their own food, and no artificial food is added. So successful has been this world's first "reef on land," that many animals including the corals, have reproduced just as they would on the reef. Through extensive displays, visitors of all ages can learn about the reef. Hands-on activities, talks, computer displays, and videos stimulate a good understanding of the reef. A multi-screen audiovisual program in the theaterette gives a good introduction to coral reef ecology. You will probably learn more on a visit here than on several visits to the reef itself.

Day trips on fast catamarans are available to various reefs and cost around A\$90-A\$120. Most include lunch, coral viewing from glass-bottom boats or semi-submersible vessels, swimming, and snorkeling. Some offer scuba diving at additional expense. Trips operate from many centers along the coast from Bundaberg to Port Douglas and from many of the islands. The largest boats carry up to 400 passengers and have excellent facilities, but some visitors prefer to travel to the reef in smaller groups. There are some opportunities to take helicopters or seaplanes to reef locations, and some islands have an airstrip. Extended cruises to the reef and islands are available from Mackay, Townsville, and Cairns.

Staying on the Reef

There are only three alternatives at present if you want to stay at a resort on a Great Barrier Reef coral cay. Lady Elliot Island and Heron Island are both in the Southern Reef region, and Green Island is in the Northern Reef region. Accommodation on Green Island is very up-market, Heron is mid-market, and Lady Elliot is lower mid-market. For further details of these resorts see the individual reef section chapters.

A number of other islands have accommodations facilities. These islands are continental-type islands, and some are quite a long way from the reef. Some, however, such as Lizard, Fitzroy, Dunk, and Orpheus have good reef reasonably close by. The majority of island resorts are located in the Central Reef region.

Camping is permitted on many islands, and some have good facilities such as running water, flush toilets, shops and supplies. Many, however, have minimal facilities, and others have virtually nothing at all. All national parks require a permit to camp. These are obtainable from the Queensland Department of Environment and Heritage offices along the coast. Some permits must be applied for at least six weeks before you want to camp, but if this is not possible it is still worthwhile calling into a local office when you are in the area to see if there is any space at one of the camp sites. Some of the major offices are:

Cairns—P.O. Box 2066, Cairns, Qld 4870 (Tel: 070-523096)
Gladstone—P.O. Box 315, Gladstone 4680 (Tel: 079-726055)
Rockhampton—P.O. Box 1395, Rockhampton 4700 (Tel: 079-276511)
Townsville—Great Barrier Reef Wonderland (Tel: 077-212399)
Whitsunday—Shute Harbour Rd., Airlie Beach (Tel: 079-467022)

Diving the Reef

The Great Barrier Reef is such a vast undersea paradise that you could dive it every day for the rest of your life and still not see it all. The warm sub-tropical and tropical climate is perfect, and local divers say the warm water at times can be as clear as air.

Graeme Kelleher, chairman of the Great Barrier Reef Marine Park Authority, says:

> The Great Barrier Reef is one of the last places on earth where people

can observe pristine nature. Here, a SCUBA diver experiences one of the world's most complex ecosystems as it was when Captain Cook first visited these shores more than 225 years ago.

Have you ever wondered what it would be like to dive over the edge of the Ribbon Reefs and look down into the black depths where the sharks cruise across the face of the continental shelf? Would you like to see some of the 1500 species of fish competing for life among the 400 species of coral? What does a crown-of-thorns starfish look like and how does it eat its coral prey?

Dive the Great Barrier Reef and find out for yourself. And remember—this is your Reef and your children's. Leave it in the same beautiful condition as you find it. Together, we can make sure that this remains the best Reef in the world.

There's a comprehensive range of dive services, dive schools, dive operators, charter boats, and dive holidays from which to choose. The variety of diving options will surprise and delight you. While some of the best sites are accessed by charter boat, and are quite a distance off-shore, on some coral cays and islands you can literally walk off the beach and dive into a coral wonderland.

The reef offers some of the best wall diving in the world. The best sites are in the outer sections, where shear walls of coral disappear into the blue void of ocean to the seabed, hundreds and sometimes thousands of meters below. There are many great locations for drift diving. Some are well known, like Dynamite Pass in the north, while others are less known but equally spectacular, like the coral rivers of the Pompey Complex southeast of Mackay. In other places you can wreck dive. You can sift the sand for souvenirs in some wrecks, while others like the S.S. *Yongala,* are "look but don't touch" zones.

The dive can also be a great educational experience. Arrange to have a marine biologist or reef guide accompany your dive to explain the rich and complex life forms of the reef. There are research stations at several locations where you can see first-hand how scientists are unlocking the secrets of the reef.

From the mainland and several island resorts, there are many one-day trips to the reef. These are on fast, safe boats which give plenty of time for a good day's diving with lunch provided. For those with more time, there are extended cruises, particularly from Townsville and Cairns, on professionally equipped and purpose-built dive vessels. Generally the food and accommodation is good, and the crews have good knowledge of all the best dive sites.

You can dive virtually anywhere on the Great Barrier Reef at any time of the year, but you will generally enjoy the best weather from May through December. The Inner Reef has a maximum depth of about 40 meters, but many dives are shallower than this, so newly qualified divers will have no problems here. On the Outer Great Barrier Reef, you can see the coral disappearing into a void which in some areas can be 8,000 meters deep. Diving here, and night and wreck diving, however, requires a greater level of skill and confidence, and normally novice divers will be accompanied on these kinds of dives by a divemaster. Diving generally is conducted using the "buddy system." Dive buddies can be arranged by the dive operator.

Almost all operators offer full rental facilities, including underwater photographic equipment. Light-style wetsuits are usually worn. All operators require an internationally recognized certification from an organization such as BSAC, CMAS, FAUI, NAUI, NASDS, PADI, SSI, and so forth. You will also have to produce details of your recent dives.

The accident rate for Great Barrier Reef diving is one of the lowest in the world, due largely to the shallow warm clear waters, and the high standards required of all operators. You will be briefed by a dive instructor before you dive. It is recommended that you use the services of a member of the Queensland Dive Tourism Association.

If you have never dived before, many resorts and charter operators run basic-training courses that allow you to shallow-dive with a group to see a little of the reef. The courses last about two hours and cost A$40-A$60. Some resorts and many mainland centers provide facilities for full accreditation, which will take five to seven days and cost A$300-A$500.

5

Southeast Queensland —Brisbane, the Gold Coast, the Sunshine Coast

1. The General Picture

Southeast Queensland is probably the fastest growing region in Australia. It is dynamic, rapidly changing, confident, but still welcoming. For many international visitors, this region is their introduction to Queensland. It may not be typical of the whole state, but it is a worthy starting point. Look around and you will see much of the best and worst in Australian life, but at least at most times, you will be seeing it in bright sunshine and sharing it with some of the friendliest Australians around.

Brisbane is the capital of Queensland and the state's largest city. Ten years ago it was called a large country town, but that image is now gone. What has emerged is a modern city that enjoys its place in the sun and is learning how to use that asset to its own advantage. The compact city center has shining glass towers standing side by side with historic sandstone churches and white heritage colonial buildings. There are good shopping, sightseeing, and entertainment possibilities. The south bank of the Brisbane River has become a visitor mecca with its parklands, attractions, restaurants, cultural facilities, and entertainment complexes. The old inner suburbs provide opportunities to see the picturesque Queenslander stilt houses with their broad verandahs, intricate fretwork, and iron roofs. Farther out, fauna reserves and theme parks let visitors experience Australian wildlife at close quarters.

The Gold Coast is a major tourist center 100 kilometers to the south. This has long been a favorite vacation spot for Australians. The region's 50-kilometer coastline from South Stradbroke Island to Coolangatta has white sand surf beaches, hundreds of accommodations options, water sports by the score, and vacation attractions in the style of Miami or Honolulu. There are world-class theme parks, international-style resorts, golf courses, marinas, canal estates, shopping and entertainment complexes, and a 24-hour casino. Surfers Paradise, with its towering highrises, is the city's hub. Just 30 minutes away, the terrain climbs to the breathtaking scenery of the Lamington National Park, Tamborine, and Springbrook. Here you can enjoy spectacular views, bush walks, and lush sub-tropical forest.

The Sunshine Coast is north of Brisbane. It has great beaches, spectacular mountains, lakes, Australian bush, villages full of craft shops and galleries, nice restaurants, rain forest, the Everglades, and birdlife. So far it has avoided an overabundance of highrise and many of the law and order problems of big cities. In places like Noosa Heads on the coast or Montville in the hinterland, it is almost perfect. Unfortunately, there are also miles of uninspiring residential subdivisions, patches of bland commercial development, and little realization that some of the best assets of the region may have already been lost. There is something for everyone on the Sunshine Coast, but it seems at present to lack a major feature which will draw and keep more international visitors in the region. For many, it is an area to see briefly on the way to further destinations up north.

There are hundreds of islands off this southeast coastline, but they are far south of the Great Barrier Reef and have no connection with it. Many are tiny and uninhabited, but there are also some that have accommodations, historical relics, and even towns. Many are national parks. South Stradbroke Island has some accommodations and restaurants. North Stradbroke Island, Moreton Island, Bribie Island, and Fraser Island all have significant tourist development. These, together with St. Helena Island, South Stradbroke Island, and Peel Island, are suitable day-trip destinations, and there are some people who will wish to stay much longer.

A note on telephone numbers. Australia is in the process of consolidating its area codes into just a few zones, and in the process it is changing to eight digit numbers. All of Queensland will ultimately be in the 07 area code zone. Brisbane and the Gold Coast are in this zone now and have new telephone numbers which are shown in this book. The Sunshine Coast has not yet changed, so telephone numbers here are presently six digits and the present area code is 074.

2. Getting There

Brisbane International Airport is one of the best in Australia. There are an increasing number of international services arriving here from around the world, and non-stop services link it with every other Australian capital city except Perth and Hobart. **Qantas,** the largest Australian international airline, has international flights from New Zealand, Singapore, and Japan direct to Brisbane. Many other international carriers also have services from many different overseas cities. Taxi, bus and limousine transfers are available from the airport to the central city. **Sunbus** (Tel: 5591-7422) has a 24-hour service from Brisbane Airport to the Gold Coast. **Sunair** (Tel: 074-782811) has 13 daily services from Brisbane Airport to the Sunshine Coast.

Coolangatta Airport, which serves the Gold Coast, is a major airport for domestic traffic. **Qantas** has several daily direct flights from Sydney, Melbourne, and Brisbane. There are taxi and bus transfers from the airport to all parts of the city. Maroochydore Airport serves the Sunshine Coast. This is smaller and has fewer services but **Qantas** or **Sunstate** have daily services from Brisbane and Sydney, and there are a few direct services from Melbourne.

Brisbane has **rail** and **long-distance bus services** from the southern areas of Australia, and there are services from here to Central and North Queensland for those wishing to see some of the mainland before visiting the reef. The **Roma Street Transit Centre** is the hub for the rail and long-distance coach transport system, including the **SkyTrans** airport transfer service.

Many Australians arrive into the region by **car,** and there are a growing number of international visitors doing the same. The international names in car rental have offices in Queensland, and there are a number of local operators as well. A further option is to rent a self-contained motor home.

3. Local Transportation

There are **taxis** available from several companies throughout this region and these are often the preferred option for short trips. Most local trips around Brisbane will cost less than A$25. Tipping is not expected, so please do not start the practice. Be careful with longer trips on the Gold and Sunshine Coasts because distances can be deceiving, and costs can quickly rise.

Brisbane has a good public transport system of electric trains, buses, and some ferries. **Citybus** operates regular all-stop services from the city to the suburbs, while **Cityxpress** operates a faster service from designated stops. (Contact **B.C.C. Transport,** Tel: 3225-4444 for information.) **Queensland Rail** (Tel: 3235-1877) operates the electric **Citytrain** services. Roverlink tickets allow you to change between most bus and rail services. Red-colored **City Circle 333** buses operate every five minutes during busi-

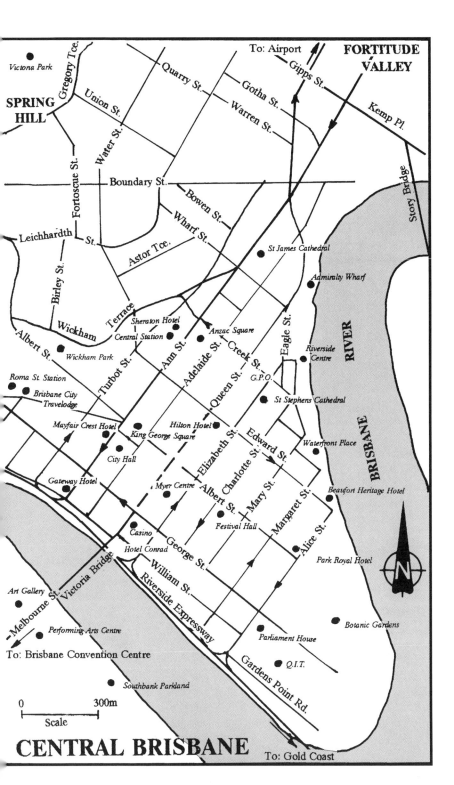

CENTRAL BRISBANE

ness hours from Monday to Friday, on a circular route around the city center for a flat fare of around 80 cents.

The Gold Coast's public transport, **Surfside Buslines** (Tel: 5536-7666), operates 24 hours, connecting most coastal suburbs with the main attractions. Rover tickets are available for one or more days. **Citybus** (Tel: 5532-6211) operates in the area between Broadbeach, Nerang, and Movie World. **Pedicabs** offer leisurely transport around central Surfers Paradise.

Sunshine Coast Coaches (Tel: 074-434555) has services seven days a week in the Landsborough, Caloundra, Maroochydore, Nambour area, and there is an Explorer pass that allows you to stop off at various attractions.

Brisbane City central business district, central Surfers Paradise, and Noosa Heads are all ideal for exploring on foot. Traveling between these centers can be done by train, bus, rental motorbike, or rental car. Some of the rental car operators are:

Brisbane

> **Avis**—Creek and Elizabeth Streets (Tel: 3221-2900)
> **Brisbane City**—47 Amelia Street (Tel: 3257-1844)
> **Budget**—21 Sandgate Road, Breakfast Creek (Tel: 3252-0151)
> **Hertz**—55 Charlotte Street (Tel: 3221-6166)
> **Low Price**—330 Vulture St., Woolloongabba (Tel: 3891-1799)
> **Network**—398 St. Pauls Tce., Fortitude Valley (Tel: 3252-1599)
> **Thrifty**—325 Wickham St., Fortitude Valley (Tel: 3252-5994)

Gold Coast

> **Avis**—Ferny & Cypress Aves., Surfers Paradise (Tel: 5539-9388)
> **Budget**—Ferny & Norfolk Aves., Surfers Paradise (Tel: 5538-1344)
> **C.Y.**—9 Tickett St., Surfers Paradise (Tel: 5570-3777)
> **Green Bicycle Rental**—(Bikes, free delivery) (Tel: 018-766880)
> **Hertz**—Surfers Paradise (Tel: 5538-5366)
> **Network**—Gold Coast Hwy & Palm Ave., Surfers Paradise (Tel: 5538-2344)
> **Red Back Rentals**—Beach Rd., Surfers Paradise (Tel: 5592-1655)

Sunshine Coast

> **Avis**—Ocean St. and Beach Rd., Maroochydore (Tel: 43-5055)
> **Budget**—Hastings Street, Noosa Heads (Tel: 47-4588)
> **Can Do**—Caloundra (Tel: 91-8788)
> — Noosa Heads (Tel: 47-2449)
> **Thrifty**—Maroochydore (Tel: 43-1733)
> — Noosa (Tel: 47-2299)

4. The Accommodations Scene

In this section I will only cover accommodations in the central areas of Brisbane, the Gold Coast, and the Sunshine Coast. Other areas of the Gold Coast and the Sunshine Coast, areas between the major centers, and island accommodations are included in Section 6 of this chapter. The following is only a selection of what is available.

Brisbane

A broad range is available. There are international chain hotels, luxury and mid-range hotels, all-suite hotels, self- contained apartments, and a few budget hotels in the central city. In the inner suburbs you can find some mid-range hotels, a variety of motels, and backpacker hostels.

EXPENSIVE ACCOMMODATIONS

Hotels with room rack rates above A$175 are included in this category. Members of airline frequent flyer clubs and similar organizations, and those eligible for corporate rates, will pay less.

The **Conrad International Hotel** (Tel: 3306-8888) is the newest luxury hotel to open in the city. It is situated in a beautifully restored old Edwardian Baroque-style building right opposite the new Treasury Casino. The 97-room hotel offers a rare blend of modern convenience and "old-world" charm. Heritage pieces are featured in all of the guest rooms, so none are exactly alike. They all have the usual five-star features. Room rates are from A$250.

The old cabinet room, last used by the government in the mid-1970s, has been restored as a meeting and dining room for guests with views overlooking Queens Park. Ryans on the Park is a restaurant featuring contemporary Australian cuisine. It has a cocktail bar, and there is also the Gallery Bar nearby. (Book with the hotel at William Street, Brisbane or Fax: 617-3306-8880.)

Sheraton Brisbane Hotel & Towers (Tel: 3835-3535) is a stylish highrise property built over the Central Railway Station. The lobby is elegant, the rooms are spacious and comfortable, and the business and sports facilities are fine. The bars and restaurants, from Denisons with its rooftop fine dining to the comfortable Sidewalk Cafe, are some of the best in the city. The Sheraton Towers is a hotel within a hotel, providing a more exclusive world of excellence complete with personal butlers. Room rates start at A$300. (Book at 249 Turbot Street, Brisbane 4000 or Fax: 617-3835-4960.)

The **Hilton International** (Tel: 3231-3131) is situated above a large shopping complex in the center of the city. The reception area is up four levels via an elevator, but once you reach it you will be impressed. Around the tallest atrium in Australia, you will find check-in, a trio of glass-walled elevators, tropical plants and palms, and several restaurants and bars. The 321 rooms are well appointed, and there are three executive floors with their separate lounge and key-operated elevator. Sporting facilities include a pool, a gym, and tennis courts. Standard rooms are from A$250. (Book at 190 Elizabeth Street, Brisbane 4000 or Fax: 617-3231-3173.)

The **Heritage Hotel** (Tel: 3221-1999), 232 rooms and 20 suites, is on the banks of the Brisbane River next to the botanic gardens. It is operated by the Beaufort Group. The atmosphere is warm, welcoming, and gracious. The lobby is small but very smart, and a grand staircase leads to a delightful lounge and bar. Some of the features of the hotel are 24-hour butler service on every floor, 24-hour laundry/dry cleaning/pressing service, pool, gym, sauna, early arrival and late departure lounge, individual facsimile numbers for each room, and TV in the bathrooms. Siggi's, the Heritage's premier restaurant, is housed in Brisbane's original post office. Room rates are from around A$250. (Book at Edward & Margaret Streets, Brisbane 4000 or Fax: 617-3221-6895.)

The **Brisbane Parkroyal** (Tel: 3221-3411) was showing its age when I last stayed there, but it has just received a multi-million dollar facelift, and I am told it has resurfaced looking just great. The location, overlooking the botanic gardens, is quiet and green, and it is within walking distance of most central business district locations. There is a respected restaurant, a cozy cocktail bar, a pool, and a sauna. Room rates are from A$200. (Book at Alice and Albert Streets, Brisbane 4000 or Fax: 617-3229-9817.)

MEDIUM-PRICE ACCOMMODATIONS

The **Carlton Crest** (Tel: 3229-9111) is a fine hotel overlooking King George Square near City Hall. There are three restaurants, five bars, and all the other facilities you would expect from a large central city hotel. There are two distinct standards of accommodations with the classically furnished Carlton Tower being the most up-market. Rooms in the newer section are generally larger, but views are probably better in the older wing. There are two pools, a gym, and a sauna. Room rates are from around A$160. (Book at Anne & Roma Streets, Brisbane 4000 or Fax: 617-3229-9618.)

The **Brisbane City Travelodge** (Tel: 3238-2222), 191 rooms, is built over the railway tracks adjacent to the Brisbane Transit Centre. The modern hotel offers good value for money, is very popular, and is always heavily booked. The rooms are comfortable and well appointed with all the usual features, but there are no particular attractions that make the hotel outstanding. The restaurants and bars are popular with Brisbane residents and hotel guests. The Jazz-N-Blues Bar features live jazz. Room rates are from A$160. (Book at Roma Street, Brisbane 4000 or Fax: 617-3238-2288.)

The **Dockside Apartment Hotel** (Tel: 3891-6644) is an attractive property on the riverbank, with something of a waterfront village atmosphere. Each apartment has a lounge and dining area, one or two bedrooms, a bathroom, a washing machine and dryer, and a full kitchen. There is a pool and other leisure facilities. A downside for some is that car access to the city is not great, and it is too far to walk; however, there is a ferry service for guests. Room rates are from A$130. (Book at 44 Ferry Street, Kangaroo Point, Brisbane 4169 or Fax: 617-3891-6900.)

The friendly **Bellevue Hotel** (Tel: 3221-6044) has come into prominence because of its location opposite the new Brisbane Casino. The hotel has comfortable rooms and a distinct Queensland atmosphere. There is a pool, a spa, and the stylish Michener's Restaurant. Room rates are from A$105. (Book at 103 George Street, Brisbane 4000 or Fax: 617-3221-7474.)

Central Apartment Hotels (Tel: 1-800-077777) operate five hotels in the South Brisbane and Spring Hill districts—Hillcrest, Summit, Ridge, Centrepoint, and SDK. Room facilities and rates vary between properties, but many are around A$120. (Book at 28 Fortescue Street, Spring Hill, Brisbane.)

Annie's Shandon Inn (Tel: 3831-8684) is a quaint 19-room bed and breakfast place. Rooms with in-suites are from A$60.

BUDGET ACCOMMODATIONS

There are many backpackers' places in or on the edge of the central business district. Some of the more popular are: **Aussie Way Backpackers** (Tel: 3369-0711) at 34 Cricket Street, Petrie Terrace; the highly rated **Balmoral House** (Tel: 3252-1397) at 33 Amelia Street, Fortitude Valley; **Sly Fox Travellers Hotel** (Tel: 3844-0022) at 73 Melbourne Street; the **YHA Brisbane City Hostel** (Tel: 3236-1004) at 53 Quay Street, not far from the Transit Centre; and the **Roma Street Travellers Hostel** (Tel: 3236-2961) at 390 Roma Street. All have dorm facilities from around A$15 a night, and many have twin/double rooms.

Two alternatives to these for budget travelers are **Elizabeth Private Hotel** (Tel: 3358-1866), a clean old-fashioned place with a kitchen, laundry, and TV in all the rooms, and rates from A$32 single, A$35 double; and **Somewhere To Stay** (Tel: 3846-2858), a beautiful Queenslander building with swimming pool on the Southside at Brighton Road and Franklin Street, West End.

Central Gold Coast

There are around 25,000 guest rooms on the coast between South Stradbroke Island and the New South Wales border, so there is a wide choice of accommodations. The majority of the luxury hotels are in or near Surfers

Paradise, but other accommodations are widespread. In this section we only consider the Broadbeach-Main Beach section of the coast. Please appreciate that the Gold Coast is a vacation spot for many Australians, so there are some excellent package rates for stays of four or more days that can reduce the daily room rate by up to 50 percent. Check these out with your travel agent.

EXPENSIVE ACCOMMODATIONS

If we use the same cost criteria as was used for Brisbane, there are only two hotels in this category, but there are several that are just under our limit.

The **Sheraton Mirage Gold Coast Resort** (Tel: 5591-1488) is generally considered the top resort on the Gold Coast. It cost a fortune to build, and it shows. The architecture is stunning, the rooms large and very well equipped, the pool and beach outstanding, and the public areas, restaurants, and bars are world-standard. The beachfront location is a big plus, but some guests complain because it is a few kilometers away from central Surfers Paradise. (You can't please everyone!) Room rates are around A$400. (Book at Sea World Drive, Main Beach, Surfers Paradise 4217 or Fax: 617-5591-2299.)

The **Marriott Surfers Paradise Resort** (Tel: 5592-9800) is a highrise property a few blocks back from the beach. As some compensation for this location the hotel has a large saltwater lagoon complete with waterfall, coral, fish, and scuba diving facilities. There is also a swimming pool, tennis courts, a fitness center, bars, and restaurants. Room rates are around A$250. (Book at 158 Ferny Avenue, Surfers Paradise 4217 or Fax: 617-5592-9888.)

MEDIUM-PRICE ACCOMMODATIONS

There are hotels, resorts, and serviced apartments in this category.

The **ANA Hotel Surfers Paradise** (Tel: 5570-1260), 403 rooms, is situated in the heart of Surfers Paradise, a short stroll from the beach. Rooms and service are good, facilities include tennis courts, a gym, pool, and sauna; and there are several restaurants and bars. Rates are around A$165. (Book at 22 View Avenue, Surfers Paradise 4217 or Fax: 617-5570-1260.)

The **Surfers Paradise Travelodge** (Tel: 5592-9900) is about two kilometers to the south. This is one of the newer hotels, and it has been very successful despite its location, a little away from the action. The rooms, facilities, and service are all good, and there is a good mix of singles, couples, and families. The pool and revolving restaurant are great meeting places. Rates are from A$150 (Book at 2807 Gold Coast Highway, Surfers Paradise 4217 or Fax: 617-5592-1519.)

The **Hotel Conrad and Jupiters Casino** (Tel: 5592-1133) is the largest hotel in the country and, for gamblers, it is paradise. The hotel is on its own small river island, but it is connected to a major shopping center and the beach by monorail train, and to the Gold Coast Highway by a bridge. There are swimming pools, spas, a sauna, a gymnasium, restaurants, and bars, and the 24-hour casino. Rates are from A$165. (Book at Broadbeach Island, Broadbeach 4218 or Fax: 617-5592-8483.)

Ocean Blue Resort (Tel: 5579-4444) is for those looking for an active holiday with other guests. The resort claims it is where "the fun never sets." The low-rise property is down-market from the previous listings, but the rooms are OK, and there are heated pools, spas, a sauna, tennis courts, a games room, restaurants, and bars. Rates are from around A$125. The **Park Regis Islander Resort Hotel** (Tel: 5538-8000) is a further step down, but many will find that the rooms, location, and facilities are satisfactory. It has a pool, spa, sauna, squash court, tennis court, bar, and restaurant. Rates are around A$80. Both resorts are on Ferny Avenue, Surfers Paradise.

Club Surfers Motel (Tel: 5531-5244) at 2877 Gold Coast Highway is popular with those looking for reasonable accommodations and facilities, at a good price. The rooms with a kitchenette are a good size, and the club has a heated pool, spa, sauna, squash court, tennis court, and barbecue. It is two blocks from the beach and a bit over one kilometer from central Surfers Paradise. Rates are around A$65.

Standard motel rooms are available in scores of small places along the highway. Near Surfers Paradise they cost around A$55-A$60, but as you go farther north or south, the price comes down below A$55. Be careful of rates that say from A$45 a night. This is usually based on a five- or seven-day stay.

BUDGET ACCOMMODATIONS

Surfers Paradise is not renowned as a budget destination, but there are a few options. **Surfers Paradise Backpackers Resort** (Tel: 5538-7250) at 2835 Gold Coast Highway; **Surfers Central Backpackers** (Tel: 5538-4344) at 40 Whelan Street; and **Cheers Backpackers** (Tel: 5531-6539) at 8 Pine Avenue, are three options.

Noosa-Coolum

Noosa and Coolum are not the largest centers on the Sunshine Coast, but they are where you are likely to find most interstate and international visitors. Noosa Heads, which is a small costal section of the Noosa urban area, is the style center of the Sunshine Coast and the most interesting location for a short stop.

EXPENSIVE ACCOMMODATIONS

The **Sheraton Noosa Resort** (Tel: 49-4888), 169 rooms, is the largest hotel in Noosa Heads. It is located in the heart of the village, but not directly on the beach. All of the extra-large rooms have a kitchenette with microwave, spa bath, video player, and verandah. There are eight two-story fantasy suites. Dining options are the stylish Charthouse, the more casual Tea Tree Cafe, and the beachfront Beach Club. I have stayed here several times, and the property seems to get better each time. Room rates are from around A$250. (Book at Hastings Street, Noosa Heads 4567 or Fax: 6174-492230.)

On the Beach Suites (Tel: 47-3444), 20 units, is an up- market version of the most common type of accommodations in Noosa—vacation apartments. The self-contained, beachfront, one-bedroom luxury suites have aircondi-tioning, room service, and private spas on the open deck overlooking the beach. Daily rates are from A$175. (Book at 49 Hastings Street, Noosa Heads 4567 or Fax: 6174-472224.)

The **Hyatt Regency Coolum** (Tel: 46-1234) is 20 minutes from Noosa, but it tries to be part of the Noosa scene by providing a complimentary shuttle service. This is a delightful resort set on 150 hectares and having several kilometers of beach frontage. Facilities include a challenging 18-hole golf course, a tennis complex, health and spa facilities, and much more. The units, restaurants, and bars are scattered over a wide area, so you use the hotel transport or bicycles to get around the resort. Room rates are from A$220. (Book at P.O. Box 78, Coolum Beach 4573 or Fax: 6174-462957.)

MEDIUM-PRICE ACCOMMODATIONS

The choice is vast. These are a few suggestions.

Ocean Breeze Resort (Tel: 47-4977) has 64 one-, two-, and three-bed-room airconditioned apartments with kitchens, room service, and 24-hour video. There are swimming pool, wading pool, spa, sauna, half-court tennis, and billiard room facilities. Rates are from A$140 nightly. (Book at Hastings Street, Noosa Heads 4567 or Fax: 6174-472170.)

Maison La Plage (Tel: 47-4400) has an absolute beachfront location in the center of Hastings Street. The rooms have a kitchen, ceiling fan, and balcony. The complex has a heated pool, a spa, gardens, a barbecue, and a restaurant. The apartments mostly rent on a weekly basis, but if there is room you can stay overnight at around A$130. A similar comment can be made of the **Jacaranda** (Tel: 47-4011), which is across the road at the end of Hastings Street. These more budget-priced apartments have motel-style units, and one-bedroom suites with kitchen. Facilities include a swimming pool, barbecue area, and laundry. Rates are from A$70.

Noosa International Resort (Tel: 47-4822), with 64 self-contained apart-ments, is set in tropical gardens on Noosa Hill. The rooms and facilities are very attractive, but it is a 15-minute walk to the beach. To compensate, there are two pools, three spas, two saunas, a games room, a bar, a restaurant, a tour desk, and a courtesy coach. Room rates are from A$115. (Book at Edgar Bennett Avenue, Noosa Heads 4567 or Fax: 6174-472025.) **Myuna Holiday Apartments** (Tel: 47-5588) are comfortable one-, two-, and three-bedroom units in the same general area. There are pool and barbecue facilities. Rates run from A$65. (Book at 19 Katharina Street, Noosa Heads 4567 or Fax: 6174-492747.)

BUDGET ACCOMMODATIONS

Noosa is not the place for heaps of budget accommodations, but there are some options. The **Koala Beach Resort** (Tel: 47-3355) at 44 Noosa Drive is one place. The **Noosa Backpackers Resort** (Tel: 49-8151) at 9 William Street, and the **Noosa Hostel** (Tel: 47-4739) at 26 Stevens Street, Sunshine Beach, are two places that specialize in budget accommodations for the young at heart. Beds are available for around A$15.

5. Dining and Restaurants

The southeast corner of Queensland has something like 2 million people, and perhaps the most dynamic tourism industry in Australia, so it is no surprise to find some excellent restaurants. Food tends to be light and fresh with much use of seafood and tropical fruit. Here are some of my personal favorite places to eat.

Brisbane

In the hotels, **Siggi's** (Tel: 3221-4555) at the Beaufort Heritage, is my recommendation. It is a formal fine dining restaurant in a beautifully restored 19th-century building. It is expensive (A$100 for two without wine), and only opens for dinner.

Michael's Riverside (Tel: 3832-5522) at 123 Eagle Street, has rightly won a heap of awards in recent years. The international menu is strong on seafood and game meat, and there is an excellent wine cellar. It opens for lunch weekdays, and dinner nightly except Sunday. Similar opening times apply to **Augustine's** (Tel: 3229-0014) at 40 George Street, which has an intimate setting in 19th-century grandeur. Both are in the upper-medium price category.

Faces Restaurant (Tel: 3368-2413) at 267 Given Terrace, Paddington, could not be considered grand as it is contained within an old shop-house. What it has, though, is a cozy atmosphere with indoor or covered courtyard dining warmed by an open fireplace, friendly attendants, and modern innovative cuisine. Prices are in the medium category. It opens for lunch Thursday to Sunday, and dinner nightly. A totally different ambience is presented at **Pier Nine** (Tel: 3229-2194) at the Eagle Street Pier. You enjoy stunning views of Brisbane while sampling some of the best seafood around.

Great seafood can also be found at the **Breakfast Creek Wharf** (Tel: 3252-2451) in Newstead. You can eat inside aboard the *John Oxley*, or outside on the deck overlooking the water. For seafood with an Asian flavor, head to the **Emperor's Palace** (Tel: 3252-3368) in Chinatown Mall, Fortitude Valley. The cooking is Cantonese or Szechuan-style. For Chinese food in an old Chinese marketplace atmosphere, visit nearby **Wang Dynasty Inn** (Tel: 3854-1700) at 302 Wickham Street, Fortitude Valley. The **Thai Orchard Restaurant** (Tel: 3808-2853) out on the Pacific Highway, Springwood, probably has the best Thai food in town.

For well-priced pizzas, pastas, and steaks try **Fiasco's** (Tel: 3236-3855) at North Quay and Turbot Streets. Similar fare is available in a casual atmosphere at **Mediterraneo Cafe** (Tel: 3368-1933) at 25 Caxton Street, Petrie Terrace. Also in this area is the attractive **Terrace House** (Tel: 3368-3824) which has good food and atmosphere at reasonable prices. Aussie-style food is served at **Ned Kelly's Bush Tucker Restaurant** (Tel: 3846-1880) in the South Bank Parklands. Two other garden restaurants are recommended. The **City Gardens Cafe** (Tel: 3229-1554) in the City Botanic Gardens is a delightful setting for breakfast or lunch. There is live entertainment, face painting, and children's games each weekend. The **Mt. Coot-tha Summit Restaurant** (Tel: 3369-9922) has emerged from what was originally a hilltop kiosk, thanks to some hard work and loving care. It is a top spot for lunch or dinner.

There are plenty of cheap eateries as well. The **Myer Centre** in the Queen Street Mall has a food hall providing all manner of fast food. For some good value lunches, look for the outdoor beer gardens or counter lunches at the pubs. You will often get a good meal for less than A$6. Try the **Breakfast Creek Hotel** (Tel: 3262-5988), a Brisbane landmark for 100 years, for great steaks; the **Caxton Hotel Char Grill** (Tel: 3369-5544) on Caxton Street, Petrie Terrace; or the **Victory Hotel** (Tel: 3221-0444) at 127 Edward Street.

The food is somewhat secondary at these final two places. **Crazies Comedy Restaurant** (Tel: 3369-0555) at Caxton and Judge Streets, Petrie Terrace, gives you a three-course meal, character waiters, and two hours of comedy, music, and choreography. *Kookaburra Queen* (Tel: 3221-1300) is a paddlewheeler that cruises the Brisbane River from the Eagle Street Pier for lunch and dinner.

Central Gold Coast

Seafood restaurants are great on the Gold Coast. My favorites are **Omeros Brothers** (Tel: 5591-5425) at The Spit Marina Mirage; the nearby **Grumpy's Wharf** (Tel: 5532-2900) at Mariner's Cove, Main Beach; the **Rusty**

Pelican (Tel: 5570-3073) at Elkhorn and Orchid Avenues, Surfers Paradise; and **Oskar's On the Beach** (Tel: 5536-4621) away down south at Greenmount Beach, Coolangatta.

Chinese food lovers will enjoy the **Imperial Palace** (Tel: 5538-5944) at 3310 Gold Coast Highway, Surfers Paradise, for yum cha from 10 A.M. to 3 P.M., and dinner from 5 P.M. One of the better Japanese restaurants is the **Tenma** (Tel: 5592-3981) at 2677 Gold Coast Highway, Broadbeach, opposite the Hotel Conrad. Not far from here, the **Thana Thai** (Tel: 5570-1500) at Surf Parade and Victoria Avenue, Broadbeach, offers the chance to dine indoors or alfresco. **Montezuma's** (Tel: 5538-4748) at 8 Trickett Street, Surfers Paradise, is where the locals go for great Mexican fare in a fun atmosphere. **Daniel's Steakhouse** (Tel: 5570-1366) at Orchid and Elkhorn Avenues in the heart of Surfers Paradise has a great selection of steaks, seafood, chicken, and other meats together with a comprehensive wine list.

Surfers Paradise is famous for its offbeat restaurants. Some of these have good food while offering other attractions. All are fun. **The Crooked House Restaurant** (Tel: 5570-1766) at Markwell Avenue and Northbound Highway is one of the most prominent. It has heaps of Australian memorabilia, "bush food," and nightly entertainment. The **Stage Door Dinner Theatre** (Tel: 5538-3484) at 2681 Gold Coast Highway, Broadbeach, is a long-running place that still manages "to pack them in." **Draculas Cabaret Restaurant** (Tel: 5575-1000) at 1 Hooker Boulevard, Broadbeach, has seen almost 1,000,000 guests horrified, scared, humiliated, terrified, fed, and entertained by a weird assortment of staff.

Noosa, Sunshine Coast

Hastings Street, Noosa Heads, is the restaurant heart of the Sunshine Coast. Along this short length there are several fine dining restaurants, a choice of cafes and brasseries, and some take-out options. Prices tend to be on the high side, but generally the quality is good, and the ambience at several is great.

La Plage (Tel: 47-3308) is charming. This has the real touch of France with its *cuisine moderne* and Mediterranean decor. Nearby **Roser's** (Tel: 47-3880) has been serving fine seafood for more than 10 years, while **Lindoni's** (Tel: 47-5111) is an authentic *ristorante* serving fine Italian cuisine for lunch and dinner. Across the road from here, **La Sabbia** (Tel: 49-2328) is a laid-back, classy place for an alfresco lunch; **Chinois** (Tel: 49-2200) has Thai and Chinese cuisine in a nice upstairs setting; the **Charthouse** in the Sheraton Noosa Resort (Tel: 49-4784) serves great seafood and other dishes most evenings; and **Touche** (Tel: 47-2222) has an eclectic blend of modern cuisine (Australian and Thai are specialities) served among terraced gardens.

There are four nice casual beachfront restaurants in the center of Hastings Street. The **Beach Club** (Tel: 49-4794) is operated by the Sheraton Hotel; under the umbrellas at **Eduardo's** (Tel: 47-5875) has style; **Beach Cafe** (Tel: 47-2740); and **Dilizo's** (Tel: 47-2855) with its char grill, all offer good value dining. All are great for breakfast overlooking the sand, the sea, and the early morning beach activity. The same can be said of **Coco's** (Tel: 47-2440), which is on the waterfront at the Noosa National Park.

Other places worth trying on Hastings Street are **Zubanibar** (Tel: 47-3337) for some unusual flavors and presentations; **Jaspers** (Tel: 74-9600) has smooth jazz, good food, and leafy dining at the roundabout; while **Cafe Le Monde** (Tel: 49-2366) is a popular outdoor place to relax in at any hour.

6. Sightseeing

I will cover some of the sightseeing attractions geographically, starting in Brisbane City, then going south, and then north.

BRISBANE

This is the third largest city in Australia, and while it is not the most exciting city imaginable, there are plenty of things to do and see. From its early European settlement as a harsh penal colony, Brisbane has grown into a dynamic modern city. This development is recorded in some of the buildings. A few buildings, such as the Old Windmill in Wickham Terrace, have survived from the convict days. The grand government buildings in George Street, and the palatial City Hall on King George Square still play an active part in today's Brisbane, while two of the city's finest buildings—The Treasury, and Old Customs House—have taken on a new lease of life as a casino and museum respectively.

Heritage Trail booklets are available from the visitor information centers in the City Hall and the Queen Street Mall, so that you can discover the city's history at your own pace. Local Aboriginal history is recorded on bush trails, such as the one at Bellbird Grove in Brisbane Forest Park, and an art trail at Mt. Coot-tha.

There are several museums and galleries to see. The **Queensland Art Gallery** (Tel: 3840-7303) is at South Bank just across Victoria Bridge. There are Australian, Aboriginal, and European collections within this modern complex. Admission is free, and it is open from 10 A.M. to 5 P.M. daily. The **Queensland Museum** (Tel: 3840-7555) is within the same cultural center complex. This museum brings together fascinating collections and information on our natural world, together with Brisbane's and Queensland's

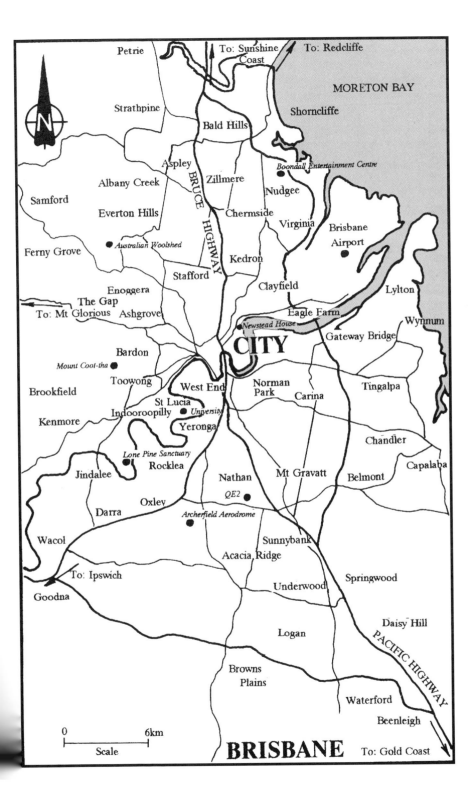

folk history. Admission is free, and it is open from 9 A.M. to 5 P.M. daily. The **Maritime Museum** (Tel: 3844-5361) is about a kilometer downriver in the South Bank Parklands area. It has a large collection of nautical memorabilia, a dry dock, and the World War II frigate HMAS *Diamantina.* The **Customs House** (Tel: 3365-8999) on the northern river bank at Queens Street, is now a gallery, bookstore, and brasserie operated by the University of Queensland.

The 16-hectare **South Bank Parklands** has become a major attraction, particularly on weekends when the locals flock here for entertainment. There are several visitor attractions, restaurants, a crafts village, a beach, entertainment, and relaxing parklands. **Gondwana Rainforest Sanctuary** has pythons, parrots, crocodiles, and koalas; then there is the butterfly and insect house; and you can take a leisurely cruise on a south ship ferry. These attractions are all included in a Parklands Discovery Ticket available on site.

Fortitude Valley is another place for exploration. This inner-city area, just two kilometers north of the central business district, is home to Brisbane's Chinatown, historic buildings, cosmopolitan outdoor cafes, art galleries, and multi-cultural restaurants. There is a market in Brunswick Street Mall every Saturday, jazz on Sunday afternoon, and a Chinese cultural show each Sunday at 11 A.M. The area has become the "hub" of contemporary art, artists, galleries, and studios, and you can visit **Bacon Galleries** (Tel: 3358-3555), **McWhirters Art Space,** and others.

Brisbane has two botanic gardens. The **City Gardens** were established in the 1820s and now have huge Moreton Bay fig trees, palms, a rain forest area, a riverside walk, and a mangrove boardwalk. The **Mt. Coot-tha Gardens,** about six kilometers from downtown, have themed sections including scented gardens, an arid climate zone, and rain forest walks with waterfalls and lush palms. A geodesic dome houses a rich variety of tropical plants, while the Sir Thomas Brisbane Planetarium treats visitors to all the wonders of the sky. While here, take the time to drive through Mt. Coot-tha Park to the lookout.

Elsewhere in the city, **Newstead House** (Tel: 3252-7373) in Breakfast Creek Road, Newstead, is the city's premier historic house occupying a commanding position overlooking the river about four kilometers from downtown. The **Australian Woolshed** (Tel: 3351-5366) at 148 Samford Road, Ferny Hills, has sheep shearing, sheep dog demonstrations, and native animals. There is a restaurant, craft shop, and drovers' camp. **Lone Pine Koala Sanctuary** (Tel: 3378-1366) at Fig Tree Pocket, is 11 kilometers west of the central city. This is the oldest and largest koala sanctuary in the world with more than 50 types of native marsupials, birds, mammals, and reptiles. **Earlystreet Village** (Tel: 3398-6866) at 75 McIlwraith Avenue, Norman Park, has a collection of Queensland's architectural and cultural heritage set in hectares of colonial gardens. There are historic buildings, a restaurant, a shop, and farm implements.

HEADING SOUTH

The major road south is the Pacific Highway through Beenleigh to the Gold Coast. This high-speed route encourages motorists to concentrate on their destination, but there are many interesting things to do on the way.

Cleveland, on the edge of Moreton Bay is one of the first diversions to consider, particularly if you are traveling on a Sunday when all the attractions are open. This was once planned as the site for Brisbane, and it still boasts some of Brisbane's finest heritage buildings. See Ormiston House, the Old Lighthouse, and Queensland's first licensed pub, the Grand View. It is a good spot to explore, picnic, dine at places like the Court House Restaurant in its 1853 setting, or shop at the weekend craft markets. There are water taxis and ferries from here to North Stradbroke Island.

Back on the highway, it is worth making a stop at **Beenleigh** to see the old rum distillery. The distillery began as an illicit operation aboard the S.S. *Walrus* back in the 1860s. The bosun found an extra use for the excess steam his small vessel generated when he installed a moonshine still. For years he cruised up the Albert River, eluding the authorities and keeping the locals supplied with the fine dark rum. When the boat became unseaworthy in 1884, the Beenleigh Rum Distillery was born with the purchase of the copper pot from the *Walrus*. Today the distillery relies on a range of modern equipment, but you can still see the original copper pot and the 100-year-old barrels used to age the rum. Tours operate each day at 11 A.M. and noon.

It is not far along the highway to **Dreamworld** (Tel: 5573-1133), the first of the major theme parks. Dreamworld appeals to all ages by providing ten themed areas, some wild rides, Australian animals, a wonderful tiger display, and family entertainment. You can step back in time to a 19th-century mining town, have your photograph taken cuddling a koala, or enjoy the six-story-high Imex Theater. Dreamworld is open every day, with adult admission around A$30.

A few kilometers farther brings you to **Warner Bros. Movie World** (Tel: 5573-3999). This brings all the fun and excitement of the movies to life with the glamour, thrills, and special effects for which Hollywood is famous. (But why in Australia?) You can start by joining Bugs Bunny and friends for a buffet breakfast then spend the rest of the day with American favorites such as Batman, Superman, and Police Academy. Movie World is open every day except Christmas Day, with adult admission around A$32.

A road off the highway to the left leads to **Sanctuary Cove,** one of Queensland's most well-known resort/residential developments. There are several reasons for visiting here. First, there are two fine golf courses, one for the public and one for members and resort guests. Second, there is the resort village, a collection of up-market shops, boutiques, and restaurants, the 400-berth marina with some of Australia's finest craft, and the boutique brewery with daily tours. Next, there is the lovely and very classy colonial-style **Hyatt Regency Sanctuary Cove Resort** (Tel: 5530-1234), which would be a great choice for those wanting some luxury in this delightful setting. (Book by Fax: 617-5577-8234.)

From here, there are roads through Runaway Bay, and Labradore to Southport and the main section of the Gold Coast.

GOLD COAST

The Queensland Gold Coast stretches 50 kilometers along the coast from South Stradbroke Island to Coolangatta. During the past few decades, the Gold Coast has changed from a popular surf haven for Australians to become an international resort city offering accommodations, a multitude of lifestyle activities, nightlife, restaurants, entertainment, and shopping to cater for all tastes. Many activities are built around the water—on more than 25 lifeguard-patrolled white sand surfing beaches, or the calm Southport Broadwater which leads to Moreton Bay, providing one of Australia's largest protected waterways.

The northern end of the coast has high-speed thrills at the **Le Mans Kart Racing Complex** (Tel: 5546-6566) at Pimpama, near Dreamworld; **Cable Ski World** (Tel: 5537-6300) and bungy jumping at Runaway Bay; and **Australia Fair,** the Gold Coast's second largest shopping center at Southport. The Broadwater offers all sorts of water sports options, and you can take a spin in a hovercraft, cruise around in a water taxi, or charter a houseboat for a vacation with a difference. Dinner cruises on the Broadwater are popular in the evening.

The Spit at Main Beach is home to **Sea World** (Tel: 5588-2222), the largest marine theme park in the Southern hemisphere. Its attractions include dolphin and sea lion shows, ski shows, an *Endeavour* replica, a monorail, and thrill rides. If you have been to Florida, you will have seen it all; otherwise you should visit. Just to the south, there are shopping villages at Fishermans Wharf, Marina Mirage, and Mariner's Cove, and **parasailing** (Tel: 5531-1091) and **bungy jumping** (Tel: 5531-1103) for the thrill seekers.

Surfers Paradise is the center of Gold Coast action. Downtown **Cavill Mall** often provides free entertainment by way of buskers, musicians, and magicians. There are attractions such as **Ripley's Believe It or Not** (Tel: 5592-0040), and fun centers such as **Funtasia. The Gold Coast City Art Gallery** (Tel: 5581-6154) at 135 Bundall Road, often has visiting exhibitions.

Broadbeach, a few kilometers to the south, offers much of the same but adds the huge **Pacific Fair** shopping center, and the 24-hour **Jupiters Casino. Carrara Markets** (Tel: 5579-9388) on the Nerang-Broadbeach Road operate every Sunday, and there is a Trash and Treasure every Saturday. **Cascade Park and Gardens**, on the Nerang River, is an historical area where you will find evidence of Aboriginal feasts and ceremonies held thousands of years ago.

Burleigh is the next major center to the south. There is a good beach, accommodations, and **Fleays Wildlife Park** (Tel: 5576-2411) where you can be introduced to Australian fauna and birdlife, amid a wetlands reserve. The center presents Aboriginal cultural talks, and offers restaurant and barbecue facilities. A little to the south at Currumbin, millions of visitors during the past 50 years have enjoyed the spectacle and experience of hand-feeding thousands of wild lorikeets. **Currumbin Santuary** (Tel: 5534-1266) continues this tradition twice daily, and also lets you come face to face with freshwater crocodiles, Tasmanian devils, koalas, wombats, dingoes, and snakes.

The twin towns of **Coolangatta** and **Tweed Heads** with their beaches and major sports and entertainment clubs are on the Queensland/New South Wales border. The **Greenmount Beach Resort** (Tel: 5536-1222), 150 rooms, is one of many accommodations options. While this area is considered to be quieter than the Surfers Paradise region, there are still good restaurant and entertainment opportunities.

Inland, there is a vast region of mountains, national parks, sub-tropical rain forest, and valleys. The area is home to thriving cottage industries, while historical charm has been preserved in some old buildings. Numerous nurseries, tea houses, craft shops, art galleries, and restaurants provide local fare as a respite from bushwalking and other activities. The **Lamington National Park** has 160 kilometers of graded walking trails. The mountain resorts of **O'Reilly's Guest House** (Tel: 5544-0644) and **Binna Burra Mountain Lodge** (Tel: 5533-3622) provide excellent accommodations, organized activities, and country-style hospitality. The area gives opportunities to try bushwalking, abseiling (descending a rock face), horse trail riding, and spotlighting of local fauna at night.

HEADING NORTH

Brisbane's northern suburbs crowd the Bruce Highway as it starts its long trip to North Queensland. The road initially winds through a mixture of new and old development with few outstanding landmarks. Off to the east are the bayside suburbs of **Sandgate, Shorncliffe,** and **Redcliffe.** Shorncliffe was once a ritzy resort, but now it's more into family picnics. The area has many elegant old Queenslander homes, and giant Moreton Bay fig trees line its streets. The focal point even today is the 1870s pier. Near here, you will find electric barbecues, picnic facilities, pony rides, and ice cream vendors. English-style Redcliffe has good seafood, water sports, fishing, and the closest sea beaches to Brisbane.

Alma Park Zoo (Tel: 3204-6566) at Kallangar, 28 kilometers north of Brisbane, is a sub-tropical zoo with a good collection of Australian and exotic animals. There are barbecues and picnic areas, a walk-through kangaroo enclosure, a friendship farm for the children, and a cafe. A few kilometers north, a road leads to **Caboolture** and its large historical village. Fruit orchards, pine plantations, and sub-tropical rain forest are common here, and just to the north are the impressive Captain Cook-named **Glasshouse Mountains.** The 13 peaks guard the southern approach to the Sunshine Coast. The national parks and state forests around here are popular for bushwalking, rock climbing, and picnicking. The Glasshouse Mountains Tourist Route leaves the Bruce Highway and travels by the small townships of Beerburrum, Glasshouse Mountains, and Beerwah to Landsborough. Near **Beerwah,** you can call at the **Queensland Reptile and Fauna Park** (Tel: 94-1134) with its daily demonstrations featuring an iguana, snakes, kangaroos, a tortoise, crocodiles, and wedge-tailed eagles.

This is the southern boundary of the Sunshine Coast region. To the right is Caloundra on the coast, to the left is Maleny and Montville on the Blackall Range.

THE SUNSHINE COAST

Here you can find something to appeal to everyone. There are great surf beaches, quiet inland waterways, picturesque mountain villages, national parks, some man-made attractions, and plenty of accommodations, restaurants, and nightlife.

Caloundra is a coastal city with great appeal to visitors who are looking for a relaxed getaway holiday. There are good accommodations options at resorts, motels, holiday apartments, guest houses, and caravan parks. The **Oasis Resort** (Tel: 91-0333) is a popular place with motel-style rooms and a pool, tennis, squash, a spa, volleyball, a games room, restaurants, and a bar. The **Gemini Resort** (Tel: 92-2200) is a highrise complex on the beach, with one- and two-bedroom self-catering units, a pool, tennis, a spa, a sauna, a games room, and a restaurant. **Raintrees** (Tel: 91-5555) is a delightful property at Moffat Beach, with 39 two- and three-bedroom self-contained holiday units set in rain forest and landscaped gardens, with two pools, a spa, and barbecues.

Caloundra has surf beaches stretching from King's Beach to Kawana Waters, but there are also calm water beaches at Golden Beach and Bulcock Beach for families. The still waters of Pumicestone Passage are a mecca for windsurfing, sailing, and fishing. The **Queensland Air Museum** (Tel:

92-5930) has a collection of 14 aircraft; the **Ben Bennett Botanical Park** is a natural bushland with walking trails; and modern **Corbould Park Horseracing Track** (Tel: 91-6788), with Saturday and public holiday racing, are all local attractions for those wanting a break from the water.

The next major center is **Maroochy,** which incorporates Mooloolaba, Alexandra Headland, and Maroochydore. You can surf, sail, ski, fish, play golf, tennis, scuba dive, or just sunbathe here. Mooloolaba is the site of the **UnderWater World/Wharf** (Tel: 44-8088) complex. This combines the largest tropical oceanarium in the Southern hemisphere, with shops, restaurants, and the chance to take a canal cruise, parasail, jet ski, or sail in a schooner. Close by are the beachfront highrise **Peninsula Apartments** (Tel: 44-4477) with self-contained one-, two-, or three-bedroom units, and a pool, saunas, a barbecue, tennis, restaurants, and shops.

Alexandra Headland is a renowned surfing beach, and there are great views both north and south. There are many self-contained holiday apartments here including **Tropicana** (Tel: 44-2888), **Alexandria** (Tel: 44-2700), and highrise **Mandolin** (Tel: 43-5011). All have pools, saunas, barbecues, and games rooms. You can also find motels and caravan parks.

Maroochydore is recognized as the business center of the Sunshine Coast, and there are major shopping centers here. Just to the north is the Maroochy River where there are parks, picnic facilities, and good fishing. Holiday apartments, motels, and holiday villages are easy to find here. The highrise **Chateau Royale Resort** (Tel: 43-0300) has up-market self-contained apartments; the **Heritage Motor Inn** (Tel: 43-7355) has ground-level motel rooms: the **Maroochy Palms Holiday Village** (Tel: 43-8611) has on-site accommodations and facilities for motor homes and camping: while the **YHA Maroochy Hostel** (Tel: 43-3151) at 24 Schirrman Drive has budget accommodations. Inland, the town of **Buderim** has some delightful gardens, restaurants, and the festival markets in the old ginger factory.

Another side of the Sunshine Coast experience is the numerous family attractions that are scattered around the region. None are world-class, but collectively they offer some interest. **Aussie World** (Tel: 94-5444) is on the Bruce Highway just north of the Caloundra turnoff. Its focal point is the weird Ettamogah Pub (an Australian legend), but there are also camel and pony rides, a reptile pavilion, a motorcycle museum, a luge ride, an opal house, a cafe, and shops. A few kilometers north, there is **Superbee** (Tel: 45-3544) where there are gardens, a bee show, children's rides, a restaurant, and barbecues; the **Bellingham Maze** (Tel: 45-2979) with its tea room, show garden, and plant nursery; and the excellent **Forest Glen Sanctuary** (Tel: 45-1274) where you can hand feed 230 deer, cuddle a koala, visit the nocturnal house, see kangaroos, emus, and wild birds, and enjoy a meal in the restaurant.

The **Big Pineapple** (Tel: 42-1333) is a few kilometers farther north. This unusual place was once the most visited attraction in Queensland, but a highway bypass and the growth of other theme parks have lessened the numbers coming here. Nevertheless, it still has appeal. See the macadamia nut factory, ride the sugar cane train, take a boat through Tomorrow's Harvest, and sample the famous sundaes and fruit salads. On the way back to the coast, you can visit **Bli Bli Castle** (Tel: 48-5373) to see the torture chamber, a doll museum, and medieval armor; **Ski and Skurf** (Tel: 94-1613) for cable water skiing; and **Nostalgia Town** (Tel: 48-7155) with its Enchanted Railway, mini-golf, mini-cars, and Albert's Time Machine.

On the coast near here, you find the **Novotel Twin Waters Resort** (Tel: 48-8000); with 374 rooms it's the largest resort on the coast. The rooms are built around a seven-hectare saltwater lagoon, and there are restaurants, bars, 1.5 kilometers of beach, and a golf course. The Sunshine Coast Airport is just north of here, then it is on to the beach centers of Coolum and Noosa.

Coolum has one of the best surf beaches along the Queensland coast, and the area is popular with day trippers from Brisbane. Sunshine Beach also has a great beach, but the main coast road is about a kilometer inland at this point, so it is much harder for casual visitors to find the waves. **Noosa** is much larger than the other centers, and it is made up of several distinct areas. Noosa Heads is where the "in-crowd" gathers, and this is where you find the Noosa National Park, the famous surf beach, the chic boutiques, restaurants, and art galleries. Noosaville is an area of canal estates, and waterfront homes and vacation apartments, much loved by the boating fraternity.

The **Blackall Range** is the perfect counterfoil to the coast. It stretches from Maleny to Montville, through Flaxton and onto Mapletown, and overlooks the coast to the east and the Mary River valley to the west. Near Maleny, Mary Cairncross Park is 41 hectares of rain forest offering spectacular views of the Glass House Mountains. Montville, a delightful village with its English cottages, Swiss chalets, classic Queenslanders, and rustic stone houses, is the creative hub of the region. Flaxton has several tea rooms and guest houses with panoramic views, while Mapletown is a lovely village with hotel, lily ponds, gardens, and some waterfalls just outside town. All these places have become arts and crafts centers with potters, painters, sculptors, leather workers, and writers all well represented.

This is a region that I particularly enjoy, and I encourage readers to visit. It is less than an hour's drive from the coast, but is light years away in atmosphere. Walk around Montville village visiting the Herb Garden, Jasmin Cottage, Black Forest Hill, Montrose, and elsewhere. Have lunch at Oma's Dutch Kitchen, Misty's Mountain Restaurant, or at half a dozen other places. Visit the **Flaxton Barn and Model Railway** (Tel: 45-7321) to see the HO gauge display in a European setting; **Miniature English Village** (Tel: 45-7225) and its brass rubbing center; walk the Senses Trail from the Village Hall in Montville; and enjoy the walks and animals in Kondalilla National Park.

For those with the time to stay longer, there is a wonderful collection of hotels, resorts, guest houses, and bed and breakfast places from which to choose. I suggest **Rowan House** (Tel: 94-1042), a rural retreat near Maleny with swimming pool and tennis court; the tudor-style **Montville Mountain Inn** (Tel: 42-9303) in Main Street, Montville; the bed and breakfast **Flaxton Inn** (Tel: 45-7157), and the **Tanderra Guest House** (Tel: 45-7179) with four in-suite bedrooms and country-style meals, both at Flaxton; and lush **Tanglewood Gardens** (Tel: 45-7100) at Mapletown with its 12 self-contained cottages set in extensive gardens containing a pool, spa, sauna, tennis court and barbecues.

The sugar town of **Nambour** provides another contrast. This is an important railway, government, and health center for the region. The Moreton Sugar Mill has tours during the June-November crushing season. Farther north, the **Ginger Factory** (Tel: 46-7100) at Yandina, lets you see the factory, then you can wander through Ginger Town with its nostalgia, doll's cottage, herb farm, and cane train. Then visit Bunya Park Wildlife Sanctuary with its koalas and other animals. **Eumundi** is an historic town a little farther north. The Village Market held every Saturday morning is one of the most popular in southeast Queensland. The Bruce Highway continues north towards Gympie and Maryborough (see Chapter 6), while a road to the east leads back to Noosa.

Cooloola is the general name for the area north of Noosa. You can take a four-wheel-drive vehicle on the ferry from Tewantin to the north shore of the Noosa River, then drive kilometers of deserted beach to the Colored Sands of Teewah, the wreck of the *Cherry Venture,* and eventually to Rainbow Beach, gateway to Fraser Island. One of the major features of the 55,000-hectare **Cooloola National Park** (Tel: 85-3245) is the Noosa River and its lakes and adjoining wet heathlands. This area is known as the Everglades, and there are popular boat trips, houseboats to rent, and fishing in the area. Lake Cootharaba is popular for sailing, and it is home to many pelicans. Boreen Point has restaurants, caravan parks, accommodations, and boats for rent.

THE ISLANDS

Moreton Bay has an archipelago of 365 islands, but only a few are inhabited or have visitor appeal. Moreton Island and North Stradbroke Island are the two largest. Farther north, Bribie Island and Fraser Island are both popular.

Moreton Island

Moreton Island is predominantly a sandy national park. Its vast tracts include Mount Tempest (280 meters), one of the tallest sand dunes in the world. There are two small settlements on the island—Kooringal in the south, and Bulwer in the north. Both have shops and a small selection of accommodations, Kooringal has an air strip, and both have vehicular ferry connections from the mainland. Permit camping is allowed on most parts of the island, and there are some campgrounds with water. There is also a major resort. Island visitors can walk through the national park, toboggan down giant sandhills, snorkel in and around the shipwrecks at Tangalooma, visit the 19th-century lighthouse, or four-wheel-drive the sandtracks that crisscross the island. The *Combie Trader* (Tel: 3203-6399) operates daily from Scarborough to Bulwer, while another service operates from Lytton to Kooringal.

Tangalooma Resort (Tel: 3268-6333) is on the west coast of the island. The resort has developed well in recent years and now offers good facilities. There are attractive gardens, a swimming pool, the Beachfront Cafe, tennis and squash courts, archery, a dolphin education center, and a nice beach. A special feature of the resort is the dolphin feeding that occurs each evening. This has been happening for some years, but it has recently been extended so that guests and some visitors can enter the water and hand feed these wild creatures. This is only one of two known places in the world where you can do this. Day trips, operated by the resort's fast catamaran, depart from a terminal at Holt Street, Pinkenba on the Brisbane River. A courtesy coach to the ferry leaves from the Roma Street Transit Centre and from many city hotels. A special Friday evening Dolphin Cruise departs Pinkenba at 5:30 P.M. This includes transport to and from the island, dolphin feeding, and dinner at the resort restaurant.

North Stradbroke Island

This is an island of white sand dunes, rocky headlands, pandanus coves, and silica beaches. There is much bird life, marine life, and native flora and fauna. Scuba diving, game and reef fishing, snorkeling, sailing, and boating are all popular. The island also has a number of land-based recreational activities such as a golf course, tennis courts, and a lawn bowls club. There are three townships, all with some accommodations and facilities, connected by paved roads. **Dunwich** is the ferry and water taxi terminal, and the island's historic and Aboriginal center. Call in to the tourist information center then perhaps visit the Aboriginal middens (burial and shell grounds), and the cemetery.

Amity Point is a peaceful little fishing haven with boating jetties, picturesque picnic areas, and calm swimming waters. The small offshore reef is popular with snorkelers. **Point Lookout** is the busiest center. There are some great surf beaches, good accommodations, restaurants, and other facilities. The **Islander** (Tel: 3409-8388) has 30 high-quality one- and two-bedroom units; the **Straddie Hotel Motel** (Tel: 3409-8188) has 26 mid-market units; the **Headlands** (Tel: 3409-8252) has budget cabins; while **Straddie Hostel** (Tel: 3409-8679) is for the backpackers. **Stradbroke Ferries** (Tel: 3286-2666) has regular vehicular ferries and water taxis from Cleveland with courtesy coach from Cleveland railway station to the ferry terminal.

Bribie Island

This sand island was inhabited long before Europeans came to Australia. Shell middens on the foreshore, and the remains of an early Aboriginal fish trap at Sandstone Point are evidence of settlement by the Joondoburri tribe. Although Captain Cook passed this way in 1770, Matthew Flinders was the first recorded visitor when he landed at what is now South Point. Flinders was accompanied by Bongaree, an Aborigine from Sydney, and they tried to befriend the native people they found on the island. They later sailed to the site of White Patch to do repairs on their ship.

The name Bribie comes from James Briby who was in this area from around 1830 and became involved with the Joondoburri tribe. Cattle were run on the island from the 1860s, and land sales using the name Bribie took place in 1887. A ferry service began in 1901, and a bridge was built in 1963. Some of this history is explained at three "talking monuments" that have been established by the Bribie Island Community Arts Society.

Since the opening of the bridge, several residential communities have developed with shopping, business, and sporting facilities. **Woorim** is on the ocean side of the island and has a surf beach, while the other centers front calm water Pumicestone Passage. Visitors find Bribie Island a quiet, relaxing place to stay. There are no luxury accommodations, but there are several options in the mid-range and budget categories. At Woorim, try **Koolamara Beach Resort** (Tel: 3408-1277) with 26 poolside units and Flinders Restaurant; **Pacific View Self Contained Flats** (Tel: 3408-1259); or the **Bribie Island Caravan Park** (Tel: 3408-1134). At **Bongaree,** try **Waterways Resort** (Tel: 3408-3000) with its 27 up-market units and Skippers Restaurant; **Placid Waters** (Tel: 3408-2122) where there are two-bedroom units, a heated pool, and a barbecue: or the **Bongaree Caravan Park** (Tel: 3408-1054) adjacent to the bowls club.

For food try intimate **Richo's** (Tel: 3408-0350), seafood at the **Golden Prawn** (Tel: 3408-1175), **Plimsoll's Water Garden Restaurant** (Tel: 3408-1676) at the Pier, or **Golden Gallery Chinese Restaurant,** all at Bongaree. Other possibilities are **Mortons** (Tel: 3408-7477) a barbecue bistro at the Bribie Island Hotel, Bellara; **Sun Lai Chinese Restaurant** (Tel: 3408-7299) at Bellara; or **Bluey's Bistro** (Tel: 3408-1004) at the Blue Pacific Hotel/Motel, Woorim.

Fraser Island

This is the world's largest sand island, covering an area of 163,000 hectares. It encompasses an amazing variety of landscapes, long surf beaches, cliffs and gorges, dense rain forests, vast desert-like sandblows, freshwater lakes perched high up in the dunes, winding streams, great basalt headlands, and salt pans with eerie mangrove forests. The clear mirror lakes and peat-colored perched lakes are some of the largest of their kind in the world. There are amazing rain forests growing in sand and surviving on nutrients from the breakdown of other plants. The beaches and forests are the habitat of more than 230 species of birds—one of the most varied communities in Australia. Fortunately the island is listed as a World Heritage site.

Fraser Island entices tens of thousands of people every year to relax and enjoy the island's scenery, and to pursue nature-based recreation activities, including swimming, fishing, camping, and walking. About half of the island is a national park, with most of the remainder a state forest. The whole island has been declared a recreation area, so there are access and camping charges for everyone. Access is by vehicular barges from **Inskip Point to Hook Point** (Tel: 074-863154), **Urangan to Moon Point** (Tel: 071-253325), **Mary River Heads to Wanggoolba Creek** (Tel: 071-241900), and **River Heads to King Fisher Bay Resort** (Tel: 071-255511). Other alternatives are private aircraft, passenger launches from **Urangan to King Fisher Bay Resort** (Tel: 071-255511), commercial tours, or private boats. There are only very limited stretches of blacktop on the island, so most travel is via the surf beach or inland sand tracks, and consequently only four-wheel-drive vehicles are permitted.

There are no towns on the island, but there is a broad range of accommodations styles. Camping is very popular, but four-star resort facilities, motels, and self-catering accommodations from caravans to apartments and luxury villas, are all available. **King Fisher Bay Resort and Village** (Tel: 071-203333) on the western side of the island provides luxury accommodations with its innovative, award-winning complex of hotel and villas. It has tennis, water sports, fishing, a swimming pool, bars, restaurants, shops, a bakery, organized activities, and a beachfront bistro and bar for day visitors. Rooms are from around A$220 a night. (Book at GPO Box 1122, Brisbane 4001 or Fax: 617-3221-3270.)

Happy Valley Resort (Tel: 071-279144) is on the central eastern coast. The timber lodges with their wide decks are attractive, they have cooking facilities, and are serviced daily. The complex has a bar/bistro, shop, swimming pool, and barbecue. (Book by Fax: 6171-279131.) **Eurong Beach Resort** (Tel: 071-279122) is on the southeastern coast. It has a wide range of accommodations from two-bedroom up-market units at A$160 a night, through various types of motel units from A$75 a night, A-frame cottages with kitchens for A$90 a night, and group cabins where beds are from A$12. It has a dining room, bistro, store, and swimming pool. (Book at P.O. Box 100, Maryborough 4650 or Fax: 6171-279178.) The resort owns a paved air strip adjacent to the Wanggoolba Creek ferry landing.

There are several developed camping areas within the national park and the state forest. These have toilets, showers (some with coin-operated hot water), cleared sites, fireplaces, and tables. They require Department of Environment and Heritage permits. There is a private camping ground at **Cathedral Beach** (Tel: 071-279177) with on-site caravans, shop, and tent sites.

7. Guided Tours

One of the best ways to see central Brisbane is on a **City Sights Tour** (Tel: 13-1230). These open tram-style buses are operated by Brisbane Transport on a circular route that passes many attractions. You can get off at any of 18 stops, then catch the next bus to a farther stop. Tours depart from Post Office Square every half hour, every day except Tuesdays, and include a commentary. Adults A$12, children A$8. Another view of the city is provided by the *Kookaburra Queen* (Tel: 3221-1300) on three scheduled daily cruises on the Brisbane River. The cost is from A$12. Several companies such as **Sunshine Tours** (Tel: 3236-3355) and **Australian Pacific Tours** (Tel: 3236-4088) have half-day and full-day bus tours around Brisbane. These companies also have day tours to the Gold Coast, the Sunshine Coast, the major theme parks, and other destinations on a daily basis.

There are one-day cruise tours from **Brisbane to Tangalooma Resort on Moreton Island** (Tel: 3268-6333), and from **Manly to St. Helena Island National Park** (Tel: 3393-3726). This latter tour provides a horse-drawn wagon ride and a guided trip around an island that was once home to Queensland's hardest criminals. Longer tours are also available from operators such as **Pacific Unlimited Holidays** (Tel: 3229-5872) to Kingfisher Bay Resort on Fraser Island, and to Heron Island Resort on the Great Barrier Reef. The **Queensland Travel Centre** (Tel: 13-1801) has a tour combining Fraser Island and Lady Elliot Island.

On the Gold Coast, the **Gold Coast Tourist Shuttle** (Tel: 5592-4167) has an all-day ticket for A$10 valid in the area between Dreamworld in the north and Currumbin Sanctuary in the south. There is a 30-minute service on the route. **Coachtrans** (Tel: 1-800-800306) has a daily series of Gold Coast tours from Brisbane, and a daily selection of Gold Coast tours, a Brisbane, and a Sunshine Coast tour, all from the Gold Coast. There are several boat cruises as well. **Island Queen Showboat Cruises** (Tel: 5592-2332) has one-hour and two-hour Surfers Paradise canal tours, a daily cruise to Sanctuary Cove with bus return, a daily South Stradbroke Island cruise tour to Tipplers Resort, and a nightly Polynesian Dance cruise. **Harley Tours** (Tel: 015-379955) has motorcycle tours from 30 minutes to six hours in duration.

On the Sunshine Coast, there are several smallish companies offering bus day tours. Try **Tropical Coast Tours** (Tel: 49-0822) or **Diana's Tours** (Tel: 94-5219). **Southern Cross Motorcycle Hire** (Tel: 45-0022) offers Harley-Davidson tours. There are numerous operators such as **Noosa Sound Cruises** (Tel: 47-3466) and **Blue Laguna Cruises** (Tel: 49-0799) running short tours on the Noosa River. There are also longer tours through the Everglades with operators such as **Everglades Water Bus Tours** (Tel: 47-1838).

Likewise, there are several operators offering day trips to Fraser Island by four-wheel-drive vehicle or air. **Skytour Scenic Air Tours** (Tel: 45-6064) has trips to Fraser Island or Lady Elliot Island. **Suncoast Safaris** (Tel: 47-2617), **Fraser Island Adventure Tours** (Tel: 47-2411), and others, have day trips by land and barge to Fraser Island. **Gemini Reef Cruises** (Tel: 92-1035) has fishing tours leaving from The Wharf, at Mooloolaba. **The Camel Company** (Tel: 42-4402) has daily one- or two-hour tours from the Lake Cooroibah Holiday Park.

8. Culture

Queensland was once described as a cultural desert, but that description is no longer true. Brisbane is rapidly developing into a sophisticated city with a wide appreciation of the arts. Rockhampton in central Queensland has been a supporter of art and theater for quite some time, while Townsville in north Queensland has developed a reputation as one of Australia's most progressive provincial cities with its own professional theater companies and a professional dance company. Today, even small centers have art galleries and theaters, and there are many touring performers and exhibitions to see.

Whether you enjoy Broadway and West End musicals or the classics, opera, and ballet; Aboriginal art or the great masters; dinosaurs or aircraft, the **Queensland Cultural Center** on the south bank of the Brisbane River should satisfy your needs. With the performing arts in the Lyric Theatre or the Concert Hall, the art gallery, the museum, and the library, there are a host of activities and events to enjoy, day or night. The nearby **Brisbane Con-**

vention and **Exhibition Centre** has regular trade fairs and exhibitions in its vast spaces.

Other places worth checking on are the 3,000-seat **Suncorp Piazza** at South Bank Parklands, the **Rotunda** and the **Topstage** in the Queen Street Mall, the **River Stage** in the City Botanic Gardens, the **Metro Arts Theatre** (Tel: 3221-1660), the **Suncorp Theater** (Tel: 3221-5177), the **ABC Music Centre** in West End, the **Brisbane City Hall Art Gallery and Museum** (Tel: 3225-4355), **La Boite Theatre** (Tel: 3369-1622) in Milton, and **Snug Harbour** (Tel: 3368-1700) at Dockside.

Brisbane hosts several festivals during the year. The prime ones are the **Brisbane Biennial International Music Festival** held in late May every second year; the **Royal National Association Show** at the Showgrounds (Exhibition) in mid-August; and **Warana,** a mardi-gras-type festival held in late September.

On the Gold Coast, the **Arts Centre** at Surfers Paradise is a popular venue for theater, ballet, musicals, and film.

9. Sports

The most popular spectator sports in Brisbane are rugby league football at ANZ Stadium and at Suncorp Stadium (April to September), Australian rules football at **The Gabba** (Tel: 3896-1777) (April to September), and cricket at **The Gabba** (October to March). Horseracing is held at **Eagle Farm Racecourse** (Tel: 3268-2171) and **Doomben Racecourse** (Tel: 3268-6800). Greyhound racing and harness racing (trotting) are held at **Albion Park Raceway** (Tel: 3862-1744). Basketball games are held at **Boondall Entertainment Centre,** while baseball fixtures are held at the **RNA Showgrounds** (Tel: 3832-4688).

There are many golf courses around southeast Queensland. Some are for members only and will only welcome guests who are club members in their home countries, but others are open to the general public. In Brisbane you can contact the **Royal Queensland Golf Club** (Tel: 3268-1127), a private club in Hamilton; the **Brisbane Golf Club** (Tel: 3848-1008), a private club in Yeerongpilly; the **Indooroopilly Golf Club** (Tel: 3870-3728); or **Victoria Park Course** (Tel: 3854-1406), a public course in Spring Hill. The Gold Coast has around 60 courses. Some you could try are **Paradise Springs** (Tel: 5593-2866) at Robina, **Palm Meadows** (Tel: 5594-2800), **Royal Pines** (Tel: 5597-8787), **Sanctuary Cove** (Tel: 5577-6031), or **Southport Golf Club** (Tel: 5532-1577). On the Sunshine Coast, the best courses are at the **Hyatt Coolum** (Tel: 46-1234), the **Novotel Twin Waters Resort** (Tel: 48-8000), and the **Tewantin Noosa Golf Club** (Tel: 74-9377).

On the Gold Coast, the **Turf Club** (Tel: 5538-1599) conducts horseracing every Saturday at the course on Racecourse Drive, Surfers Paradise. **Greyhound racing** (Tel: 5532-2611) is held Wednesdays at the Parklands complex, Southport. This is also the venue for **harness racing** (Tel: 5532-1222) on Tuesday evenings. The **Sunshine Coast Turf Club** (Tel: 91-6788) meetings are at the Corbold Park course in Caloundra.

10. Shopping

Because of the relative weakness of the Australian dollar against major North American, European, and Asian currencies, shopping has become something of a bargain "Down Under." Southeast Queensland may not have the best range of goods in Australia, but prices are generally better than Sydney or Melbourne, and it is certainly the best shopping place in Queensland, so you could well find that you are giving your credit cards some exercise and yourself some overdue indulgences. Being compact and less frenetic than some cities, Brisbane is user-friendly for shopping, and fortunately the central business district is still a major shopping area. City shopping hours are Monday to Thursday 8:30 A.M. to 5:30 P.M., Friday 8:30 A.M. to 9 P.M., Saturday 9 A.M. to 4 P.M., and Sunday 10:00 A.M. to 4 P.M.

The shopping district centers on **Queen Street Mall.** Leading off the mall are some stylish shopping galleries and arcades. The largest is the **Myer Center** with the Myer department store and over 200 other shops and food outlets. The **Wintergarden Center** has 150 shops specializing in fashion and jewelry, while the **Broadway on the Mall** is a fresh modern gallery of fashion shops and cafes. Major department stores such as Myer and David Jones provide multi-lingual staff to assist international visitors.

Duty-free shopping in Australia is good value. You can choose from a wide variety of goods in duty-free shops in the city center, or in the departure lounge of the international airport. Goods can be collected from the airport on your departure. Alcohol and perfumes can be purchased by international visitors and returning residents on arrival at Brisbane International Airport before passing through customs.

One of the most popular purchases for international visitors is an Australian opal. These come in a variety of colors, and they can be purchased tax free from several excellent opal specialists such as **Quilpie Opals** (Tel: 3221-7369) or **Bensons of Brisbane** (Tel: 3229-3869), both in Lennons Plaza, Queen Street Mall. The unique arts of the Aboriginal people are another good option. There are some genuine articles and much imitation rubbish, so go to a reputable shop such as **Queensland Aboriginal Creations** (Tel: 3224-5730) at 135 George Street. Bush fashion icons such as Akubra hats, kangaroo skin belts, and Driz-a-bone oilskin jackets are available from several shops around the city. The **Billabong Bookshop** (Tel:

3229-2801) at Queen Street and North Quay, and the **National Trust Gift Shop** (Tel: 3221-1887) have Australian books, gifts, posters, and cards.

Shopping in Brisbane takes on a new dimension on weekends with open-air arts and crafts markets operating in several locations. The largest and most colorful are at **South Bank Parklands,** and on the river terraces of Eagle Street. Opening times are South Bank, Fridays 5 P.M. to 10:30 P.M., Saturday 11 A.M. to 5 P.M., Sunday 9 A.M. to 5 PM., and Eagle Street, Sundays 8 A.M. to 4 P.M.

On the Gold Coast, **Pacific Fair** (Tel: 5539-8766) at Broadbeach, and **Australia Fair** (Tel: 5532-8811) at Southport have over 250 stores within each complex. There are reasonable shopping facilities in the main area of Surfers Paradise, on the Spit around Marina Mirage, and at several other centers.

11. Entertainment and Nightlife

Brisbane and the Gold Coast have both developed a reasonably vigorous nightlife in recent years.

Brisbane's **Conrad Treasury Casino** (Tel: 3306-8888) at the top end of the Queen Street Mall opened in mid-1995 with three levels of gaming excitement, and it now operates 24 hours a day. This has brought a new dimension to Brisbane. There are seven bars and three restaurants, 102 gaming tables, and 1,224 machines.

Live concert performances by national and international stars can be seen at several venues around the city. For details contact **Ticketworld** (Tel: 13-1931). Brisbane has numerous clubs, discos, and pubs offering live or recorded dance music. Try the **Brisbane Underground** (Tel: 3236-1511) at 61 Petrie Terrace; the **Caxton Hotel** (Tel: 3369-5544) on Petrie Terrace; **Grand Orbit,** Eagle Street Pier (Tel: 3236-1384); or **Margaux's** (Tel: 3231-3131) at the Hilton Hotel in the Queen Street Mall.

The **Jazz and Blues Bar** (Tel: 3238-2222) at the Brisbane City Travelodge is a popular venue for great jazz. The **Brisbane Jazz Club** (Tel: 3391-2006) at 1 Annie Street, Kangaroo Point, is also worth checking out on a weekend. There are several theater-restaurants worth visiting, including **Dirty Dick's** (Tel: 3221-1750) at the Britannia Inn; **Brentleigh Theatre Restaurant** (Tel: 3857-3857) on Gympie Road, Kedron; and **Crazies Comedy Restaurant**(Tel: 3369-0555) at Petrie Terrace. The **Sit Down Comedy Club** (Tel: 3368-1700) operates from Thursday to Saturday at Snug Harbour, Dockside.

On the Gold Coast, **Jupiters Casino** (Tel: 5592-1133) has lead the way for several years with a 24-hour operation and big-show extravaganzas nightly in the International Showroom. Coolangatta/Tweed Heads is famous for its clubs where well-known performers appear regularly. The

Twin Towns Services Club (Tel: 5536-1977) or **Seagulls** (Tel: 5536-3433) are two of the best operations. There are several theater-restaurants, intimate bars, dinner and party cruises, nightclubs (try **Cocus** at Broadbeach, Tel: 5592-4433), and discos.

Nightlife on the Sunshine Coast is more relaxed and low-key, but there is some activity. The **Galaxy Nightclub** (Tel: 43-1811) at Stewarts Hotel, Alexandra Headland, often has top performers, or you can dance the night away at the adjacent **Connections Nightclub.** At Noosa, **Artis Cafe** (Tel: 47-2300) has jazz and blues from Wednesday to Sunday, while the **Laguna Bay Beach Club** (Tel: 49-4794) has live dance music from Thursday to Sunday. At Mooloolaba, try **Illusions** (Tel: 44-1048) or **Rock On** (Tel: 78-3422), both on the Esplanade.

12. The Southeast Queensland Contact List

Brisbane

Ambulance—(Tel: 3364-1222)
Banks—National Australia Bank, 308 Queens St. (Tel: 3234-5222)
Bus Service Information—69 Ann Street (Tel: 3225-4444)
Churches—Anglican, St. John's, Ann St. (Tel: 3835-2231)
          —Catholic, St. Stephen's, Elizabeth St. (Tel: 3229-4058)
          —Uniting, Albert and Ann Streets (Tel: 3221-6788)
Consulates—British, 193 North Quay (Tel: 3236-2575)
          —Japanese, 12 Creek Street (Tel: 3221-5188)
          —New Zealand, 288 Edward Street (Tel: 3221-9933)
          —USA, 383 Wickham Terrace (Tel: 3831-3330)
Credit Cards—American Express (Tel: 3229-2022)
          —Diners Club International (Tel: 3221-6005)
Dental Services—Emergency, 160 Wharf St. (Tel: 3830-4157)
Emergency Calls—Ambulance, Fire, Police (Tel: 000)
Fire Service—(Tel: 3896-3533)
Hospital—Royal Brisbane, Herston Rd., Herston (Tel: 3253-8111)
          —Princess Alexandra, Ipswich Road (Tel: 3240-2111)
Immigration—Commonwealth Centre, 295 Ann St. (Tel: 3405-4799)
Lifeline—24-hour counseling service (Tel: 3252-1111)
Mayor's Office—City Hall, King George Sq. (Tel: 3225-4400)
Medical—Travellers, Coles Bld., 210 Queens St. (Tel: 3221-8083)
Police—100 Roma Street (Tel: 3364-6464)
Pharmacy—Delahunty's Day & Night, 245 Albert (Tel: 3221-8869)
Post Office—261 Queen Street (Tel: 3405-1202)
Qantas Airlines—247 Adelaide St., Domestic (Tel: 3131-313)

—Post Office Sq., International (Tel: 3234-3833)
RACQ—Breakdown service (Tel: 3340-1122)
Rail Services—Central Station, Ann Street (Tel: 3235-1877)
Taxi—Black & White Cabs (Tel: 3238-1000)
        —Yellow Cabs (Tel: 3391-0191)
Telephone calls—international operator (Tel: 0101)
        —international direct dial (Tel: 0011)
Tourist Information—Queens Street Mall (Tel: 3229-5918)
        —Qld. Gvt. Travel Centre (Tel: 3221-6111)

Gold Coast

Ambulance— (Tel: 5531-2121)
Bus Service—Surfside Busline (Tel: 5536-7666)
        —City Bus (Tel: 5532-6211)
Churches—Anglican, 73 Salerno St., Surfers Paradise (Tel: 5592-1543)
        —Catholic, Fairway Drive, Surfers Paradise (Tel: 5531-5366)
        —Uniting, Scarborough St., Southport (Tel: 5539-6889)
Dental Services—(Tel: 5539-8945)
Emergency Calls—Ambulance, Fire, Police (Tel: 000)
Hospital—Southport General (Tel: 5571-8211)
Lifeline—24-hour counseling service (Tel: 5539-9999)
Mayor's Office—(Tel: 5531-9211)
Medical—24-hour clinic (Tel: 5538-8823)
Pharmacy—24-hour service (Tel: 5592-1321)
Police—Gold Coast H.Q. (Tel: 5581-2800)
Post Office—Surfers Paradise (Tel: 5592-1184)
Qantas Airways—(Tel: 5591-0361)
Queensland Dept. of Environment & Heritage (Tel: 5535-3032)
RACQ—(Tel: 5532-0311)
Taxi—Surfers Paradise (Tel: 5532-0311)
Tourist Information—Visitors Bureau (Tel: 5538-4419)

Sunshine Coast

Ambulance—(Tel: 41-1333)
Churches—Anglican, 29 Sunshine Ave., Tewantin (Tel: 49-8009)
        —Catholic, Elizabeth St., Coolum (Tel: 46-3422)
        —Uniting, Werin Street, Tewantin (Tel: 49-9029)
Dental Services—Bay Village, Noosa Heads (Tel: 47-2266)
Emergency Calls—Ambulance, Fire, Police (Tel: 000)
Fire Service—(Tel: 74-9911)
Hospital—Nambour Public (Tel: 41-9600)
        —Noosa District (private) (Tel: 47-6022)

—Caloundra District (Tel: 91-1888)
Medical—after hours, Noosa (Tel: 42-4444)
    —Maroochydore (Tel: 43-7622)
Police—Langura Street, Noosa (Tel: 47-5888)
Post Office—79 Noosa-Tewantin Road, Noosa (Tel: 47-3280)
Qantas Airways—Domestic services (Tel: 13-1313)
RACQ—breakdown service, Noosa (Tel: 47-3455)
Taxi— Suncoast Cabs (Tel: 13-1134)
Tourist Information—Sunshine Coast (Tel: 43-6400)
    — Noosa Info. Center (Tel: 47-4988)

6

Bundaberg, Gladstone, Rockhampton, and the Southern Great Barrier Reef

1. The General Picture

Humpback whales, loggerhead turtles, rainbow-colored parrot fish, and giant clams call this region home. Heritage buildings, undeveloped beaches, wonderful recreational fishing, and interesting cities and towns add to the appeal. The pace and atmosphere is quite different from that of southeast Queensland. Here there is more time, less pressure, and better communication with the visitor.

The Great Barrier Reef reaches its southern extremity at Lady Elliot Island. From here, a group of reefs and islands runs north to just above the Tropic of Capricorn, a distance of some 200 kilometers. Relatively speaking, this southern reef is small, but it is an important tourist region because this section of reef is closest to the Brisbane international gateway and the big population centers farther south. Many visitors reach here by road, so the coastal centers of Bundaberg, Gladstone, and Rockhampton are important destinations and gateways to the islands and reef. At the same time they serve as regional industrial and commercial centers.

Don't expect modern, high-powered sophistication, though. These centers think of themselves firstly as solid commercial centers, and they make few concessions to the whims of international visitors. That, of course, becomes one of their charms. You see the real Australia rather

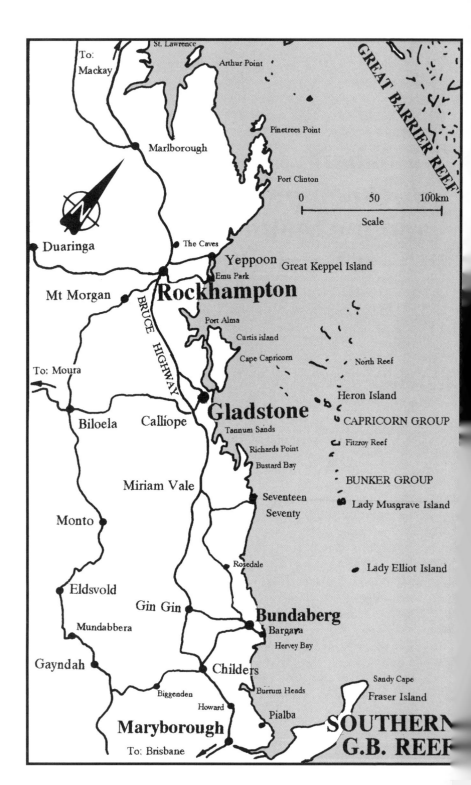

than some tourist imitation. Accommodations are adequate, restaurants are plentiful, although the variety is somewhat limited, tourist operators are low-key and friendly, and family fun is more important than all-night partying.

The region starts at Maryborough and Hervey Bay in the south. Maryborough has charm and serenity, and it is proud of its colorful history. Much of the character of the place has been preserved in its heritage buildings. Nearby Hervey Bay has a reputation as a safe, relaxing family aquatic playground. In recent years it has developed a thriving whale-watching industry as huge humpbacks play in waters close by.

Bundaberg is a city of 45,000 people with an attractive central area, several interesting parks and gardens, history associated with famous aviator Bert Hinkler, sugar, and rum. The district produces one-fifth of Queensland's sugar crop, so throughout the year the green mosaic of fields is constantly changing as the crop is planted, matured, and harvested. The district is also an important producer of tomatoes, melons, squash, capsicum, and macadamia nuts. There are flights to Lady Elliot Island, and day boat trips to Lady Musgrave Island. To the east of the city there are several relatively pristine beaches with permanent communities that welcome holiday visitors.

The industrial city of **Gladstone** has one of Australia's major ports, a huge alumina smelter, and Queensland's largest electric power generating station. Despite this, there are numerous recreational areas in the region, the city is a major gateway to Heron Island, and there is access to Lady Elliot Island and other parts of the Great Barrier Reef. To the south there is history, beaches, swimming and fishing, national parks, and a sense of discovery at the Town of 1770 and surrounding areas.

Rockhampton is the gateway to the tropics. The city of 60,000 people sits on the Tropic of Capricorn and is known as the beef capital of Australia. One-third of Queensland's beef cattle graze in the region. The city is a solid blend of old and new. Quay Street has been classified by the National Trust because of its historic significance, while the Aboriginal Dreamtime Cultural Center shows something of a civilization that has existed here for at least 40,000 years. The Capricorn Coast to the east is a popular destination for western Queenslanders wanting the water, and southern Australians seeking the sun. Accommodations, attractions, and sporting facilities are provided for the visitor. Great Keppel Island and the Great Barrier Reef are accessible from here.

A note on telephone numbers. Within the next few years all of Queensland will be in a single area code region, and all telephone numbers will contain eight digits. The process has started and will continue progressively over four years. At present, however, there are a variety of area codes. All areas covered by this chapter currently have numbers with six digits, and you must use the area code when calling between different zones, e.g. Maryborough to Gladstone, or Bundaberg to Rockhampton.

2. Getting There

Rockhampton Airport is connected to Brisbane by several daily jet services as well as smaller commuter planes. There are also direct commuter connections to Gladstone, Mackay, and Townsville, and some of these services continue to Bundaberg, Brisbane, and Cairns. Gladstone, Bundaberg and Maryborough are not on the main jet routes, but all have commuter aircraft links to Brisbane and other Queensland coastal centers. For further details contact **Qantas Airways** (**Sunstate**). There are air connections from Rockhampton to Great Keppel Island, from Gladstone to Heron Island and Lady Elliot Island, and from Bundaberg and Hervey Bay to Lady Elliot Island.

Maryborough, Bundaberg, Gladstone, and Rockhampton are all on the electrified north coast railway line from Brisbane. They are served by the **Spirit of Capricorn** and the **Sunlander** trains. These centers are also served by the **long-distance bus companies** on their Brisbane-Cairns services.

The **Bruce Highway** provides good access to these centers. Maryborough is only three hours drive from Brisbane, while Bundaberg is around four and a half hours, Gladstone is about five and a half hours, and Rockhampton is six and a half hours for those in a hurry.

3. Local Transportation

All of the main centers have **taxis** that are available 24 hours a day. Fares within cities are reasonable. Trips to local beaches or outlying centers can quickly become expensive, however.

Local **bus services** operate in the major centers, but frequencies can be poor, and after-hours services almost non-existent. Some resorts and hotels have courtesy buses, and these are recommended to visitors.

Rental cars are readily available. If you do not have your own vehicle these are highly recommended in this region because of the large distances that many people end up traveling. Here are some of the operators.

Bundaberg (Tel. area code 071) has operators clustered in Takalvan Street Try: **Avis** (Tel: 52-1877), **Hertz** (Tel: 55- 2755), and **Thrifty** (Tel: 51-6222) **Network** (Tel: 52-3818) and **Reasonable** (Tel: 51-3058) are two other operators.

Gladstone (Tel. area code 079) car rental options include **Avis** (Tel

78-2633), **Budget** (Tel: 72-3755), **Gladstone Car Rentals** (Tel: 72-6900), **Hertz** (Tel: 78-1687), **Network** (Tel: 73-3066), and **Thrifty** (Tel: 72-5999).

Rockhampton (Tel. area code 079) car rental options include **Avis** (Tel: 27-3344), **Budget** (Tel: 26-4888), **Hertz** (Tel: 22-2500), **Network** (Tel: 22-2990), **Rockhampton Car Rentals** (Tel: 22-7802), and **Thrifty** (Tel: 27-8755).

4. The Accommodations Scene

In this section I will only cover accommodations in Bundaberg, Gladstone, and Rockhampton. For island accommodations see Section 8 within this chapter. For accommodations at other mainland centers see the relevant part of Section 6 within this chapter. The following is a selection of what is offered. It is divided into three categories—expensive, medium-price, and budget.

Bundaberg (Tel. area code 071)

EXPENSIVE ACCOMMODATIONS

There are no accommodations in Bundaberg in the expensive category.

MEDIUM-PRICE ACCOMMODATIONS

The **Bougainvillea Motor Inn** (Tel: 51-2365), 40 rooms, is one of the largest and best motels in the city. There is a good choice of rooms from doubles, triples, suites, and self-contained with kitchens. All are well equipped with the normal features, and some have spas. There are restaurant, swimming pool, spa, tour desk, and laundry facilities. Room rates are from A$70. (Book at 73 Takalvan Street, Bundaberg 4670 or Fax: 6171-531866.) The **Bundaberg City Motor Inn** (Tel: 52-5011), 17 ground-level rooms, is another of the better places in the city. The accommodations are typical motel-style, but there are a few extra touches that set this apart from the average. It has a swimming pool, barbecue, and children's playground. Rates are from A$60 double. (Book at 246 Bourbong Street, Bundaberg 4670 or Fax: 6171-525516.) The **Alexandra Park Motor Inn** (Tel: 52-7255) is something quite different. Here the elegance of a bygone era is recaptured in this gracious old home which has been lovingly restored but with the addition of modern-day comforts. Rooms have all the usual features, some even have spas, plus the unique atmosphere of the past. The motor inn has a pool, and the adjoining Hog's Breath Cafe is popular for its cuisine and atmosphere. Rates are from A$60. (Book at 66 Quay Street, Bundaberg 4670.)

There are many motels down-market from here. They provide the usual room facilities but generally do not have pools or restaurants. You could try the **Matilda Motel** (Tel: 51-4717) at 209 Bourbong Street, the **Rum City Motel** (Tel: 52-5722) at 52 Takalvan Street, or **Coral Villa Motel** (Tel: 52-4999) at 56 Takalvan Street. Rates here are around A$45 double. **Lyelta Lodge** (Tel: 51-3344) at 8 Maryborough Street is a little different. Here there are two motel rooms and 16 guest rooms all containing reasonable facilities. Bed and breakfast is available from around A$35 double. The **Appollo Gardens Caravan Park** (Tel: 52-8899) at 83 Princess Street has in-suite cabins for A$35.

BUDGET ACCOMMODATIONS

The caravan parks, older-style hotels, and backpackers lodges are the choices here. The **Bundaberg Caravan Park** (Tel: 55-1969) is situated on the southern approaches to the city at 20 Childers Road. Facilities are not wonderful, but there are cabins and on-site vans from a reasonable A$22. Facilities are better at the **Midtown Caravan Park** (Tel: 52-2768) at 61 Takalvan Street, but the price goes up. The cabins are in landscaped gardens, and there is a pool. Normal units are around A$28, and those with in-suite bathrooms are around A$35. The **Riverdale Caravan Park** (Tel: 53-6696) at 6 Perry Street beside the river on the north side of the city has cabins for A$28. The **Grand Hotel** (Tel: 51-2441) is right in the center of town. Rooms are available from around A$20 single and A$28 double.

Bundaberg Backpackers & Travellers Lodge (Tel: 52-2080) is adjacent to the bus terminal at 2 Croften Street. It has a laundry, games room, kitchen, television, kiosk, and barbecue. Double rooms are available for around A$25 and shared facilities are A$12. **City Centre Backpackers** (Tel: 51-3501) at 216 Bourbong Street has shared or twin accommodations, laundry, common room with TV, and kitchen. Rates are around A$12 per person. The **Federal Guest House** (Tel: 53-3711) at 221 Bourbong Street is also around A$12. All are backpacker job centers for those wanting work as seasonal fruit and vegetable pickers.

Gladstone (Tel. area code 079)

EXPENSIVE ACCOMMODATIONS

Only one property comes into this above A$100 category. The **Highpoint International** (Tel: 72-4711), 54 rooms, has good facilities and atmosphere. The suites are spacious and well equipped with extras such as lounge suites and laundry facilities, and they have balcony views. The Magzeenz Restaurant has an extensive menu and an intimate bar, and there is 24-hour room service. The swimming pool and terrace is a popular place to relax. A courtesy van will transport you around the city. Room rates are around

A$120 double. (Book at 22 Roseberry Street, Gladstone 4680 or Fax: 6179-724940.)

MEDIUM-PRICE ACCOMMODATIONS

The **Country Plaza International** (Tel: 72-4499) is situated in the center of town. The 72 units include some two-bedroom suites. All have a full range of facilities. A licensed restaurant is open seven days, and there are lounge, piano bar, swimming pool, barbecue, laundry, and courtesy van facilities. Room rates are from around A$90 double. (Book at 100 Goondoon Street, Gladstone 4680 or Fax: 6179-724921.)

There are a few large motels a little down-market from here. The **Gladstone Country Club Motor Inn** (Tel: 72-4322) is a popular place a little way from the center of the city. The 36 rooms are in a two-level building set in gardens, and it is within walking distance of the golf course. Facilities include a pool and spa, water views from some units, a nice restaurant, a bar, a laundry, and room service. Rates are from around A$70. (Book at Far Street and Dawson Highway, Gladstone 4680 or Fax: 6179-724352.) Alternatively, there is the **Gladstone Reef Hotel-Motel** (Tel: 72-1000) near the city center. This 48-room property has views, rooftop pool, in-house movies, several bars, and a restaurant featuring fresh seafood. Rates are around A$70. (Book at 38 Goondoon Street, Gladstone 4680 or Fax: 6179-721729.)

Then there is a group of smaller motels with good room facilities at a cheaper price. The **Gladstone Village Motor Inn** (Tel: 78-2077), 26 rooms, at Chapman Drive near the airport; the **Mid City Motor Inn** (Tel: 72-3000), 25 rooms, at 26 Goondoon Street; **Why Not? Motor Inn** (Tel: 72-5479), with motel and self-contained units at 23 Coon Street; and **Mawarra Motel** (Tel: 72-1411), 32 rooms, at 6 Scenery Street are typical of this group. Room rates start at around A$50. There are a few motels below this price, but it is becoming harder to find a bargain.

BUDGET ACCOMMODATIONS

The caravan parks with cabin accommodations is the next area to look. **Auckland Caravan Park & Holiday Cottages** (Tel: 78-1419) on the Dawson Highway has self-contained cottages with kitchen, shower, and TV for around A$40. The complex has a pool, laundry, children's playground, and barbecue. The **Clinton Van Park Holiday Village** (Tel: 78-2718) is on the Dawson Highway, nearby. There are self-contained cabins and camp-o-tels. The facilities include tennis, pool, laundry, and kitchen. Rates are from A$35. **Barney Beach Caravan Park** (Tel: 72-7549) at Barney Beach, is not too far from the city center, and there are in-suite beachside cabins, on-site vans, and caravan and tent sites in a shady setting.

Dorm beds are available at the **Gladstone Backpackers Hostel** (Tel:

72-5744) at 12 Rollo Street and at **Harbour Lodge** (Tel: 72-6463) at 16 Roseberry Street.

Rockhampton (Tel. area code 079)

EXPENSIVE ACCOMMODATIONS

There are no accommodations in Rockhampton in the expensive category.

MEDIUM-PRICE ACCOMMODATIONS

The **Country Comfort Inn** (Tel: 27-9933) is arguably the best accommodations in Rockhampton. The 76 rooms are of excellent quality, and the facilities at the property include pool, barbecue, laundry, two bars, a coffee shop, conference facilities, and a high-class restaurant specializing in reef seafoods and tropical fruits. Rates are now approaching A$100. (Book at 86 Victoria Parade, Rockhampton 4700 or Fax: 6179-271615.) **Duthies Leichhardt Hotel** (Tel: 27-6733) is a well-established property that is a favorite with western Queensland people coming to the city. There is a range of accommodations available here. The best rooms in the tower are good, the west wing less so. Facilities include restaurants and bars, laundry, convention rooms, and 24-hour reception, room service, and coffee shop. Rates start at around A$50 and rise to near A$100. (Book at Denham & Bolsover Streets, Rockhampton 4700 or Fax: 6179-278075.)

The next group of accommodations can be described as the up-market motel. There are several of these. The **Regency on Albert Street** (Tel: 22-6222) is a good example. The 37 single, double, and family units and one-, two-, and three-bedroom self-contained apartments are all completely equipped. Motel facilities include pool, laundry, restaurant, lounge, room service, and conference rooms. Rates are around A$65. (Book at 28 Albert Street, Rockhampton 4700 or Fax: 6179-222573.) The nearby **Archer Park Motel** (Tel: 27-9266), 26 units, has similar facilities, standards, and prices. (Book at 39 Albert Street, Rockhampton 4700 or Fax: 6179-225750.) The **Bridge Motor Inn** (Tel: 27-7488), 32 units, is a few blocks closer to the river and has most of the same facilities, but the rate here is around A$50. (Book at 31 Bolsover Street, Rockhampton 4700 or Fax: 6179-224161.)

There are cheaper motels than these. You mostly find them on the north and south approaches to the city. You may be lucky and find a room for A$45. The **Tropical Wanderer Holiday Village** (Tel: 28-2621) on the Bruce Highway in North Rockhampton has a range of accommodations from Melanesian units, through motel units and cabin vans, to safari tents. There are restaurant, pool, games room, laundry, barbecue, tennis, and camping facilities on site. Unit rates start at around A$35. In the same area you will find **Ramblers Motel Caravan Park** (Tel: 28-2084). Options are airconditioned villas, serviced units, cabins (some with in-suite bathrooms), caravans, and camping. The **Criterion Hotel-Motel** (Tel: 22-1225) on the corner of Quay and Fitzroy Streets overlooking the Fitzroy River offers a further alternative. There are conventional motel units, hotel rooms, and hotel suites. The building has considerable style, and there are bars, a restaurant, a lounge, and entertainment. Hotel rooms start at around A$25.

BUDGET ACCOMMODATIONS

Backpackers accommodations are the only option under A$25. The **YHA Rockhampton Hostel** (Tel: 27-5288) is at 60 MacFarlane Street in North Rockhampton. This is typical of hostels with cooking and laundry facilities, and a courtesy coach to pick you up from the train or bus station. Dorm beds (around A$12) and twin rooms (around A$28) are available. The other options are **Southside Caravan Village** (Tel: 27-3013) on the Bruce Highway near the information office, or **City Heart Backpackers** (Tel: 22-2414) at 170 East Street near the mall.

5. Dining and Restaurants

As with accommodations, I will only discuss Bundaberg, Gladstone, and Rockhampton restaurants in this section. See Section 6 for dining options in other areas.

Bundaberg

The region grows some excellent fruits and vegetables in the rich red volcanic soils. Bundaberg is known as the tomato capital of Australia, and local zucchini, squash, cucumber, capsicum, beans, lychees, melons, and pineapples are also good. Try these while you are here, with the local fish, prawns, scallops, crabs, pork, and beef. Bundaberg ginger beer or local tropical wine will add to the pleasure of a meal, and a Bundaberg royal rum liqueur is ideal with coffee.

The **Bacchus Restaurant** (Tel: 52-2524) at 47 Takalvan Street is hailed by many as the best in the city. It has been popular for over 20 years, so it is obviously doing something right. There is a friendly relaxed atmosphere and a cocktail bar, and the menu features fresh seafood and char-grilled steaks. It is open for lunch and dinner. The **Spinnaker Stonegrill Restaurant and Bar** (Tel: 52-8033) at 1A Quay Street is another favorite. The location overlooking the river is excellent, and lunch on the deck can be memorable. Lunch prices are very attractive, while the seafood dinners are reasonable. It is open seven days. **Charley Magees** (Tel: 59-2081) on Perry Street (North) is also worth a visit for lunch or dinner.

Other cuisines are also available. The best Chinese food is probably at the **Eastern Pearl Restaurant** (Tel: 51-5145) at 268 Bourbong Street. **De George's Restaurant** (Tel: 53-1770) at 238 Bourbong Street serves Greek and Australian cuisine, and there is a special blackboard menu. **Numero Uno** (Tel: 51-3666) at 167 Bourbong Street has Italian favorites, pasta, pizza, and espresso. The **Mexican Border** (Tel: 52-1675) at 27 Elliott Heads Road has a selection of Mexican, Australian, and vegetarian favorites. **Stockman's Australian Cafe** (Tel: 53-4774) on Bourbong Street and a second one at Sugarland Shopping Center are self-explanatory. **Hog's Breath Cafe** (Tel: 53-5777) at 66 Quay Street has some of the best steak in town. The **Art Gallery Restaurant** (Tel: 51-2365) at 73 Takalvan Street combines good food and service with fine art. **Beaches** (Tel: 53-2255) at the Reef Gateway Motor Inn, 11 Takalvan Street, and **Rendezvous** (Tel: 53-1747) at the Sugar Country Motor Inn, 220 Bourbong Street, are two of the popular motel eateries.

Several hotels have meals in bistros, beer gardens, or bars. Try the **Federal** (Tel: 53-1390) at 221 Bourbong Street for lunch specials, the **Club Hotel** (Tel: 51-3262) at Bourbong and Tantitha Streets for lunches and dinner in the Sidewalk Garden Bistro, the **East End Hotel Carvery** (Tel: 52-6388), or the **Railway Hotel** (Tel: 51-3247) at 87 Perry Street, North Bundaberg, for the super daily specials. The **Coach's Inn** (Tel: 51-6106) at 66 Targo Street is proving popular with bus passengers and backpackers.

Gladstone

I have never found Gladstone to be a culinary capital, but the city does have some worthwhile offerings particularly with fresh seafood. **Swaggy's Australian Restaurant** (Tel: 72-1653) at 56 Goondoon Street has what is claimed to be the most comprehensive Australian menu in the country. It has damper, kangaroo tail soup, witchetty grub soup, emu, crocodile, kangaroo, beef, seafood, and much more. It is open for lunch Monday to Friday and dinner Monday to Saturday. **Le Beaujolais Restaurant** (Tel: 72-1647) at 28 Tank Street is the city's only French a la carte restaurant. It has an intimate cocktail bar and is open for dinner Monday to Saturday.

Other options are the **China Garden Restaurant** (Tel: 72-5044) at 19 Tank Street; **Amicci's Pizza & Pasta Restaurant** (Tel: 72-2082) for Italian favorites; **Lily's Oriental Kitchen** at Philip Street (near McDonald's and Big Rooster) has Thai, Malaysian, Indonesian, and Chinese either dine-in or take-out; **Flinders Restaurant and Brasserie** (Tel: 72-8322) at Flinders Parade and Oaka Lane; and **Sailors Restaurant** (Tel: 72-6833) at the Gladstone Marina for seafood. Home-cooked Russian and Australian fare is available at the **Selah Kiosk** (Tel: 79-3322) in the visitor's center at the Toondoon Botanic Gardens. In the motels, the **Brass Palm Restaurant** (Tel: 72-4499) at the Country Plaza International has a cocktail bar, seafood specials, and entertainment most evenings, while the **Klickity's Restaurant** (Tel: 72-4322) at the Gladstone Country Club Motor Inn has a wide menu and is justifiably popular.

Rockhampton

This is not the beef capital of Australia for nothing, so it would be appropriate to try the local product. You can do this at almost every restaurant and at many hotel bistros. One of the most popular of the latter is the **Tropical Garden Bistro** (Tel: 22-1225) at the National Trust classified Criterion Hotel in Quay Street. Apart from steak, Rockhampton offers cuisines from around the world available in a range of restaurants.

Excellent Chinese food is to be found at the **Chung San Restaurant** (Tel: 28-6316) at 392 Dean Street, North Rockhampton, and at the **Hong Kong Seafood Restaurant** (Tel: 27-7144) at 98A Denham Street, south of the central business district. Both are open seven days. The taste of India can be experienced at **Indian Tandoori & Curry House** (Tel: 27-4182) at 39 East Street. For Japanese food try **Taste of Japan** (Tel: 26-2269) at 386 Dean Street, North Rockhampton. Fresh seafood is the specialty of **Cascades** (Tel: 22-6631) at Fitzroy and Campbell Streets, while **Malaysia Hut Restaurant** (Tel: 27-7511) serves Asian fare for lunch and dinner at 7 Wandal Road (west of the central business district).

Those seeking Italian favorites will enjoy **Italian Graffiti** (Tel: 22-6322) at 147 Musgrave Street, North Rockhampton. Mexican fanciers are drawn to **Crazy Cactus** (Tel: 22-8132) at Alma and Derby Street near the city center, or to **Amigos** (Tel: 27-2699) at Club Tavern, Kent and Denham Streets. **Club Tavern** actually has two restaurants, the other being **Spinnakers** (Tel: 27-2699), which features seafood. Seafood lovers also head for **Skylites Uptown** (Tel: 22-2882) at East and Williams Streets on the mall for a variety of a la carte dishes. The same J. J's complex also offers cheaper meals at **Strutters Uptown** where you find a buffet, snacks, and entertainment, or **Al Fresco** with its casual atmosphere, cheap eats, and coffee.

This doesn't exhaust the possibilities by any means. **Chow Quay** (Tel: 22-8228) on Quay Street has a well-regarded buffet with Chinese, Australian, and seafood dishes on offer. A little to the west, **Shangri-La** (Tel: 27-5334) overlooks the river at 28 Victoria Parade. In this same area, **Restaurant 98** (Tel: 27-5322) at 98 Victoria Parade has an extensive a la carte menu and a good reputation. **Craving's Bar & Grill** (Tel: 28-5666) at Water Street and Lakes Creek Road in North Rockhampton has a char grill, seafood, and a chalkboard menu.

Rockhampton is a city with a large number of motels and many of these have restaurants. They generally provide good quantities of standard fare at reasonable prices. Some have attached bars, and a few offer poolside dining. The **Altimos** (Tel: 22-6222) at the Regency Motel at Albert and Campbell Streets is one of the better ones. **Greenhouse** (Tel: 27-8866) at the Country Lodge Motor Inn at Larnach Street and Gladstone Road is another with a good reputation. You will often find locals in the restaurant at the **Albert Court Motel** (Tel: 27-8261) at Albert and Alma Streets, and also at the restaurant at the **Central Park Motel** (Tel: 27-2333) at 224 Murray Street behind the Central Park Fountain. That is always a good sign of quality and good value.

6. Sightseeing

The Central Queensland, or Southern Reef Region, stretches along the coast for around 400 kilometers. For those traveling from southeast Queensland by land, I have arranged this section in a south to north direction starting at Maryborough and going through to the Capricorn Coast just north of Rockhampton. The islands are covered separately in Section 8 of this chapter.

MARYBOROUGH

Maryborough was first settled in 1847 as a wool port on the broad Mary River. It is one of Queensland's oldest cities. Remarkably, much of the city's early character has been preserved in its public buildings and houses, so it is reaping the benefits of a booming tourism industry focusing on history.

Maryborough's special charm is best discovered through the city's **Heritage Walk** which takes in 28 key buildings in the central business district. A longer driving tour takes in almost 80 of the city's architectural jewels, historic sites, and points of interest. The highlight is probably the **Wharf Street Precinct** where there are many historic buildings and an atmosphere of old-world charm. Bygone memories of sailing ships, greasy wool, and bewildered immigrants can be recaptured by a stroll around the buildings, or a drink in one of the original pubs. Entering **Brennan and Geraghty's Store** is like stepping into a time capsule thanks to wonderful restoration work by the National Trust. The **Bond Store Port** of **Maryborough Heritage Museum** is a growing part of this precinct. **Historic Baddow House** (Tel: 23-1883) at 364 Queen Street is open for tours and Devonshire teas.

Heritage Market Day is held each Thursday in Kent and Adelaide Streets. There are arts and craft stalls, homemade baked goods, sidewalk cafes, and fresh produce together with some colorful characters and entertainment. The "Time Cannon" is fired at 1 P.M. under the supervision of the town crier and the tourism ambassador "Mary Heritage." On market day you can visit **Olds Engine House** (Tel: 21-3649) at 78 North Street where some of the famous collection of models built by the late William Olds are on display.

There are products and souvenirs for sale, and you can visit the adjacent engineering works and foundry and see an operating steam engine.

Take time to stop and feed the black swans at **Ululah Lagoon Wildlife Sanctuary** while you have a picnic or barbecue in the parkland. In September and February, visit **Elizabeth Park** at Kent and Tooley Streets to see and smell the 2,500 rose bushes. **Queens Park** in Sussex Street was established more than a century ago. There is a fernery, waterfall, lily pond, lace-trimmed band rotunda, and a 13-centimeter model railway that comes alive on the last Sunday in each month. There is a **Sugar Museum** at Lower Kent Street on the river bank, a **Railway Museum** (Tel: 21-2451) at the railway station in Lennox Street, the **Old Waterhouse Gallery** (Tel: 22-4408) on Wharf Street, and the **Maryborough Historical Society Display** in the foyer of the **School of Arts Building,** Kent Street.

The best accommodations in town are probably at the **McNevins Parkway Motel** (Tel: 071-222888) at 188 John Street. There are 50 high-quality units with good facilities and a pool, spa, restaurant, bar, room service, laundry, and children's playground. Rates are from around A$65 double. The smaller **Maryborough Motor Inn** (Tel: 071-222777) at Ferry and Queen Streets has similar facilities and prices. Cheaper rooms are available at the **Wallis Motel and Caravan Park** (Tel: 071-213970) at 22 Ferry Street, and at **Kellys Roadhouse Motel and Caravan Park** (Tel: 071-214681). Old-style hotel rooms are found at the **Criterion Hotel** (Tel: 071-213043) in Wharf Street, and the **Federal Hotel** (Tel: 071-224711) at 270 Kent Street.

Most of the motels and hotels have restaurants or you could try **Mimosa Restaurant Down Under** (Tel: 23-1459) at 389 Kent Street for crepes and Mexican food, or the **Timber City Cafe** (Tel: 23-1349) at 375 Kent Street, for light meals, snacks, and coffee. The **Colonial Kitchen Restaurant** (Tel: 23-2700) in the heritage-listed Engineers Arms Hotel on March Street has simple home-style meals in attractive surroundings, while **Feelgoods Family Restaurant** (Tel: 21-2241) at 340 Kent Street, is a well-priced all-you-can-eat buffet that is open for lunch and dinner seven days.

Some useful contacts are **Maryborough Taxis** (Tel: 21-2533). **Starline Taxis** (Tel: 22-2311), **Avis Rent-a-Car** (Tel: 22-3644), **Maryborough Promotions Bureau** (Tel: 21-4111), **RACQ** (Tel: 22-4655), **hospital** (Tel: 21-2222), **post office** (Tel: 21-2918), **Qantas information** (Tel: 21-5623), and **city council** (Tel: 21-2431).

HERVEY BAY

This region, 35 kilometers from Maryborough, has established itself as one of Queensland's premier family holiday destinations. The area has sheltered waters and attractive beaches, boating and fishing opportunities, water sports, and a growing number of man-made attractions. There are whale watching cruises from August to October, barge and ferry access to Fraser Island, and a two-week **Whale Festival** in August. This is no night-bird's heaven or thrill-seeker's paradise. Life here is relaxed and unhurried, but visitor facilities are good and improving.

The Hervey Bay urban area stretches for about 10 kilometers along the coast from Urangan to Point Vernon. The population here now outstrips that in Maryborough, but the new city has not yet developed a true heart, although Pialba is likely to emerge as the center. Tourist interest stretches from the tourist boat terminal at the huge **Great Sandy Straits Marina Resort** (Tel: 28-9999), to the 1.4-kilometer-long **Urangan Pier**, which is very popular for fishing, the **Hervey Bay Historical Museum** (Tel: 28-4804) at Scarness, **Vic Hislop's Shark Show** (Tel: 28-9137) on the Esplanade at Uran-gan, **Neptune's Marine Aquarium** (Tel: 28-9828) at Dayman Point, Urangan, and **Natureworld** (Tel: 24-1733) on the main road at the entrance to Hervey Bay. All these places fit the "laid-back" style of the region.

Visitors might like to drive the coast road and check out the accommo-dations offered. A few suggestions are **Hervey Bay Resort** (Tel: 071-281555) on the Esplanade, Pialba (around A$70 a night); **Playa Concha Motor Inn** (Tel: 071-251544) at 475 Esplanade, Torquay (around A$65 a night); **Kon-dari Resort** (Tel: 1-800-072131) with its 10 hectares of lush grounds at 49 Elizabeth Street, Urangan; and the **Delfinos Bay Resort** (Tel: 071-241666) at 383 Esplanade, Torquay. The **Great Sandy Straits Marina Resort** (Tel: 071-289999) has two-bedroom apartments from A$130 nightly or A$500 weekly. Budget travelers have the choice of the excellently situated **Koala Backpackers On the Beach** (Tel: 071-253601) at 408 Esplanade, Torquay; **Beaches Backpackers** (Tel: 071-281458) at 195 Torquay Terrace, Torquay; and **Colonial Backpackers Resort** (Tel: 071-251844) at Boat Harbour Drive, Urangan.

Some of the better-rated restaurants are **Don Camillo** (Tel: 25-1087) at 486 Esplanade, Torquay, for Italian cuisine; **Marina's By the Bay** (Tel: 25-4522) in the Riviera Resort, 385 The Esplanade, Torquay, for French/Mediterranean Food; stylish **Gatakers on the Waterfront** (Tel: 24-2480) for good food and a great outlook; and **Slaughterhouse** (Tel: 25-5466) at Bideford and Freshwater Streets, Torquay, where the outback comes to the coast, and the steaks are just great.

Sporting opportunities include **ten pin bowling** (Tel: 28-4200), **mini-golf** (Tel: 25-1166), **jet skis** (Tel: 28-9758), **lawn bowls** (Tel: 28-1093), **golf** (Tel: 24-4544), and **squash/tennis** (Tel: 28-9147). Major new shopping com-plexes have been developed at **Condor Lakes Shopping Village** (Tel: 28-3690) at Pialba, and **Pialba Place Shopping Village** (Tel: 28-4306). The **Sunset Market** every Friday at 5 P.M. at the Seafront Oval, Pialba, has arts, crafts, clothing, food, and fun.

There is a road that takes you back to the Bruce Highway at **Howard,** where gracious old **Brooklyn House** (Tel: 29-4943) is well worth visiting. There is a craft shop and Devonshire teas. Historic **Childers** is a National Trust town with many of the buildings coming from the late 1800s. The highway passes along the main street, and it is worth stopping to walk the sidewalk and visit the **Pharmaceutical Museum** and the **Regional Art Gallery.** It is 53 kilometers from here to Bundaberg.

BUNDABERG

Much acclaim greeted the refurbishing of Bundaberg's central business district. Bourbong Street has become a true sub-tropical streetscape with bright flowers blending with fountains, restored buildings, and leafy green trees. Dominating the scene is a charming central pavilion that provides a venue for entertainers, and the amazing Whaling Wall painted by internationally acclaimed environmental marine artist, Wyland. This mural covers the western wall of a six-story office block and is No. 23 in a planned series of 100 world-wide. The wall shows the region's close association with the humpback whales that visit during the August-October period each year.

The **Burnett River** flows through the city, providing recreation facilities for locals and visitors. There are fishing, boating, rowing, and waterskiing facilities. **Anzac, Alexandra,** and **Queens Parks** are along the banks. Alexandra Park has a Victorian-era band rotunda and a free zoo. **Baldwin Swamp** in East Bundaberg is an environmental park with walking trails and boardwalks to take you through the paper bark tea tree forest, vine scrub, and eucalypti forest. The **Millaquin Sugar Mill** and the **Bundaberg Rum Distillery** (Tel: 52-4077) are a little farther downriver. Bundaberg is the only place in Australia where the entire range of sugar production activities occur; growing, machinery manufacture, milling, refining, research, and distilling. You can visit the distillery on tours that depart weekdays at 10 and 11 A.M. and 1, 2, and 3 P.M., and weekend mornings.

Without a doubt, Bundaberg's favorite son is Bert Hinkler. In a lifetime of 40 years, Bert Hinkler became one of the world's greatest pioneer aviators. The **Tourist Information Centre** (Tel: 52-2333) at Bourbong and Mulgrave Streets displays a replica glider and models of his aircraft. **Hinkler House Memorial Museum** (Tel: 52-0222) in the Botanic Gardens, North Bundaberg, is housed in Hinkler's Southhampton, England, home. The building, which was under threat of demolition, was dismantled and brought to Bundaberg in 1983. The **Botanic Gardens** also house the fascinating **Bundaberg & District Historical Museum** (Tel: 52-0101), and the **Bundaberg Steam Tramway Preservation Society**'s coal-fired steam cane train (Tel: 59-3341) which runs on its one-kilometer track. The **Rose Garden Tourist Complex & Restaurant** (Tel: 53-1477) provides snacks, meals, and souvenirs for those who are enjoying the gardens. Also here is **Fairymead House,** a huge plantation home that now houses the sugar museum.

There are a number of what might be called "secondary attractions" close at hand. The **Bundaberg Art Gallery** (Tel: 52-3700) in the School of Arts Building is open weekdays. **Boyd's Antiquatorium** (Tel: 52-2576) at 295 Bourbong Street has vintage cars, early cameras, farm machinery, rare music boxes, and pianos. It is open from 2 to 4 P.M. daily. Out on the Childers Road in the vicinity of the airport, you will find the **Dreamtime Reptile Reserve** (Tel: 55-1015) with its crocodiles, snakes, lizards, and tortoises; **Paradise Park** (Tel: 55-1085) with its excellent bird collection, koalas, and gardens; and the **Pennyroyal Herb Farm** (Tel: 55-1622) with its display gardens, sales office, and herbal treats and snacks in the Culinary Corner.

Schmeider's Cooperage & Craft Centre (Tel: 52-8573) in Alexandra Street lets you see the age-old tradition of barrel making, and you can buy a unique gift. **Tropical Wines** (Tel: 51-5993) at 78 Mt. Perry Road, North Bundaberg, produces dessert wines from fruit. Out at **Calavos, Avocado Grove** (Tel: 59-7367) is a forest of ferns, orchids, rare fruit trees, and birds, with lunches, snacks, and souvenirs available.

There are a number of beach communities within 15 kilometers of the city. **Elliott Heads** is the most southerly, and here there is swimming, fishing, catamaraning, picnicking, and camping. There is a caravan park, cabins, and holiday apartments. **Riverview** is a quiet spot a little upstream where there are small fishing boats for rent. **Innes Park** has a beach and a golf course (Tel: 59-3489). **Bargara,** with Kelly's Beach to the south and Neilson Park beach to the north, is the major center. There are good shopping facilities and excellent accommodations. The **Don Pancho Beach Resort** (Tel: 59-2146) is a Spanish-style building with gardens, a pool, and a restaurant, situated between the beach and an 18-hole golf course. Rates are from around A\$60. **Kelly's Beach Resort** (Tel: 59-1222) is another alternative. There are many motels and apartments such as **Shoreline** (Tel: 59-1180) at 104 Miller Street.

Mon Repos, a few kilometers north, is famous as the largest and most accessible turtle rookery in mainland Australia. This is an environmental park where access is limited during the November to March period. Rangers conduct guided tours each night from the visitor center (Tel: 59-2628) during this period. **Burnett Heads** is at the mouth of the Burnett River. This is also the port of Bundaberg. There is a sugar terminal, and it's the departure point for boats to Lady Musgrave Island.

NORTHWARDS TOWARDS GLADSTONE

The coastal road is paved the 60 kilometers to Rosedale. On the way there are several local roads to the right leading to delightful, isolated coastal fishing villages. **Rosedale** is a small rural center with a friendly country hotel, a general store with a model railway in the garden, and a caravan park. Eight kilometers north, a multitude of gravel roads branch to various points. It's 30 kilometers from here to the highway, but many visitors take a road to the right which leads 60 kilometers to **Agnes Waters.** This has the distinction of being the most northerly surf beach in Queensland. As well as the beach, there is a small museum, some shops, and motel, caravan park, and bed and breakfast accommodations. The **Town of 1770,** named after James Cook made his second landing in Australia here, is six kilometers north. **Round Hill Head** provides excellent views, and the local fishing is good. There is a jetty with trips to **Lady Musgrave Island,** the unusual amphibious vessel environmental tour aboard *Sir Joseph Banks* (Tel: 74-9422), and motel-style and caravan park accommodations.

The main road north from Bundaberg does not follow the coast but rejoins the Bruce Highway at **Gin Gin.** This is an agricultural and pastoral town with shade trees, picnic tables, and gardens in its central area. The **Residence** (Tel: 57-2625) on Mulgrave Street houses the district's pioneering memorabilia, and **Euston House** has arts and crafts. **Lake Monduran,** 24 kilometers to the north, has toilets and barbecues and is popular for water-skiing.

It's another 80 kilometers to **Miriam Vale.** This is the northern gateway to Agnes Waters and Seventeen Seventy. Drop into the new **Discovery Coast Tourist Information Centre** for maps, brochures, and good advice. It's 40 kilometers farther to a turn off to **Tannum Sands.** This and its twin, **Boyne Island** to the north, are developing into popular beach settlements. There are swimming, fishing, boating, and water sports opportunities. The beaches are good, shopping and accommodations are adequate, and it is only 20 kilometers from Gladstone. The huge **aluminium smelter** (Tel: 73-0642) is located nearby, and it offers tours at 10 A.M. each Tuesday and Thursday.

By taking this route, we have bypassed picturesque **Lake Awoonga** with its swimming, picnicking, boating, fishing, walking, and camping possibilities. This area has been extensively developed in recent years and is very attractive. It is eight kilometers west of the Bruce Highway, near **Benaraby,** about 30 minutes from Gladstone.

GLADSTONE

Industrial development is not the ideal base for a great tourism industry and, frankly, Gladstone is not a world-beater in the tourism stakes. Some areas are barren and dusty, but there are also some things well worth seeing. The **marina, Auckland Hill lookout and waterfall, Happy Valley Park** on Glenlyon Street, the **lookout** overlooking the Queensland Alumina plant, and the **Regional Art Gallery and Museum** (Tel: 72-2022) in its handsome white Georgian building in Goondoon Street are worth a quick look.

More time should be allocated to the 55-hectare **Toondoon Botanic Gardens.** This is one of Australia's few totally native botanic gardens. There is an area that specializes in the native plants of the Gladstone region and another that concentrates on North Queensland rain forest. Self-guiding trails take visitors throughout the gardens to points of interest. All start at the orientation shelter.

Potters Place (Tel: 72-4030) at 35 Dawson Road opposite the high school has displays of paintings, pottery, porcelain, jewelry, beadwork, and so on from around 80 local artists. It is open seven days. Back out on the highway, the **Calliope River Historical Village** (Tel: 75-7428) has a range of lovingly restored historical buildings all fitted out with period furniture. This is the scene for regular market days, and vintage car rallies.

It is 107 kilometers from here to Rockhampton.

ROCKHAMPTON

The village started as a makeshift port site. With the help of gold it developed into a thriving town. Now it is a solid city, rich because of grain crops, cattle, and mining. For visitors, Rockhampton has several man-made attractions, impressive cultural facilities, and some of the best heritage buildings in the state.

One of the best ways to walk back through time is to take a stroll on the banks of the **Fitzroy River** along Quay Street. The whole street has been classified by the National Trust. The oldest building is the Australian Estates building at 184. It was erected in 1861. A special **Heritage Walk** has been designed to show visitors some of the best examples of early architecture. Away from Quay Street, other monumental buildings are the **post office** (from 1892), **St. Joseph's Catholic Cathedral** on Gladstone Street, **St. Paul's Anglican Cathedral** on William Street, and the old **Borough Chambers** (from 1885) in North Rockhampton now the headquarters of the Rockhampton Historical Society. Three further glimpses of the past are provided by the 1870s **Rockhampton Heritage Village** (Tel: 27-5676) on Canoona Road near the airport where there are cottage shops among huge trees; the 1850s **Glenmore Homestead** (Tel: 36-1033) on Belmont Road about 12 kilometers north of the city with its family items from last century; and the **Gangalook Heritage Village** about 20 kilometers north of the city, where there are old shops, equipment, coach rides, a dairy, sheep shearing demonstrations, and tours held daily.

Back in the city, Australia's first 40,000 years of civilization is well documented at the country's largest Aboriginal cultural center, **Dreamtime** (Tel: 36-1655) on the Bruce Highway, North Rockhampton. Here you can see a sandstone cave replica, burial sites, rock art, gunyahs (Aboriginal shelters), and a tree-lined billabong (old river).

The **Rockhampton Botanic Gardens** (Tel: 22-1654) in Spencer Street about 1.5 kilometers behind the Capricorn Information Center at the Tropic of Capricorn is one of the best provincial gardens in Australia. The 40-hectare gardens were established in 1869 and now have stunning displays of tropical foliage, a fernery, an orchid house, a Japanese garden, a flight aviary, a fauna park, and the Koala Research Centre. The **Cliff Kershaw Native Botanic Gardens** (Tel: 22-1654) Charles Street, North Rockhampton, is a rapidly developing area of Australian wetlands and rain forest flora, with a scented garden and a spectacular waterfall.

The **Rockhampton City Art Gallery** (Tel: 27-7129) beside the Pilbeam Theater in Victoria Parade has a good collection of Australian contemporary art. **Spirals Gallery** sells Aboriginal art, and **The Attic** (Tel: 22-5831) on the mall has a huge range of local arts and crafts. The **Fitzroy Ski Gardens** just upstream of the river barrage has picnic facilities, a children's playground, barbecues, boating, and fishing.

Visitors interested in spectacular natural history will find the limestone caves about 20 kilometers north of the city of great interest. There is a small community beside the Bruce Highway called **The Caves**, and there are two private operators, **Cammoo Caves** (Tel: 34-2774), and **Olsen's Capricorn Caverns** (Tel: 34-2883).

CAPRICORN COAST

Beaches, islands, space, and laid-back enjoyment are the hallmarks of this region. **Yeppoon** is the major center, but there are 45 kilometers of coastline south to Keppel Sands to provide many options. **Keppel Sands** is regarded as one of the best fishing spots in Queensland. **Emu Park** is home to *The Singing Ship,* a free-form spire designed to interpret the spirit of Captain Cook's ship the HMS *Endeavour.* **Rosslyn Bay Boat Harbour** is the base for the charter vessels to Keppel Islands and the Great Barrier Reef.

The area has some man-made attractions, but none of them are in the "world-beater" category. **Coral Life Marineland** (Tel: 39-6581) has sharks, stingrays, and turtles at Kinka Beach. **Kooorana Crocodile Farm** (Tel: 43-4749) between Keppel Sands and Emu Park lets you get close to these formidable creatures. **Camel Jaunts** (Tel: 39-3248) gives you a peaceful bush trek at Yeppoon. The **Cooberrie Park Fauna Sanctuary** (Tel: 39-7590) is 10 kilometers north of Yeppoon.

Accommodations here are mainly in motels and holiday apartments. The notable exception is the large **Capricorn International Resort** (Tel: 079-390211) on the beach amid huge grounds, a few kilometers north of Yeppoon. This was planned as Australia's largest resort development, but it

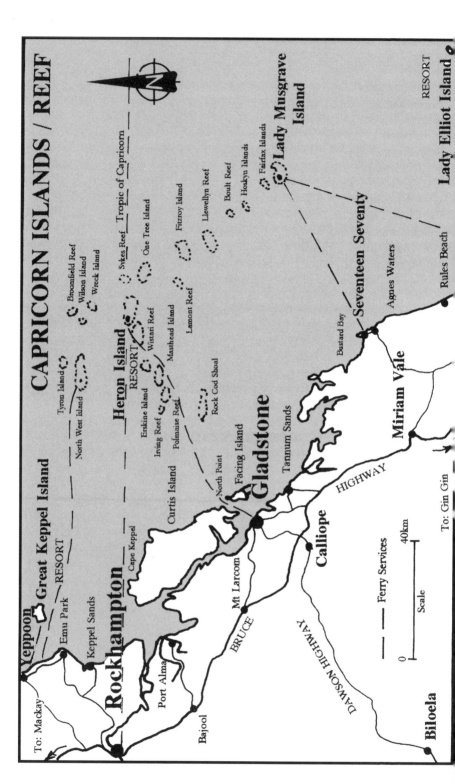

has had a mixed history and has not developed as intended. Nevertheless it offers good facilities at the room rate of A$130 for two. There are two 18-hole golf courses, a large pool, restaurants, bars, tennis, and water sports. Other options are the **Rosslyn Bay Resort** (Tel: 079-336333) with restaurant, pool, tennis, and putting green for A$70 double; **L'Amor Holiday Apartments** (Tel: 079-336255) at Lammermoor Beach for A$65 double; and bushland-set **Gumnut Glen** (Tel: 079-393988) at South Tanby Road, Yeppoon, with 12 airconditioned self-contained cabins and a pool, tennis, barbecues, and wildlife.

A different experience is offered by the **Byfield State Forest** farther to the north. There is some lush flora, native fauna, and various picnic areas. Accommodations and food are provided by **Ferns Hideaway** (Tel: 079-351235), and the **Nob Creek Pottery** is worth a visit.

7. Guided Tours

There are only limited land touring opportunities in this region. In Bundaberg, **Rum City Tours** (Tel: 071-514409) operates a day tour with light lunch, visiting many of the district attractions. Cost is around A$40. **Adina Tours** (Tel: 018-798126) operates both full- and half-day trips, a day trip to Fraser Island each Wednesday, and extended tours to the hinterland. Three- and five-day tours are offered by **Bundaberg Coach Tours** (Tel: 071-531037). Joy flights in vintage aircraft are available from the **Bundaberg Airport** (Tel: 018-797828). There is a half-day guided tour of the extensive wetlands from the **Capricorn International Resort** at Yeppoon for A$20 adults.

On the water it is a different story. From Hervey Bay there are many vessels offering fishing trips and, in the season, whale watching trips. One of the most popular is *Spirit of Hervey Bay* (Tel: 25-5131). Most services leave from Urangan Harbour. Catamaran services operate from the Kingfisher Bay Marine Terminal to the resort on Fraser Island, while barges operate from River Heads to the resort, from Urangan to Moon Point on Fraser Island, and from River Heads to Wanggoolba Creek. Barge fares are around A$60 for four-wheel-drive vehicle and driver. **Top Tours** (Tel: 25-3933) have one- and two-day tours to Fraser Island. **Harry's Air Charter** (Tel: 25-3054) has a variety of offerings. **Fraser Island Cruiser Charters** (Tel: 018-797719) lets you rent your own 10-meter cruiser for a holiday afloat. **Krystal Klear** (Tel: 28-9537) has daily coral viewing trips from Urangan for around A$45.

8. The Reef and Islands

This is the most southerly coastal region to offer reasonable access to the Great Barrier Reef. Here are some of the options.

From Bundaberg, day trips are operated to Lady Musgrave Island by **Lady Musgrave Barrier Reef Cruises Catamaran** (Tel: 1-800-072110) from Port Bundaberg Jetty, and by **Bundaberg Seaplane Tours** (Tel: 071-552068). There are trips several days a week from Seventeen Seventy to Lady Musgrave Island by **Great Barrier Reef Cruises** (Tel: 74-9077). From Gladstone a two-day trip to Heron Island including launch transfers, three meals, and overnight accommodations is available at around A$220. A day tour to Lady Elliot Island by air is available from Gladstone (Tel: 72-2288) for A$130.

From Rosslyn Harbour near Yeppoon, there are trips to Great Keppel Island, Middle Island Underwater Observatory, North West Island, and the Great Barrier Reef. Try **Reefseeker Cruises** (Tel: 079-336744), **Australis Cruises** (Tel: 079-336865) or **Island Taxi** (Tel: 079-395095).

THE ISLANDS

There are a large number of islands off this coast, but most of them have no development and are not readily accessible. From Seventeen Seventy north, there are several coral cays that can be visited, and off the Capricorn Coast there are some mainland-type islands with visitor facilities. I will cover these islands in a general south to north direction.

Lady Elliot Island

This small coral cay is at the very southern end of the Great Barrier Reef. It has good fringing reef and is popular with divers. The fringing reef has been the undoing of many vessels over the past 150 years, and remains of wrecks are seen on the reef flat, the beach, and in various items around the resort. Some of the island has good vegetation cover, but other areas are barren. This is due to guano mining that occurred last century and to later overgrazing by goats that were put ashore as food for possible shipwrecked sailors. The island has an 1870s lighthouse, two graves in a tiny graveyard, and a growing number of permanent and migratory birds.

The **Lady Elliot Island Resort** (Tel: 1-800-072200 or in the USA Tel: 1-800-531-9222) is low-key but comfortable. There are four levels of accommodations; tent cabins with electric power, covered patio, and four bunk beds; a 10-room lodge with verandah and four bunk beds per room; motel-style reef units with attached bathroom; and larger, better equipped island suites. No accommodations are airconditioned or luxurious. There are two bars, a restaurant with straightforward food, a dive shop, a souvenir shop, a children's playground, and the Reef Eco Center.

Activities center around diving, snorkeling, reef walking, and swimming. There is excellent diving straight off the beach on the western side of the island. The coral gardens are good, and you can often see huge manta rays, sharks, and turtles. Snorkeling is good near the resort, and there are fish here that will take food from your hand. There is a glass-bottom boat, fishing trips, a small par-3 golf course, archery, and bowls. Sometimes there is nighttime entertainment.

Access is by air from Bundaberg, Hervey Bay, or Gladstone. The island is the only coral cay along the coast to have an air strip. **Day trips** are possible (Tel: 1-800-072200) at around A$130, but it is better to stay longer. A two-day/one-night package including transfers, accommodations, and two meals is from around A$220. (Book accommodations at Lady Elliot Island, via Torquay, Hervey Bay 4655.)

Lady Musgrave Island

This is a tiny uninhabited national park about 40 kilometers north of Lady Elliot Island. The 14-hectare coral cay rests on the edge of an accessible deep-water lagoon, so it is ideal for boats and day-trippers. A small resort was established here in 1939, but it soon folded. The whole island became a national park in 1967, and in 1979 the surrounding waters became part of the Great Barrier Reef Marine Park. The open vegetation of the southeastern side gives way to rambling stands of pisonia and sandpaper fig in the center, then higher density pisonia forest towards the sheltered northwestern side. The beach here is backed by graceful coastal she oak trees.

The island is very important as a breeding ground for seabirds. Shearwaters nest in burrows, and black noddies build messy, flimsy nests in the pisonia trees. Green and loggerhead turtles nest on the island in summer. Permit camping is allowed on the island, and there are bush toilets provided, but there is no water, and firewood must not be burned. Day trips operate from Bundaberg on *M.V. Lady Musgrave* (Tel: 1-800-072110) and from Seventeen Seventy with **Captain Cook Cruises** (Tel: 079-749077). Both trips provide lunch, coral viewing, and a chance to walk the island.

Quoin Island

This is very different from the previous islands. It is a native fauna reserve, a mainland-type island within Gladstone harbor. Bushwalking is very popular, and you are likely to see wallabies, guinea fowl, and wild turkeys. The **Quoin Island Resort** (Tel: 079-722255) provides accommodations for up to 60 guests. Cabin-style self-contained rooms have airconditioning, TV, radio, refrigerator, tea/coffee-making facilities, and a private deck. Breakfasts and evening meals are included in the tariff. There are wading and swimming pools, a spa, a sauna, tennis, canoeing, sailing, fishing, a library, kite-flying, and sailboarding. Day visitors are welcome. Access is 20 minutes by private ferry from Gladstone Marina, but it should be noted that the island was not operating at the time of this writing (late 1995), and its future is uncertain.

Forty-kilometer-long **Curtis Island** is across the channel, and at times there is a weekend ferry service from Gladstone to Southend where there are lodge accommodations and some camping facilities. This was not operating in late 1995.

Heron Island

This is one of the best-known coral cays right on the reef. It is virtually on the Tropic of Capricorn about 70 kilometers northeast of Gladstone. The island is surrounded by 24 square kilometers of reef, and this is its big attraction. It was named in 1843 by Joseph Jukes because of the many reef herons that he saw. Today the island is home to tens of thousands of noddy terns, and every tree is laden with their ramshackle nests. Two-thirds of Heron was declared a national park in 1943, and it was the first coral reef in Australia to be declared a Marine National Park (1974).

The **Heron Island Resort** (Tel: 079-781488) is owned by P&O Resorts. It seems that Heron is better known overseas than it is in Australia, and over half of the guests are international visitors. Most are divers or "wannabe" divers. There has been a resort here since 1932, and although nothing remains from that time, there is quite a range of accommodations from different eras. The cheapest accommodations are the lodges, which sleep four and have shared bathroom facilities. Next are the motel-style Reef Suites, which have refrigerators, radios, tea/coffee-making facilities, a ceiling fan, and bathroom. The Heron and Point Suites are up-market from here.

Resort facilities include pool, restaurant, coffee shop, dive shop, tennis, semi-submersible vessel for coral viewing, and giant chess. There are many activities including dive tuition, day and night dive trips, snorkeling trips, reef walks, fishing, guided walks, helicopter joy flights, and entertainment. The University of Queensland has a research center on the island, which can be visited, and there is a Marine Parks Information Centre run by a park ranger. Access is about two hours by high-speed catamaran from Gladstone (about A$130 round-trip) or **Lloyd's Helicopters** (Tel: 079-781177) will get you there in 30 minutes (about A$300 round-trip). Daily rates at Heron start at around A$150 per person, meals included, but standby rates (within 48 hours of arrival) can reduce this to around A$115. (Book at Heron Island Resort, via Gladstone 4680 or P&O Resorts, Fax: 612-9299-2477).

P&O, from time to time, also operates nearby **Wilson Island** where there are eight canvas tents on wooden platforms, communal hot showers, a central dining area, and peace and privacy. The beach is excellent, the snorkeling is sensational, and the sense of being an exotic beachcomber will appeal to many. The cost is around A$150 a day with meals; however, this was not operating in late 1995, and its future is uncertain.

North West Island and Others

North West Island, due west of Wilson Island, is the largest cay in the Great Barrier Reef region. For the white-capped noddy and the wedge-tailed shearwater, it is the largest breeding site on the reef. It is also a major green turtle nesting site and a particularly beautiful place for visitors. The island is a national park with no resort facilities, but permit camping for up to 150 people is allowed. (Contact P.O. Box 1362, Rockhampton, or Tel: 079-276511 for permit inquiries.) Pit toilets are provided, and there is a hut, the "Tanby Hilton," containing several small water tanks which are fed from roof runoff, although it is recommended that you bring your own supply. Access is provided from Rosslyn Bay by the **Capricorn Reefseeker** a few days a week (about A$100 for day trip), and there are also trips from Gladstone (contact **P&O Marine Division,** Tel: 72-5166).

Masthead Island and **Tyron Island** are two others in this area where camping is permitted, although there are no regularly scheduled boat connections to either. Charter operators from Gladstone and Seventeen Seventy are happy to take visitors there. They are both important bird and turtle nesting islands. Neither island has any constructed camping facilities, so campers must be completely self-sufficient.

Great Keppel Island

This relatively large mainland-type island has lovely beaches, some decent hills, and a long history of settlement. It was named by Captain Cook in 1770 but was probably occupied by Aborigines for long periods before that. The first whites settled in 1906, and the island was used during the 1920s and Thirties by the Leeke family to graze sheep. Their restored house can be visited today. A resort was established in 1967. and today there is a variety of accommodations on the island.

The Qantas-operated **Great Keppel Resort** (Tel: 079-395044) is by far the largest complex on the island. It is promoted as an active resort, and there are many facilities and activities to keep guests busy. There are around 200 guest rooms and a choice of three levels of accommodations. The older beachfront and garden units are motel-style with fan, TV, telephone, refrigerator, tea/coffee-making facilities, and verandah. The ocean-view villas are newer, more stylish, and have airconditioning. Activities which are included in the room rate include tennis, golf, squash, windsurfers, catamarans, archery, aerobics, volleyball, and the swimming pools.

Restaurant choices are the main dining room, a char grill for steak or fish, and a cafe for burgers, pies, pizzas, and snacks. Guests can buy a meal package if they wish. The cocktail bar is a popular place for a drink, while the Anchorage Bar has a live band or disco most nights. Room rates start at around A$250 double, but most people are on some sort of package, which reduces the cost considerably. Ask about stand-by rates if you have not booked ahead. (Book at Great Keppel Island Resort, Queensland 4702 or by Fax: 6179-391775.)

Keppel Haven (Tel: 079-391907) is much more down-market, but it is relaxed, friendly, and popular. There are cabins, with kitchens and laundry but no bathrooms, which sleep up to six. This has recently been bought by one of the cruise boat operators, so they are keen to promote packages inclusive of transfers. Cost for two people is around A$120. There are also permanent safari tents with mattresses at A$84 per double, and beachfront camping for those with their own equipment. Facilities include a popular kiosk/store with some supplies, an evening restaurant, a bar for light meals and drinks, a dive shop, and a kitchen with refrigerator and barbecue.

The **YHA Hostel** is known as the **Captain Cook Memorial Camp.** Bookings are made by the **Rockhampton Hostel** (Tel: 079-275288) and are strongly recommended because the Great Keppel Hostel is a very popular place. It has a guest kitchen, barbecue facilities, and a volleyball court. There are two dorms and two eight-bed units with bathrooms. Bed costs are from A$12. **Keppel Lodge** (Tel: 075-394251) is another alternative. There are four motel-style rooms with a central lounge and kitchen. Rates are around A$80 double.

Keppel Watersports, which is run by the resort, has equipment for rent on Fishermans Beach. Some of this is free to resort guests, but it is all available to everyone else for a fee. There are jet skis, snorkeling gear, windsurfers, catamarans, motorboats, paraflying, and waterskiing. Some of these activities are also available from the Beach Hut on Putney Beach. There are regular trips to the **Middle Island Underwater Observatory** (Tel: 39-4191) and to the Great Barrier Reef at North West Island. Everyone is welcome to visit the **Shell Shop** with its pleasant tropical garden and excellent Devonshire teas, and the **Island Pizza** with its pizzas, pastas, sandwiches, and hot dogs. Access is provided by several vessels from Rosslyn Bay (try **Reefseeker,** Tel: 33-6744, or **Australis,** Tel: 33-6865) and by **Sunstate Airlines** (Qantas) (Tel: 13-1313) from Rockhampton.

Middle Island, west of Great Keppel, is a national park and the site of an underwater observatory. **North Keppel Island** is a reasonable-size national park island about 10 kilometers north of Great Keppel. It has a campground at Considine Beach with toilets and well water. Tiny **Pumpkin Island,** just a few hundred meters from North Keppel, has a few cabins with stove, refrigerator, bathroom, solar electricity, and water. They sleep up to five for a cost of A$100 a night (Tel: 39-2431).

9. Sports

There are good sporting facilities at all the major centers. Most clubs welcome visitors to their facilities. Here are a few suggestions.

Golf

The **Bundaberg Golf Club** (Tel: 52-6765) is at One Mile Road, the **Bargara Golf Club** (Tel: 59-2221) is on Millar Street, and the **Innes Park Country Club** (Tel: 59-3489) is on Innes Park Road. The **Maryborough Golf Club** (Tel: 21-3717) is on Queens Street.

In Gladstone, the **Gladstone Golf Club** (Tel: 78-1200) is close to the center of town on Hickory Avenue. The **Boyne Tannum Country Club** (Tel: 73-7377) on Jacaranda Drive has a nice nine-hole course.

At Rockhampton, the **Rockhampton Golf Club** (Tel: 27-3311) is on Anne Street Extension, and the **Capricorn Country Club** (Tel: 27-7766) is on Richardson Road, North Rockhampton. The **Capricorn International Resort** (Tel: 39-0211) at Yeppoon has two 18-hole courses. The **Emu Park Golf Club** (Tel: 39-6804) is on Rockhampton Road, as is the **Yeppoon Golf Club** (Tel: 39-1056).

Bowling

Maryborough has the **Sugar Coast Lanes** (Tel: 22-3100) and Hervey Bay, the **Bay City Ten Pin Bowl** (Tel: 28-4200). In Bundaberg, the **Bundy Bowl** (Tel: 52-4334) is in Heidke Street. The **North Rockhampton Squashbowl** (Tel: 27-1555) has both bowling and squash.

Diving

Facilities are good from the resort islands, and the following also have services.

Anglo Diving Services—200 Bourbong St., Bundaberg (Tel: 51-6422)
Bundaberg Dive Centre—22 Quay Street (Tel: 52-6707)
Capricorn Reef Diving—189 Musgrave St., Rock. (Tel: 22-7700)
C.Q. Fishing & Diving—16 Goondoon St., Gladstone (Tel: 72-4658)
Rockhampton Diving—61 High St., Nth., Rockhampton (Tel: 28-0433)
Tropicana Dive—12 Anzac Parade, Yeppoon (Tel: 39-4642)

Horseracing

The **Bundaberg Race Club** (Tel: 53-1416) and the **Bundaberg Greyhound Racing Club** (Tel: 52-2033) share facilities in Maynard Street. Gladstone has horse racing under the control of the **Gladstone Turf Club** (Tel: 72-1493).

The Rockhampton Jockey Club holds races each Saturday at the **Callaghan Park Track** (Tel: 27-1300) in North Rockhampton. This is also the venue for meetings held by the **Rockhampton Greyhound Racing Club** (Tel: 22-5793) and the **Rockhampton Harness Racing Club** (Tel: 27-1633).

Sailing

There are clubs in most centers. Traveling north, the **Maryborough Sailing Club** (Tel: 21-3436), the **Hervey Bay Sailing Club** (Tel: 25-3980) at the Esplanade, Torquay, and the **Bundaberg Sailing Club** (Tel: 59-4424) at Port Bundaberg, are all active. The **Gladstone Yacht Club** (Tel: 72-2294) is involved in the annual Brisbane to Gladstone Yacht Classic and the accompanying Harbour Festival that fills the marina parklands each Easter. **Keppel Isle Yacht Charters** (Tel: 39-4949) has facilities for bareboat or crewed charters.

Other Sports

Information on a wide range of other sports is best obtained from the local telephone books, the local newspapers, or from the local tourist offices (see Section 12 of this chapter for names and contacts).

10. Shopping

There are good shopping facilities in the major centers but little to buy that is not available elsewhere in Australia. Most of the major centers have regional shopping plazas that compete with the central business districts. **Rockhampton Shopping Fair** in North Rockhampton is one of the largest.

The **Maryborough Heritage City Markets** each Thursday in Kent and Adelaide Streets bring back the pleasure of old-time shopping. The **Bundaberg Craft and Treasure Markets** (Tel: 52-6549) are held every Sunday at Shalom College. The **Rocky Markets** (Tel: 22-2400) at 132 Denison Street, Rockhampton, have food, plants, antiques, jewelry, clothes, and handicrafts each Saturday and Sunday from 8 A.M. to 2 P.M.

11. Entertainment and Nightlife

Rockhampton and Gladstone both have very active theaters which stage local productions and present visiting groups and artists. None of the cities are "big" on nightlife, although most have pubs with weekend entertainment, sports clubs, and others with gambling machines, discos, and at least one nightclub.

In Bundaberg, **Caseys Cabaret** (Tel: 52-8266) at 17 Electra Street is a popular place. In Gladstone, **Gattor Bar** (Tel: 72-2847) and **Visions Night Club** (Tel: 72-6333) are both at 6 Goondoon Street. Rockhampton has more action with **Pinocchio's Nite Club** (Tel: 22-5344) at 189 East Street,

Flamingo (Tel: 27-9988) at Quay and William Streets, and **Strutters Uptown** (Tel: 22-2882) at East and William Streets, all drawing crowds.

12. The Bundaberg, Gladstone, and Rockhampton Contact List

Bundaberg

Ambulance—7A Maryborough Street (Tel: 522455)
Bus Terminal—66 Targo Street (Tel: 529700)
Churches—Anglican, 233 Bourbong Street (Tel: 512467)
  —Catholic, Holy Rosary, 70 Woongarra St. (Tel: 516666)
  —Uniting, Woongarra Street (Tel: 532201)
Emergency Calls—Ambulance, Fire, Police (Tel: 000)
Fire Services—19 Woongarra Street (Tel: 512233)
Mayor's Office—City Council, Bourbong St. (Tel: 524588)
Police—Quay Street (Tel: 521211)
Post Office—157B Bourbong Street (Tel: 532700)
Qantas Airways (Sunstate)—167B Bourbong St. (Tel: 522322)
RACQ—92 Bourbong Street (Tel: 523377)
Rail Services—McLean Street (Tel: 539709)
Taxi—56 Boundary Street (Tel: 512345)
Tourist Information—Bourbong & Mulgrave Sts. (Tel: 522333)

Gladstone

Ambulance—(Tel: 721722)
Churches—Anglican, 70 Auckland Street (Tel: 724754)
  —Catholic, 38 Herbert St. (Tel: 726611)
  —Uniting, 13 Waratah St. (Tel: 781778)
Emergency calls—Ambulance, Fire, Police (Tel: 000)
Fire Service—Charles St. (Tel: 721011)
Mayor's Office—101 Goonboon Street (Tel: 722022)
Police—Yarroon St. (Tel: 721122)
Post Office—69 Goondoon St. (Tel: 722413)
Qantas Airways (Sunstate)—81 Goondoon St. (Tel: 723488)
RACQ—Glenlyon Street (Tel: 723911)
Rail Services—Tooloona St. (Tel: 764211)
Taxi—27 Chappel St. (Tel: 721800)
Tourist Information—56 Goondoon St. (Tel: 729922)

Rockhampton

Ambulance—(Tel: 278333)
Churches—Anglican, St. Paul's (Tel: 276555)

—Catholic, St. Joseph's, 170 William St. (Tel: 278898)
—Uniting, 15 Bowen Terrace (Tel: 221026)
Emergency calls—Ambulance, Fire, Police (Tel: 000)
Fire Service—113 Kent St. (Tel: 271488)
Mayor's Office—Bolsover St. (Tel: 311311)
Police—Denham St. (Tel: 321500)
Post Office—80 East St. (Tel: 276566)
Qantas Airways—107 East St. (Tel: 221033)
RACQ—134 William St. (Tel: 272255)
Rail Services—George St. (Tel: 320453)
Taxi—163 East St. (Tel: 227111)
Tourist Information—The Spire (Tel: 272055)
            —Riverside, Quay St. (Tel: 225339)

7

Townsville and the Central Great Barrier Reef

1. The General Picture

The sun shines brightly on the seemingly endless Great Barrier Reef and the surrounding flat blue sea. Sleek high-speed boats leave shimmering wakes as they head out into the stunning Coral Sea with sightseers, scuba divers, fishing folk, and adventurers. All is warm, clean, and fresh.

This is North Queensland, one of Australia's most popular playgrounds for those seeking lush tropical islands, white beaches, dense rain forest, boating, diving, and relaxation in the sun.

Townsville is the "big city" here. You have to travel 1,400 kilometers south to find anything larger, but by many standards its population of around 130,000 still makes it "small." Townsville is graced by a pace that is slower, a feeling that time is perhaps not too important, and a friendliness now missing from much of the rest of the world.

Australian Aborigines have lived here for thousands of years, but Western knowledge of the area started with Captain Cook, who sailed this coast in 1770. Cook named many islands, capes, and bays, but some of the other place names you hear today are developed from the Aboriginal languages that existed centuries before.

Even today, there are more black faces here than in most parts of the country; Aborigines, Torres Strait Islanders, and South Sea Islanders. These

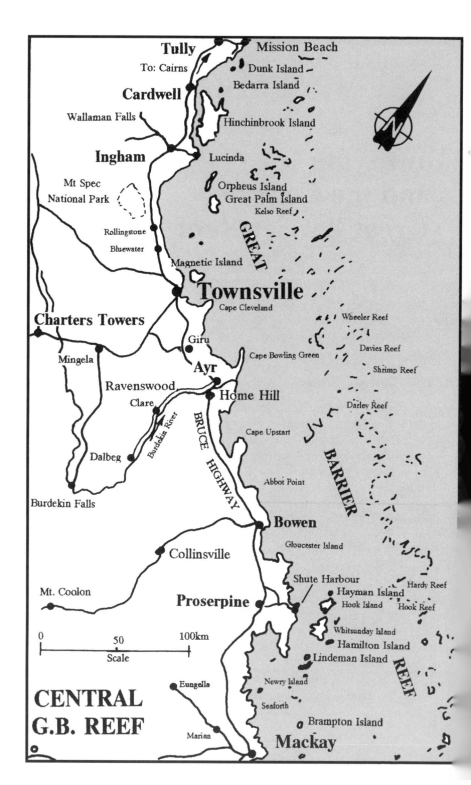

people have been joined in more recent times by sizable communities of Italians, Greeks, Filipinos, and others to provide an interesting mix in the population.

Townsville is keen on tourism, but it is also a significant center for research, education, government, business, and industry. The international airport and the rapidly expanding port are supported by one of the richest and most diverse regions in Australia. In the central city, highrise towers stand tall beside century-old colonial buildings, amid palm trees and brilliant bougainvillea. Huge, shady old homes on stilts, guarded by laden mango trees, live on in near pristine condition in the older inner suburbs.

Tourists come to this region because of the reef, the islands, and the weather. There is a perfect warm-to-hot winter climate from April to October, with clear days and balmy nights. Sunshine is guaranteed; in fact, Townsville receives more sunshine hours than any other large city in Australia.

Elsewhere, there are many smaller places to enjoy along the coast. **Mackay** is an attractive city serving the sugar, cattle, coal, and tourism industries. Major investments in resorts and cruise facilities in recent years have resulted in large increases in tourist numbers. Mackay's northern beaches and Brampton Island are particularly popular. Farther north, the Whitsunday mainland and islands are some of the best places in Australia to spend a vacation on or near the water. The principal mainland center is **Airlie Beach** (now part of Whitsunday), a small, attractive, waterfront town with a significant tourism infrastructure.

Bowen, Ayr, Ingham, and **Cardwell** are all small local centers that provide low-key tourism opportunities. For those looking for uncrowded beaches, an unhurried lifestyle, and reasonably inexpensive facilities, any of these towns would suffice. **Mission Beach,** in the northern part of the region, is less of a natural center and more of a tourist destination. It has long, clean beaches, walking trails through the rain forest, Aboriginal culture, arts and crafts, interesting restaurants, and nearby islands.

The Central Great Barrier Reef is considered by many to be one of the most interesting and diverse sections of reef. In the south, it is still quite a way off the coast, so it is better protected than some other sections. In the north, it becomes readily accessible and is a popular playground for swimmers, snorkelers, divers, and boating enthusiasts.

2. Getting There

Townsville International Airport has had a checkered history of international services over recent years. There have been scheduled services from the United States, New Zealand, Singapore, Indonesia, and Papua New

Guinea, but all have struggled to survive. At present it is only charter operators that are providing international services. Domestic flights are a different matter. Direct services wing in from Sydney, Brisbane, Mackay, Proserpine, Rockhampton, Mount Isa, and Cairns with increasing frequency. **Qantas,** for instance, has three direct jet services a day from Brisbane, four services a day from Cairns, two from Mackay, and one from Sydney.

Mackay has air services from Brisbane, Townsville, and Rockhampton. **Proserpine** has services from Sydney, Brisbane, and Townsville. **Hamilton Island** has services from Sydney, Brisbane, and Cairns.

Mackay, Proserpine, Bowen, Home Hill, Townsville, Ingham, Cardwell, and Tully are all on the north coast rail line from Brisbane. They are serviced by both the **Sunlander** and **Queenslander** passenger trains with a choice of economy and luxury seating and sleeping berths. These centers are also on the Bruce Highway and are served by **long-distance buses** from Brisbane and Cairns. Many bus fares are in the budget range.

Several tour companies offer one-way or round-trip coach tours to North Queensland from Brisbane with accommodations, sightseeing, and some meals included.

Or why not drive? The **Bruce Highway** from Brisbane has been upgraded, accommodations are readily available, and the attractions on the way are numerous. Brisbane to Townsville can take two days, two weeks, or two months.

3. Local Transportation

All of the main centers have **taxis** that are available 24 hours a day. Within urban centers, distances are relatively short, so fares are usually below A$15. Be careful with longer trips to outlying beaches or elsewhere.

Local **bus services** are available in some centers but, except in Townsville, frequencies are usually poor. Fares are reasonable. Some resorts and hotels have shuttle services for guests, and these are recommended when they are available. Bus services operate between airports and many accommodations facilities.

Commuter air services link several islands with mainland centers. Dunk, Hinchinbrook, Great Palm, and Orpheus Islands are linked with Townsville. Brampton Island is connected to Mackay. Hamilton and Lindeman Islands have services from the Whitsunday air strip, and from Mackay.

There are extensive **boat services** in the Whitsundays, and from Mackay to Brampton Island, Townsville to Magnetic Island, and Mission Beach to Dunk Island.

Rental cars are readily available. Townsville has branches of all the national operators plus several local outfits. Some of the locals operate older and cheaper vehicles for use within the local area only. These can save you considerable money. Some operators have four-wheel-drive vehicles, sports models, and recreational vehicles for those who want something different. Here are some of the operators:

Allcar Rentals—12 Somer St., Hyde Park (Tel: 723311)
Australian Rent-a-Car—Mercure Inn, Currajong (Tel: 256621)
Avis Australia—Townsville Airport (Tel: 752888)
Budget Rent-a-Car—293 Ingham Rd. (Tel: 252344)
Four Wheel Drive Hire—711 Flinders St. (Tel: 212404)
Hertz—321 Sturt St., City (Tel: 716003)
National Car Rental—614 Sturt St., City (Tel: 725133)
Rent A Rocket—14 Dean St., South Townsville (Tel: 726880)
Thrifty Car Rental—Dean St., South Townsville (Tel: 724600)
Townsville Car Rentals—12 Palmer St., South Townsville (Tel. 721093)

There are several national and local operators in **Mackay**. Try **Avis** (Tel: 511266), **Budget** (Tel: 511400), **Cut Rate** (Tel: 531616), **Hertz** (Tel: 572662), **Network** (Tel: 531022), and **Thrifty** (Tel: 573677). **Proserpine** has outlets for **Avis** (Tel: 466318), **Budget** (Tel: 451833), and **Hertz** (Tel: 467401), while in **Airlie Beach** you can find **Avis** (Tel: 466318), **Budget** (Tel: 466499), **Hertz** (Tel: 467401), and **Thrifty** (Tel: 467727).

Bicycles and **motorcycles** are available for rent from most centers.

4. The Accommodations Scene

In this section I will only cover accommodations in Townsville and Mackay. For island accommodations see Section 8 within this chapter. For accommodations at other mainland centers see the relevant part of Section 6 within this chapter. The following is only a selection of what is available.

Townsville (Tel. area code 077)

The city has an excellent range of very reasonably priced accommodations from luxury through to budget.

EXPENSIVE ACCOMMODATIONS

The value of Townsville accommodations is seen when I put anything above A$115 in the expensive category. No wonder many visitors decide to stay longer than they planned.

The **Sheraton Breakwater Casino Hotel** (Tel: 222-333), 193 rooms, is the standard-setter for Townsville hotels. The hotel is on a waterfront site about one kilometer from the central business district. All rooms have water views. The rooms are typical five-star, and the hotel has several bars and two excellent restaurants. Melton's, an a la carte restaurant, only opens for dinner. Sails on the Bay has a buffet or a la carte service for about 18 hours a day (24 hours on weekends). The pool area is particularly attractive, and there are tennis courts and other sporting facilities. Of course, the casino is a big attraction to some people. Even if you don't gamble, it is fun to wander around and watch the action. Room rates start at around A$165. (Book at Sir Leslie Theiss Drive, Townsville 4810 or Fax: 6177-724741.)

The **Townsville Travelodge** (Tel: 72-2477), 134 rooms and 52 suites, is the other hotel in this category. The 20-story circular building is in the heart of the central business district. All rooms have sweeping sea or city views. Hotel facilities include a rooftop swimming pool and barbecue area, two restaurants, three bars, 24-hour room service, in-room video rental, hair dryers and irons, and all the other usual features. Free covered valet parking is provided. Room prices start at A$115 for standard rooms. Suites and two-bedroom family rooms with kitchenettes are also available. (Book with the hotel at 334 Flinders Mall, Townsville 4810 or Fax: 6177-211263.)

MEDIUM-PRICE ACCOMMODATIONS

Aquarius on the Beach (Tel: 72-4255), 156 rooms, has an excellent beachfront position about two kilometers from the center of the city. All rooms in this highrise, all-suite hotel have vibrant-colored decor, kitchenettes, nice balconies, and water and island views. Facilities include a ground-level, palm-enclosed swimming pool, a poolside cafe, a top-floor restaurant, a bar, in-house movies, and a guest laundry. Room rates start at A$105. (Book with the hotel at 75 The Strand, Townsville 4810 or Fax: 6177- 211316.)

A viable alternative to this is the nearby family-run **Townsville Reef International** (Tel: 21-1777). This is a low-rise development with 45 quality rooms with balconies, covered parking, swimming pool and spa, 24-hour reception, and licensed restaurant and bar. There is a nice feel to this Best Western property. Room prices start from A$100. (Book with the hotel at 63 The Strand, Townsville 4810 or Fax: 6177-211779.)

Southbank Motor Inn (Tel: 21-1474) is close to the city on the south side of Ross Creek. The 98 rooms are all well appointed, and many have good views over the creek and city. A licensed restaurant, bar, 24-hour reception, in-house video, a children's playground, and covered parking are some of the attractions. The inn belongs to the Flag Group. Room rates start at A$95. (Book with the inn at 23 Palmer Street, Townsville 4810 or Fax: 6177-212010.)

The **Mercure Inn Townsville** (Tel: 25-2222), 200 rooms, is a lakeside resort about three kilometers from the city center. The inn has a large free-form swimming pool, spa, sauna, and tennis court. Some units have kitchens, some have balconies, and all are serviced daily. The inn is part of the largest hotel group in Australia. Room rates start at A$100. (Book with the hotel at Woolcock Street, Currajong, Townsville 4810 or Fax: 6177-251384.)

Seagulls Resort (Tel: 1-800-079929) is another delightful alternative. The 70-room low-rise property has lush landscaping, and there are some sea views through the trees. A palm-studded island in the free-form swimming pool mimics the view of Magnetic Island across the bay. Attractions include a tropical-style restaurant, a pool bar, compact tennis, guest laundry, a barbecue area, a children's playground, and in-house video. Some units have a kitchen, and some have a balcony. Room rates start at A$75. (Book with the resort at 74 The Esplanade, Belgium Gardens, Townsville 4810 or Fax: 6177-213133.)

Back in the city, the **Plaza Hotel** (Tel: 1-800-653598) has 70 recently renovated rooms right on the mall. The hotel has a popular restaurant, lobby bar, pool, sauna, spa, guest laundry, and 24-hour in-house movies. Rates are from A$65. (Book at Stanley Street, Townsville 4810 or Fax: 6177-721299.)

Robert Towns Motel (Tel: 71-6908) is a Greentrees Inn a little farther up Stanley Street. The 47 rooms and suites are adequate, and facilities include a popular licensed restaurant and bar, a swimming pool, barbecue facilities, in-house video, and guest laundry. Room rates are from A$60. (Book with the hotel at 261 Stanley Street, Townsville 4810 or Fax: 6177-211492.)

The **Rex Inn The City** (Tel: 71-6048) is just around the corner. This recently renovated motel has a saltwater pool, heated spa, and barbecue area. The location is a three-minute walk from the center of the city. There is no restaurant, but breakfast and dinner can be ordered to eat in the room. Room rates are from A$55. (Book with the inn at 143 Wills Street, Townsville 4810 or Fax: 6177-215076.)

A further option in this area is the **Town Lodge** (Tel: 71- 2164). There are 10 standard motel units, 10 self-contained units with kitchenettes, and four two-room self-contained units. The location is quiet and secluded, and some of the units have excellent views. There is a pool and also a barbecue area. Room rates are from A$60. (Book with the motel at 15 Victoria Street, Townsville 4810 or Fax: 6177-721270.)

Historic Yongala Lodge (Tel: 72-4633) has nine rooms and 10 self-contained units. The location is within walking distance of the city and the beach, and the Greek restaurant in the old house is a real delight. The lodge has a pool, room service, a barbecue, and a laundry. Room rates are from A$60. (Book with the hotel at 11 Fryer Street, Townsville 4810 or Fax: 6177-211074.)

For those with transportation, there are cheaper accommodations along Bowen Road, about six kilometers from the city center. This is the main route into the city from the south and west, and there are around a dozen motels in an 800-meter length. Prices start from around A$40, and some are very good value. The **A1 Motel** (Tel: 79-3999), 31 rooms at 107 Bowen Road, is a well-priced older-style property with covered parking, pool, grill room, bar, and in-house video. Room prices start at A$40. The 43-room **Monte Carlo Motor Inn** (Tel: 25-2555) at 45 Bowen Road, is newer and has two pools, a spa, a playground, in-house video rental, a barbecue, and laundry. Room rates are from A$50.

BUDGET ACCOMMODATIONS

Below A$40 there is still considerable choice. **Coral Reef Lodge** (Tel: 71-5512) is a recently renovated heritage guest house close to the city center. Single rooms are A$35, and doubles and self-contained rooms are also available. There is a guest kitchen, barbecue area, and laundry. You find it at 32 Hale Street.

Civic Guest House (Tel: 71-5381) is also in the central city area. The accommodations are clean and homely. Facilities include TV rooms, two kitchens, a barbecue area, and laundry. Single rooms are from A$28. Self-contained rooms are from A$37. Shared rooms are available at A$13 a person. (Book at 262 Walker Street, Townsville 4810 or Fax: 6177-214919.)

Reef Lodge (Tel: 21-1112) has similar facilities. Don't expect heaps of style, but the property is clean and friendly. You will find a kitchen, laundromat, barbecue, and a choice of fans or airconditioning. Single rooms are from A$26 and doubles A$32. You can get shared accommodations from A$10. (Book at Wickam Street, Townsville 4810 or Fax: 6177-211405.)

Adventurers Resort (Tel: 21-1522) at 79 Palmer Street, South Townsville, is the YHA Hostel in Townsville. The modern multi-story development is only three minutes from the bus terminal, and it overlooks a marina and the city. Accommodations are in dorm, single, or double rooms, and there are restaurant, barbecue, pool, spa, guest kitchen, laundry, tour desk, and common room facilities. Rates start at A$12. **Globetrotters** (Tel: 71-3242) is a modern, tropical-style building close by. Facilities include a swimming pool, landscaped gardens, a kitchen, barbecue, and laundry. Single rooms are from A$24 and shared accommodations are A$12. The location is 45 Palmer Street, South Townsville 4810.

You find **Andys backpackers** at the Transit Centre (Tel: 21-2322) in the same area. This is situated within the Townsville long-distance bus terminal. All rooms are airconditioned, and there are restaurant, bar, and take-out food facilities within the complex. Other attractions are the large TV room, the free bus to the ferry terminal, a nightly city tour, and bicycle rental. The center is at Palmer and Plume Streets, South Townsville 4810. Bed rates are from A$12.

Some visitors may prefer accommodations in one of the old central city hotels. Most rooms have a hand basin but no bathroom. Try the renovated **Newmarket Hotel** (Tel: 21-1377) at 499 Flinders Street from A$20 a room; the **Great Northern** (Tel: 71-6191) at 500 Flinders Street from A$18 a room; or the **Tattersalls Hotel** (Tel: 71-3428) at the other end of town at 87 Flinders Street East, from A$15.

A further choice is provided by many of the caravan parks where on-site vans or cabins are available. The **Rowes Bay Caravan Park** (Tel: 71-3576) is on the beach and is one of the more attractive available.

Mackay (Tel. area code 079)

EXPENSIVE ACCOMMODATIONS

There are no accommodations in Mackay that are in the expensive category.

MEDIUM-PRICE ACCOMMODATIONS

The bulk of these accommodations are on Nebo Road (Bruce Highway from the south) or at one of the beaches.

On Nebo Road, the **Alara Motor Inn** (Tel: 51-2699) with 34 ground-level units would be a good choice. Facilities include a nice restaurant which offers the option of poolside dining, room service, pool, hot spa, sauna, and guest laundry. Rates are from A$65. (Book at 52 Nebo Road, Mackay 4740 or Fax: 6179-514785.) An alternative would be the **White Lace Motor Inn** (Tel: 51-4466), a two-level property with excellent restaurant and bar, pool, 24-hour service, and 24-hour in-house movies. Rates here are from A$70. (Book at 73 Nebo Road, Mackay 4740 or Fax: 6179-514942.) A further choice is **Miners Lodge Motor Inn** (Tel: 51-1944). This is a Best Western property with bistro, pool, and barbecue facilities. Rates are from A$65. (Book at 60 Nebo Road, Mackay 4740 or Fax: 6179-572737.)

Illawong Beach, in the southern part of the city, has two noteworthy properties. **Ocean International Hotel** (Tel: 57-2044) has several levels of accommodations, and the popular Galleons Restaurant and Bar. The hotel has 24-hour reception, pool, spa, and sauna. Room rates are from A$110. (Book at 1 Bridge Rd., Mackay 4740 or Fax: 6179-572636.) Almost next door is **Ocean Resort Village** (Tel: 51-3200) where there are 34 airconditioned, self-contained, ground-level apartments with full-size cooking stoves. The village has a swimming and wading pool, tennis, pitch and putt golf, kiosk, and barbecue. Rates are from A$65. (Book at 5 Bridge Road, Mackay 4740 or Fax: 6179-513246.)

My favorite place on the northern beaches is **Ko Huna Beach Resort** (Tel: 54-8555) at Bucasia Beach. There are 60 self-contained bures amid four hectares of lush beachfront gardens. Facilities include Monsoon's Restaurant, the poolside Barefoot Bar and Bistro, three swimming pools, a spa, nightly entertainment, a boutique, tennis, sailboards, and catamarans. Room rates are from A$85. (Book at The Esplanade, Bucasia Beach, Mackay 4750 or Fax: 6179-546080.) **Dolphin Heads Resort** (Tel: 54-6666) is a little to the south. This is also a beachfront property, and it advertises that boredom is banned. There are facilities for tennis, table tennis, mini-golf, and water sports, and it has a Kids Klub. A pool, hot spa, restaurant, coffee shop, and disco help to fill in the hours. Rates are from A$70. (Book at Beach Road, Dolphin Heads, Mackay 4740 or Fax: 6179-548341.) The **Shores Holiday Apartments** (Tel: 54-9444) are farther south again. These were designed for longer-term stays, but they are available for overnight. The beachfront, air-conditioned villas and townhouses are self-contained, and the complex has a pool, spa, tennis court, and barbecue. Rates are from A$70. (Book at 9 Pacific Drive, Blacks Beach, Mackay 4740 or Fax: 6179-548580.)

BUDGET ACCOMMODATIONS

There are a variety of budget accommodations. Some of the motels on Nebo Road or in North Mackay have competitive rates. The **Paradise Lodge Motel** (Tel: 51-3644) near the bus terminal has room rates from A$40. Two backpacker lodges are nearby. **Larrikan Lodge** (Tel: 51-3728) at 32 Peal Street is the Mackay YHA Hostel. **Backpackers Retreat** (Tel: 51-1115) at 21 Peal Street is the other alternative. Rates are from A$12 for dorm beds. The **Tropical Caravan Park** (Tel: 52-1211) has cabins, on-site vans, a shop, a recreation room, and a pool. Rates are A$30. The **Beach Tourist Park** (Tel: 57-4021) is at Illawong Beach. The large site has self-contained cabins, on-site vans, on-site tents, a pool, a kiosk, barbecues, and a camp kitchen.

Out at Bucasia, **Loafers Lodges** (Tel: 54-6308) has self-contained two-bedroom units with a pool and barbecue area. Also popular is the **Bucasia Beachfront Caravan Resort** (Tel: 54-6375) where there are shade trees, a pool, cabins, on-site vans, and a pool room. Rates are from A$30.

5. Dining and Restaurants

I will only discuss Townsville and Mackay restaurants here. See Section 6 of this chapter for dining options in other mainland areas, and Section 8 for island information.

Most visitors to this region are immediately attracted by the great seafood available. You will find fresh king prawns, mud crabs, and two great local fish—barramundi and coral trout. Then there are the tropical fruits—mango, paw paw (papaya), pineapple, lychees, and star fruit. Most restaurants feature dishes based on seafood and fruit, while some specialize in them. Don't forget that the region also has locally grown beef, chicken, crocodile, kangaroo, and emu, so these are also good.

Many visitors are surprised by the quality of the ethnic cuisine available in the area, but this can be explained by the many large ethnic communities here, and the attraction of the easy-going lifestyle of the ethnic Thai, Greek, French, Japanese, and Italian chefs who may otherwise have made the "big time" in the major cities.

Townsville

The major hotels offer excellent dining choices. The award-winning **Melton's** at the Sheraton serves *haute cuisine* in an elegant, formal, yet friendly atmosphere. It only opens for dinner, and reservations are recommended.

Margeaux is the popular signature restaurant at the Travelodge, while **Flutes** at the Townsville Reef International has a friendly atmosphere and is in a similar top a la carte category. The **New Horizons Restaurant** on the 14th floor of the Aquarius has fine cuisine and great views.

Other hotel restaurants with good reputations include **Seagulls** at the Seagulls Resort (open for breakfast, lunch, and dinner seven days a week); **Kelli's** at the Mercure Inn with similar hours and nightly theme buffets; **Stanley's Restaurant** with its casual, friendly restaurant at the Robert Towns; and **Omar's** for steak, seafood, and pasta at the Newmarket Hotel.

Sails on the Bay at the Sheraton has all-day dining either buffet style or a la carte. You find many locals here, particularly for the seafood buffets on Friday and Saturday nights. There is a special menu for children. The Sheraton also has casual dining outside the main building at **Quarterdeck on the Marina.** There is an airconditioned area and a delightful outdoor deck with some of the best views you will find anywhere. **Raffles on the Mall** is the all-day restaurant/coffee shop at the Travelodge. There are good value meals together with happy faces. Lovers of Greek food will head for **Historic Yongala Lodge** with its seafood and international menu served on the wide verandahs or inside the 110-year-old building.

Outside the hotels, the correct choice depends on the type of cuisine you fancy. Lovers of French food have several alternatives. I'm conservative, so I can't go past the tried and tested **Affaire de Coeur** (Tel: 72-2742) at Sturt and Denham Streets, or the **L'Escargotiere** (Tel: 72-3435) with its tropical garden at 3 Palmer Street, South Townsville. Both have been operating for at least 15 years.

It is no surprise that **The Pier** (Tel: 21-2567), on Sir Leslie Thiess Drive, specializes in seafood. It is open for lunch daily except Saturday, and dinner nightly. **Fisherman's Wharf** (Tel: 21-1838) beside Ross Creek in Ogden Street has a popular well-priced seafood smorgasbord, fish and chips, and steaks. **Admiral's Restaurant** (Tel: 21-1911), at Blackwood and Sturt Streets, has a seafood smorgasbord with live entertainment in an airconditioned setting Tuesday to Sunday evenings.

There seems to be an inordinate number of Chinese restaurants in Townsville. The **Dynasty Seafood Restaurant** (Tel: 72-7099) at 228 Flinders Street East is one of the best Chinese restaurants in Queensland. When I took a group of Singapore visitors there a few years ago, they were so impressed that they went back three nights in a row. The **Capital Restaurant** (Tel: 71-3838) at 187 Flinders Street East has the same owners, but prices are cheaper. It has an a la carte menu, while the adjacent outlet has a buffet lunch Sunday to Friday and a family smorgasbord on Sunday evening. The **Sun Doo Chinese Restaurant** (Tel: 71-4642) is another favorite at 110 Charters Towers Road, Hermit Park, about three kilometers from the center of the city.

There are two excellent Thai restaurants in the city center. The **Thai International Restaurant** (Tel: 71-6242) is open for dinner seven nights a week at 235 Flinders Street East, while the **Reef Thai Restaurant** (Tel: 21-6701) at 491 Flinders Street (West) has weekday lunches, and dinner every night.

Other Asian cuisines are also available. The award-winning **Jun Japanese Restaurant** (Tel: 72-3394) at 436 Flinders Street is open seven nights. **Satay Mas** (Tel: 75-2633) at 234 Charters Towers Road has Malaysian charcoal-grilled satays and curries, yum cha lunches, and a smorgasbord on Friday and weekend nights. **Asian Delights** (Tel: 75-6122) at 219 Charters Towers Road combines Japanese, Malaysian, and Chinese cuisines. In the same area, **Taste of India** (Tel: 79-6875) at 279 Charters Towers Road specializes in curries and tandoori seven nights a week.

Australian food is offered at **Larrikans** (Tel: 72-5900), 95 Denham Street. Try seafood, beef, kangaroo, crocodile, emu, and buffalo. Modern Australian cuisine is offered each evening in an elegant casual indoor, balcony, or garden setting at **Somewhere Nice** (Tel: 72-4765) at 81 Bundock Street, Belgian Gardens. It is hard to go past the **Hog's Breath Cafe** (Tel: 71-5747) at 247 Flinders Street East for prime rib steak, homemade deserts, and ice cold beer. It is open weekdays for lunches and seven nights for dinner. A few doors away, **Covers** (Tel: 21-4630) at 209 Flinders Street East has a big reputation with the locals for fine food and good airconditioned or balcony atmosphere.

The choice still goes on. The **Pompeii Restaurant** (Tel: 72-7353) at 519

Flinders Street opposite the railway station is my favorite Italian restaurant. **Casa Blanca** (Tel: 79-4289) at 164 Charters Towers Road has Spanish and other Mediterranean cuisine. **Norma's** (Tel: 21-4555) at 58 The Strand, North Ward, has Lebanese favorites for lunch and dinner from Tuesday to Sunday. **Cactus Jack's** (Tel: 21-1478) at 21 Palmer Street, South Townsville, is a fun place for a beer and Tex-Mex cooking.

I have one or two more recommendations. The **George Coates Restaurant** at the Townsville College of TAFE (Tel: 71-8248) is at Fulham Road and Hugh Street and is worth the search. This is a training restaurant for hospitality students, so prices are very attractive. The **Garden of Eating** (Tel: 72-2984) at 11 Allen Street, South Townsville, has a small constantly changing menu and a delightful courtyard. **Michel's Cafe** (Tel: 24-1460) at 7 Palmer Street, South Townsville, has an open kitchen, a flare grill, attractive dishes, and indoor and sidewalk tables.

For those who must have fast food, be cheered by the fact that there are several outlets of **McDonald's, KFC, Red Rooster,** and **A Kebab.** You will also find **Pizza Hut** and **Sizzler** for those needing a little more. If nothing appeals so far, take a walk down Flinders Street East and make your own choice from at least 20 outlets.

Mackay

There are several good restaurants attached to hotels and motels. Some of the best are the **Valencia Restaurant** (Tel: 51-1244) at the Coral Sands Motel, 44 MacAlister Street; the restaurant at the **White Lace Motel** (Tel: 51-4466); **Galleons Restaurant** (Tel: 57-2044) at the Ocean International; and the **Monsoons Restaurant** (Tel: 54-8555) at the Kohuna Beach Resort.

The city also has several good restaurants and bistros located in older hotels. The **Balcony** (Tel: 57-2241) at Victoria & Gregory Streets; **Tennysons** at the Langford's Hotel, Tennyson Street; and the **Anchor Bar** (Tel: 53-1545) at the Crown and Anchor Hotel, River Street, are three good examples.

For specialty food, there is **Hog's Breath Cafe** (Tel: 57-7799) at Victoria and Wood Streets for great steaks; **Mandarin Restaurant** (Tel: 51-3303) for a fine selection of Chinese dishes; **Lychee Gardens** (Tel: 51-3939) at Victoria and Wellington Streets, for its popular Chinese buffets; **Sergios** (Tel: 57-3262) for Italian fare; **Mariner Restaurant** (Tel: 57-3279) in Victoria Street, for evening seafood buffets; and **Creperie** (Tel: 51-1226) for a range of crepes.

Other options include the **Mango Tree Garden** (Tel: 57-7266) on Wood Street, for vegetarian and Mexican fare; **Pippi's Italian Bistro** (Tel: 51-1376) at Grendon and Palmer Streets in North Mackay; the well-known buffets at **Crossroads Diner** (Tel: 57-2468) at 142 Nebo Road; and **Cafe Kebab** (Tel:

57-3333) at 73 Victoria Street. The **Arts Restaurant** (Tel: 53-5835) at 53 Sydney Street, is open long hours and is always good for croissants, coffee, and late supper. **Eagle Boys Dial-a-Pizza** (Tel: 53-1533), **Pizza Hut** (Tel: 57-2481), and **McDonald's** (Tel: 42-3999) are all here.

6. Sightseeing

The Central Reef region is an area stretching along the coast for around 600 kilometers, so unless you have your own transportation it is difficult to see it all. I have arranged this sightseeing section by starting in Townsville then traveling south as far as Mackay. We then travel north from Townsville as far as Mission Beach. The islands are covered separately in Section 8 of this chapter.

TOWNSVILLE

Flinders Mall is the perfect introduction to Townsville. The two-block pedestrian precinct is crowded with palms, fountains, street games, eateries, benches, stalls, and children's playground equipment. Here too are the fashion boutiques and shopping arcades, the Visitor Information Center, the post office, and the **Perc Tucker Art Gallery** (Tel: 22-0289) with its good collection of paintings, sculptures, and other works by North Queensland and international artists. In common with many cities, the growth of major suburban shopping centers has reduced the number of shops in the central city in recent years, so fewer locals shop here now.

Flinders Mall leads to **Flinders Street East,** an area of restaurants, art galleries, souvenir shops, and nightclubs. There are many beautifully restored buildings from the late 19th century adorned with wrought-iron lacework. Most times it is casual and quiet, but on Friday and Saturday evenings the whole area is crowded with fun-loving people out for a good time. At the far end of the street is the **Great Barrier Reef Wonderland.**

This is Townsville's premier man-made attraction. The excellent aquarium is operated by the Great Barrier Reef Marine Park Authority. The huge walk-through seawater complex, with its waves and tides, holds the world's largest living coral reef on land. It provides one of the most spectacular views of living coral that can be seen anywhere. Associated displays and touch tanks provide excellent educational opportunities. You should also see the Great Barrier Reef film at the adjacent **Omnimax Theater.** Then you can visit the Great Barrier Reef itself with sufficient knowledge to appreciate fully what you see.

Great Barrier Reef Wonderland also has several fast food outlets, news and souvenirs shops, a dive shop, ferry and cruise terminals, a national parks office, and the Museum of Tropical Queensland. You can easily spend several hours here, and there are some good photo opportunities.

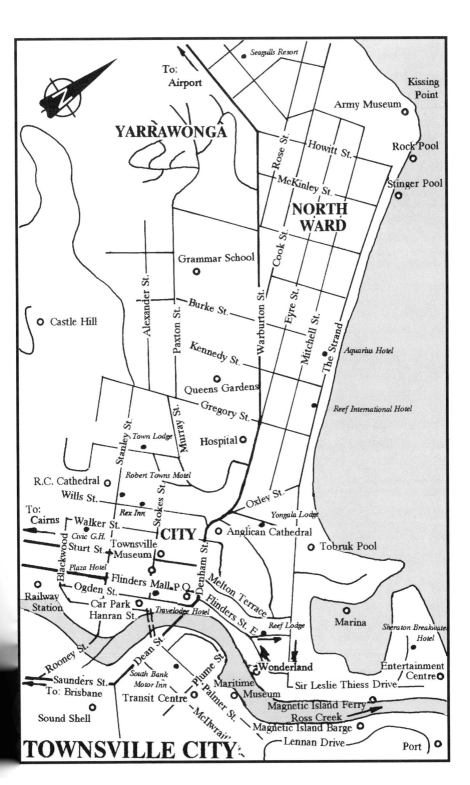

Walk 200 meters north and you are in **Anzac Park** by the edge of the Breakwater Marina. Look at the old Customs House, the television studio that was once the famous Queens Hotel, the various war memorials, and the band rotunda. From here you can go along Sir Leslie Thiess Drive to the **Magnetic Island ferry terminal,** the **casino,** and the **Entertainment Center.** Alternatively you can head along The Strand and you come to the **waterfall, Tobruk swimming pool,** and **St. Patrick's College** with its Queensland-style architecture. Farther still, there is a nice beach, a netted swimming enclosure to protect against marine stingers that may be in the sea from November to April, and the adjacent rock pool with its changing rooms and kiosk.

Castle Hill dominates the central city. There is a walkway from Stanley Street to the top, but it's best to drive the road or take the long-talked-about cable car. The top has spectacular views, walking tracks, and places to relax.

The **Townsville Environmental Park** (often known as the Common), between the airport and Pallarenda, is recognized as one of the world's most important urban water bird sanctuaries; however, a series of failed wet seasons has caused the bird population to dwindle and development works to be curtailed. The best time to visit is early in the morning or late in the afternoon. **Pallarenda** is worth visiting for its long, deserted beach, the picnic facilities, and the old Quarantine Station which is now a park and museum.

Elsewhere in the city, you will find several other museums and gardens. The **Townsville Museum** (Tel: 72-5725), at Sturt and Stokes Street, has displays of early history showing the development of the city since 1865. The **Maritime Museum** (Tel: 21-5251), in Palmer Street, South Townsville, preserves the North Queensland nautical tradition. The **National Trust homes** (Tel: 72-5195), in West End, and the **Jezzine Military Museum** at Kissing Point, contain historic memorabilia and preserve a part of history long gone. The **Townsville Palmetum** (Tel: 25-5202), near James Cook University, has a world-class collection of palms in attractive surroundings.

GO SOUTH

The Bruce Highway takes you through the southern suburbs, and past the Murray sports complex and the Cluden horse racetrack before skirting the coastal range on the way to **Ayr. Billabong Sanctuary** (about 17 kilometers) (Tel: 78-8344) is a nine-hectare wildlife refuge where Australian native animals live happily in a carefully recreated natural environment. Billabong is an Aboriginal word for water hole, and this place is well named. Here's your chance to hand feed a kangaroo, wrap yourself in a python, learn about estuarine crocodiles, take a photo with a koala, hold a fruit bat, or hug a wombat. There are various wildlife shows throughout the day, a swimming pool, restaurant, and gift shop. It is open from 8 A.M. to 5 P.M. daily.

The turnoff to the Mount Elliot section of the **Bowling Green Bay**

National Park is another eight kilometers along the highway. There are picnic areas, camping facilities, abundant wildlife, freshwater swimming in Alligator Creek, and walking trails. On the way along the access road, you pass **Melville's Pioneer Park** (Tel: 78-8288) where every Sunday there are sheep shearing displays, whip cracking, horseshoe throwing, and vintage car and horse-drawn coach rides.

The **Australian Institute of Marine Science** (Tel: 78-9211) is located at Cape Ferguson. The turnoff is 31 kilometers from Townsville. This is one of the world's premier marine research institutions, and it draws scientists from around the globe. Guided tours are by appointment on Friday.

Giru is a small town with a sugar mill and an active local community, but it is regularly inundated by flood waters from the nearby Haughton River. The swampy coastal plain provides great fishing opportunities, with Barrattas Creek being the popular access to kilometers of fishable water. From Giru, a road goes west to **Woodstock** on the Townsville to Charters Towers and Mount Isa road.

Ayr and **Home Hill** are twin towns on either side of the Burdekin River. They have a combined population of around 12,000. The highway and the railway cross the river on the 1,100-meter-long steel bridge. This is one of the largest sugar producing areas in Australia, and with the development of the huge Burdekin Irrigation Scheme, it is expanding rapidly. There are three sugar mills and a rice mill in the immediate area. Local points of interest include the **Burdekin Theatre** and its "living lagoon" sculptures in the main street of Ayr; the **Ayr Nature Display** (Tel: 83-2189) at 119 Wilmington Street, Ayr; **Alva Beach** about 18 kilometers from Ayr; **Ashworth's Tourist Centre** with its displays of minerals, fossils, stones, gems, and perhaps the finest agate display in the world; and **Groper Creek,** a fishing paradise. There are small hotels and motels in both towns.

Twenty kilometers south of Ayr, a narrow paved road leads to the summit of **Mount Inkerman** for nice views and picnic facilities. The next 60 kilometers of highway is through uninteresting, flat, open cattle country. Abbot Point provides a deep-water anchorage for huge coal carriers which take Collinsville coal to overseas markets, but there is little for the visitor to see. The final 10 kilometers from Merinda to Bowen is through rich small crop development, which produces some of the best mangoes, tomatoes, rock melons, capsicums, and sweet corn in Australia.

Bowen was the first town established in North Queensland, but it has never reached the potential hoped for by the early pioneers. The Bruce Highway touches the desolate outskirts of the town, and many travelers will be tempted to keep going straight on. That is a pity because Bowen is an interesting center, and there are things to do and places to see. Wall-size paintings are a feature of the town thanks to the work of the **Bowen Shire**

Festival of Murals Society Inc. A map showing the mural locations is available from the information center. The **Bowen Historical Museum** (Tel: 86-2035) at 22 Gordon Street, has Aboriginal artifacts, shipwreck relics, records of the region's white pioneers, and a 125-year-old slab cottage. The town's beaches are some of the best around. Horseshoe Bay is my favorite, but others like Murray Bay, Rose Bay, and Queens Beach are also nice. **Porters Horseshoe Bay Resort** (Tel: 86-2564) is a popular, reasonably priced place, while the budget-minded will head to **Bowen Backpackers Hostel** (Tel: 86-3433) at 56 Herbert Street.

Fifty kilometers south of Bowen, a road to the left is signposted Whitsunday. One kilometer along this road, there is an intersection with a road to the north which leads to **Dingo Beach** and **Earlando Beach.** These are pretty places, but they are off the tourist route, and facilities are somewhat limited. This, of course, is their attraction to some people. The **Earlando Beach Resort** (Tel: 079-457133) has some self-contained cabins, a bar and dining room, on-site vans, a shop, and rental dinghies and canoes.

The next center farther south is **Proserpine.** This is another sugar and cattle town, but it is also a major gateway to the Whitsunday area. Jet aircraft arrive daily from the south with holiday-makers heading for the coast or the islands. The coastal towns of Cannonvale, Airlie Beach, Jubilee Pocket, and Shute Harbour are collectively known as Whitsunday, but few people and businesses use this name. The local council has gone about removing Airlie Beach from most of the road signs, so visitors are often confused about where they are heading.

THE WHITSUNDAYS

Airlie Beach is 25 kilometers from Proserpine. This is the center for most of the action, and it is where most of the resorts, restaurants, and nightspots are situated. The town is nicely located between the ranges and the sea, and it has managed to retain some of its natural charm as it has grown. **Whitsunday Wanderers Resort** (Tel: 079-466446), 127 rooms, is one of the most popular accommodations places, particularly with families. There are seven hectares of tropical gardens, four swimming pools, tennis courts, mini-golf, archery, a bar, a bistro, and live entertainment. Room rates are from A$65 depending on the time of the year. (Book at Shute Harbour Road, Airlie Beach 4802 or Fax: 6179-466761.) An alternative is the **Coral Sea Resort** (Tel: 079-466458), an up-market motel-style property with ocean frontage, and room rates from A$100. (Book at 25 Oceanview Avenue, Airlie Beach 4802 or Fax: 6179-466516.)

Many other options are available. **Whitsunday Terraces Resort** (Tel: 079-466788) has a choice of self-contained luxury studio units or one-bedroom suites set on a hillside above the town, priced from A$100 including breakfast for two. (Book at Golden Orchid Drive, Airlie Beach 4802 or Fax: 6179-467128.) The **Island Gateway Holiday Resort** (Tel: 079-466228) has 55 units with seven types of accommodations covering self-contained aircon- ditioned units, cabins, on-site caravans, and camping sites. Facilities include tennis, mini-golf, and a TV and video area. Rates start at around A$35 for the cabins. (Book by Fax: 6179-467125.)

There are several good budget resorts in town. **Beaches** (Tel: 1-800-636630) features airconditioned dorm rooms with in-suite bathrooms, bar, restaurant, two pools with sun decks and tropical gardens, laundry, and games and video room. Rates are from A$14 per person. (Book at 356 Shute Harbour Road or Fax: 6179-467764.) **Whitsunday Village Resort** (Tel: 46-6266) with its self-contained cabins set in gardens, is close by. There are two pools, an entertainment area, popular Magnums Bar and Grill, and a fun atmosphere. Dorm beds are from A$14 and rooms from A$35. (Book at P.O. Box 313, Airlie Beach or Fax: 6179-465980.) Also in this same area is the **YHA hostel Club Habitat** (Tel: 46-6312). This is a smaller hostel with motel-style rooms offering dorm, double, and family rooms. Facilities include a pool, kitchen, lounge, reading room, laundry, and tour desk. (Book at 394 Shute Harbour Road, Airlie Beach or Fax: 6179-467053.)

Two kilometers away at **Cannonvale, Club Crocodile** (Tel: 079-467155) has been successfully marketed as a fun resort. Facilities include a large pool, nice grounds, tennis, a spa, and a choice of restaurants and bars. The resort's Beach Club has windsufing and paddle skis. Rates are from A$75. (Book at Shute Harbour Road, Cannonvale 4802 or Fax: 6179-466007.) Also in Cannonvale is **Bush Village Resort** (Tel: 1-800-809256), a budget-style resort with 18 fully self-contained cabins, a pool, spa, barbecue, tour office, and free breakfast. Dorm beds are from A$10, doubles from A$32. (Book at 2 St. Martins Road or Fax: 6179-467227.)

Airlie Beach has heaps of restaurants within a small area. **La Perouse** (Tel: 46-6262), in the Beach Plaza, is open for lunch Tuesday to Saturday then has intimate French dining by candlelight at night. The **Brasserie** (Tel: 46-7448) in the same complex has an international menu and a balcony overlooking the esplanade. Seafood with a Mediterranean flavor, great pasta, and maybe a view of the moon rising over the water is offered by **The Italian Kangaroo** (Tel: 46-6337). Asian food is offered at the **Spice Island Bistro** (Tel: 46-6585), the **Wok Inn** (Tel: 46-6713), and the **Satay Court** (Tel: 46-5865).

If you tried the Townsville **Hog's Breath Cafe,** you are sure to head for its Airlie Beach namesake (Tel: 46-7894) for prime beef, seafood, and Cajun-style delights. Steaks and serve-yourself salads are offered at **K.C's Chargrill and Bar** (Tel: 46-6320), while **Charlies Round The Bend** (Tel: 46-6250) has prawns, beef, and pasta, and a great piano bar. There are plenty of outlets offering pizza, spaghetti, burgers, sandwiches, salads, and coffee.

Activities in the Whitsunday region center very much on the water, but there are a few other things to do. The **Whitsunday Information Centre,** three kilometers past Airlie Beach on the Shute Harbour Road, is worth a visit for the displays and information on the natural history of the area. It is open from 9 A.M. to 5 P.M. Monday to Friday. The **Australian Wildlife Park** (Tel: 46-1354), on the Proserpine side of Cannonvale, has 700 animals and various shows throughout the day. Much of the forested hill country you see around here is contained within the **Conway Range National Park,** and there are picnic areas, walking tracks, and some great lookouts. Local transportation is provided by a **bus service** (Tel: 45-2377), **rental bicycles, minicars** (Tel: 46-5311), or regular **car rental** (see Section 3 of this chapter).

The other notable component of Whitsunday is **Shute Harbour.** There are some accommodations here, but its main claim to fame is as a setting-off point for visits to the island resorts and the reef, and as a bareboat charter base. Visit Shute Harbour around 9 A.M. and you will not be surprised to learn it is the second busiest passenger port in Australia.

FARTHER SOUTH

It is 120 kilometers from Proserpine to Mackay. About 18 kilometers along the highway, a road leads to the left to Midge Point. Before you reach the point, you pass the luxury **Laguna Quays Resort** (Tel: 079-477777) on its 1,750-hectare site. This is a delightful place with excellent facilities, but it has been struggling to establish itself due primarily to its relatively isolated location. You will find a manicured golf course, tennis courts, a pool, a children's club, and a restaurant, bar, and marina. Accommodations are in the full-service deluxe Golf Lodge or in a variety of serviced condominiums. Room rates start at around A$150. (Book at Kunapipi Springs Road, Repulse Bay, Whitsundays 4799 or Fax: 6179-477701.)

Midge Point is way down-market from here, but it is a good place for fishing. The **Travellers Rest Camping and Caravan Park** (Tel: 079-476120) has units, on-site vans, camping sites, and a store.

The next major point of interest is the **Seaforth/Halliday Bay/Cape Hillsborough** area. This is about 20 kilometers off the highway, but it is an interesting region offering several small low-key resorts. **Cape Hillsborough Resort** (Tel: 079-590152) is perhaps the most interesting accommodations. There is nothing up-market about this place, but the beachfront rain forest location surrounded by a national park is very picturesque. There are hotel-style units, cabins, on-site vans, backpacker accommodations, a caravan park, a swimming pool, a restaurant, a small supermarket, tame kangaroos, and scrub turkeys. Prices start from A$20. (Book by Fax: 6179-590500.)

It's now just 40 kilometers to Mackay, but there is one other attraction worth mentioning. **Eungella National Park** is one of the largest rain forest parks in the state and also one of the most popular. The park straddles the Clark Ranges about 85 kilometers west of Mackay. The park's appeal is the unspoiled beauty of its waterfalls, streams, rain forest and lookouts, and the opportunity to see the shy Australian platypus. These egg-laying mammals with their fur coats and duck bills live in creeks and rivers and are most active at dawn and dusk. The Broken River in the heart of the park is an ideal habitat. The park information office and kiosk are open seven days a week. **Eungella village** has some basic facilities, and there are arts and crafts shops in the area. The **Eungella Chalet** (Tel: 079-584509) has hotel accommodations and self-contained cabins, a restaurant, pool, and tennis court. The **Broken River Mountain Retreat** (Tel: 079-584528) has motel units, self-contained cabins, a restaurant, and a special platypus-viewing platform.

MACKAY

This city of around 60,000 people is the center for a region rich in primary industry. Sugar, coal, cattle, and grain have been the lifeblood of the city, and now they are joined by tourism. The climate, the reef, the islands, and the forests are bringing visitors in increasing numbers. It is a destination that appeals to a wide cross-section of people because it doesn't seek to do anything other than portray itself in a natural way.

The city has a number of attractions. The **Commonwealth Bank, Mackay Courthouse, Customs House,** and **Seymore** and **Alman Houses** are superb examples of century-old architecture that has been maintained and restored. A **Heritage Walk** brochure is available from **Mackay Tourism** (Tel: 079-522677). **Mackay Harbour** is said to be one of the finest man-made harbors on the east coast of Australia. There is a huge sugar terminal here, and it's also the departure point for island and reef trips. The adjacent **Harbour Beach** has pine trees and picnic facilities.

Illawong or **Far Beach** is on the south side of the Pioneer River. Swimming is safe most times from May to October, and there are picnic grounds, a children's playground, and a kiosk. Farther south, there is the huge **Hay Point coal loading facility.** There are a string of beaches to the north of the city—Slade Point, Black's Beach, Dolphin Heads, Eimeo, Bucasia. Some offer good swimming, fishing, and picnicking facilities, and most have accommodations.

GO NORTH

The country to the north of Townsville is quite different from that to the south. As you leave the city you pass the huge Garbutt Air Force base, then you drive through some of the industrial areas which help to make this

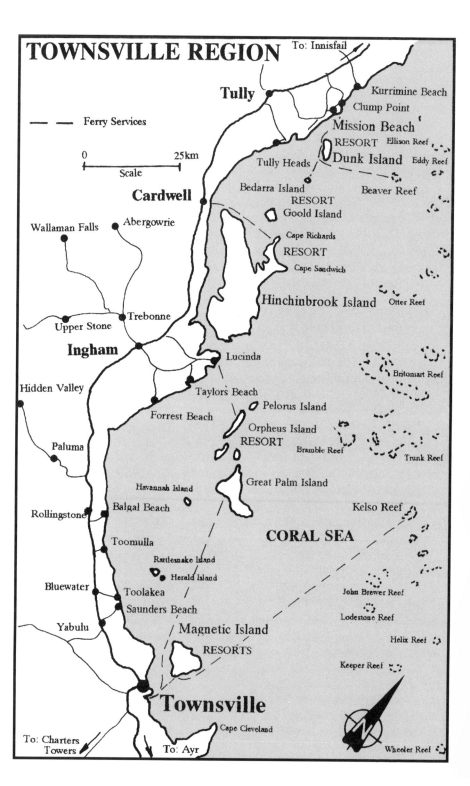

the "Capital of North Queensland." For the next 50 kilometers, roads head off the highway to the right to various beachside suburbs and villages. On the highway just past **Yubulu,** you can visit **Butterfly World** (Tel: 78-6003).

About 65 kilometers north of Townsville, a road climbs the spectacular Paluma Range to the town of **Paluma** and the **Mount Spec National Park.** Part way, make a stop at **Little Crystal Creek** for a swim or a walk along the stream, then drive on to **McClelland's Lookout** for panoramic views of Halifax Bay. **Paluma** has picnic facilities, arts and crafts, refreshments, charm, and some accommodations. Back near the highway, **Paradise Waterhole** on Big Crystal Creek has barbecues, toilets, tables, drinking water, and excellent swimming.

Jourama Falls National Park is 78 kilometers north of Townsville. It is an excellent place to picnic, walk, swim, and camp in the natural surroundings of open forest and rain forest-fringed creeks rich in wildlife. Several falls and cascades add to the park's natural beauty.

Ingham is a town in the center of a sugar-growing district. There are two mills—Victoria, the largest in the Southern hemisphere, and Macknade, the oldest operating mill in Australia. One of the major attractions here is **Wallaman Falls**—at 305 meters it is the highest sheer drop waterfall in the country. **Broadwater Park** has swimming, a 1.6-kilometer interpretative rain forest walk, and picnic and camping facilities. Call into the **Hinchinbrook Visitors Centre** (Tel: 077-765211), on the highway in the main street of Ingham, for directions and more information on the district and the **Wet Tropics World Heritage Area**. Lucinda, Taylors Beach, and Forrest Beach are all northeast of Ingham, and all have stinger net-protected swimming areas. From Lucinda, you can rent a **houseboat** (Tel: 077-763466) or be taken on a conducted safari up the Hinchinbrook Channel. The fishing in this region is great. There are small hotels, motels, and caravan parks in Ingham, and some accommodations and caravan parks at most of the beaches.

Cardwell, the village by the sea, vies with Bowen as the oldest settlement in North Queensland. There has been some new development in recent years, but the town hasn't been overwhelmed with commercialism. The beach is nice, there are some great views to Hinchinbrook Island, and the fishing is outstanding. Trips are available to some of the islands. Accommodations are good and varied, and prices are generally reasonable. Even if you are not staying overnight, Cardwell is an excellent place to break your journey and to sample the local "fish and chips."

Kennedy is a small, neat, mainly Aboriginal and Islander settlement on the highway, 11 kilometers farther north. Spectacular **Blencoe Falls** is two hours inland from here. Farther north, **Murray Falls** is an interesting diversion off the highway, then it's on to **Tully,** one of Australia's wettest towns. The area is famous for sugar, bananas, and other tropical fruit, and inland there is cattle grazing. A paved road follows the Tully River upstream to **Cardstone** and the Kareeya power station, and provides access to one of the best whitewater rafting rivers in Australia. On the coast you can visit the small settlements of **Hull Heads** and **Tully Heads.** The turnoff to Mission Beach is two kilometers north of Tully.

MISSION BEACH

Positioned midway between Townsville and Cairns, the **Mission Beach** region offers a chance to explore an unspoiled environment of rain forest, sandy beaches, and lowland scrub forest while still enjoying the comforts and convenience of modern man-made facilities.

Fishing, sailing, and swimming are some of the popular Mission Beach diversions, but to these you can add crocodile spotting in estuarine rivers, Aboriginal cultural experiences, tandem skydiving, helicopter joyrides, horseback riding, night walks in the rain forest, and daily trips to islands and the reef. The picture of Mission Beach is not complete, however, without huge brightly colored, near-extinct cassowary birds, iridescent blue Ulysses butterflies, an abundance of accommodations from luxury to budget, small restaurants tucked into flamboyant foliage, shops and boutiques selling local works of art and imported necessities, well-maintained jungle walks leading from smooth paved highways, a weekend market, and a host of friendly residents.

Mission Beach is a region covering the communities of South Mission Beach, Wongaling Beach, Clump Point, Bingil Bay, and Mission Beach itself. Each center has accommodations and some shopping facilities, but the main shopping and restaurant facilities are in Mission Beach township. **Castaways Beach Resort** (Tel: 070-687444), 54 rooms, is on the beach in Mission Beach town. The three-story building has standard rooms, some self-contained units, a nice restaurant, bar, and shop, and there are beach barbecue, pool and a covered terrace, large grounds, and water sports facilities. Room rates are from around A$100. (Book at Seaview Street, Mission Beach 4854 or Fax: 6170-687429.) **Mission Beach Resort** (Tel: 070-688429), 76 rooms, is a one-level complex that sprawls through nice gardens at Wongaling Beach. There is nothing memorable about the rooms, but resort facilities include a good restaurant, a bistro, a bar, a playground, four pools, tennis, spas, barbecues, and a shop. The complex is across one road from the beach. Room rates are from around A$85. (Book at Wongaling Beach, Mission Beach 4854 or Fax: 6170-688429.)

The most expensive accommodations are actually in some of the self-contained apartments on the beach. **Wongalinga Apartments** (Tel: 070-688221) on Wongaling Beach are stylish and spacious. Rates start at A$130 for two people and rise to A$210 for six. (Book at 64 Reid Road, Wongaling Beach

4854 or Fax: 6170-688180). The **Lugger Bay Apartments** (Tel: 070-688400) at South Mission Beach are top of the heap. There are six three-bedroom polehouse units dramatically elevated into the rain forest canopy, to provide Coral Sea views. A free-form swimming pool is suspended over a forest gully. Units rent at A$175 a night. (Book at 18 Explorers Drive, South Mission Beach 4854 or Fax: 6170-688586.)

Cheaper accommodations are also available. There are motels, less up-market self-contained units, caravan parks with cabins and on-site vans, and backpacker hostels. Try **The Village Motel** (Tel: 070-687212) at Mission Beach from A$55, **Del Rio Apartments** (Tel: 070-688270) at South Mission Beach from A$45, **Beachcomber Coconut Village** (Tel: 070-688129) at South Mission Beach with cabins from A$36 and camp-a-tel units from A$18, and **Mission Beach Backpackers** (Tel: 070-688317) with bunkhouse beds from A$12 and units from A$26.

7. Guided Tours

The range of tours within this area is mind-blowing. Here are a selection of the land tours from the various centers. Tours to the reef and the islands are covered in the next section of this chapter.

Townsville

A city tour is a good way to orientate yourself in Townsville. **Detours Coach Tours** (Tel: 077-215977) has a very reasonably priced tour that takes you past the central city heritage buildings, then it travels through the suburbs to take in the Townsville Palmetum, the Military Museum on Kissing Point, and the panoramic view from the top of Castle Hill. An alternative is offered by **Acacia Luxury Transport** (Tel: 077-714441). This is not as extensive, but it includes morning or afternoon tea on the 14th floor of the Aquarius Hotel. Townsville taxi tours are offered by **Standard White Cabs** (Tel: 077-131008). **Tour de Townsville** (Tel: 21-2026) has half-day bicycle tours of the city, which include a meal.

Detours also has a range of day trips from the city. The Billabong Tour goes to the Billabong Sanctuary to see unique Australian animals and feeding shows, and to enjoy a Devonshire tea. The Tropical Rainforest Tour visits the Butterfly Farm then travels to the Mount Spec National Park for swimming and rain forest walking. On the return journey you stop off at Frosty Mango to have an exotic fruit tasting. The Outback Tour takes in all the major points of interest in the old gold mining center of Charters Towers and introduces you to the taste of traditional Australian billy tea and damper. Tours operate to the Australian Institute of Marine Science each Friday.

Aboriginal culture is displayed on the **Gubinbara Indigenous Cultural Heritage Tours** (Tel: 077-715483). One tour takes in the Town Common; walks the bush tucker trail; demonstrates fire-making and spear and boomerang throwing; has a barbecue with kangaroo, emu, and crocodile meat; introduces visitors to dreamtime storytelling; and finishes with a guided tour of the Museum of Tropical Queensland. Others cover natural history and birdwatching on a Bohle River cruise, and there are fishing tours using the knowledge and experience of local Aboriginal guides.

Adventure seekers can take a trip to the Tully River for a day of **whitewater rafting** (Tel: 077-215977), or can stay in Townsville for the **To The Limit Tour** (Tel: 077-212619), which includes a visit to the Omnimax Theatre, a Harley-Davidson ride, parasailing, abseiling, and lunch. Air tours are offered by the **Townsville Aero Club** (Tel: 077-792069), **Sky Gold Aviation** (Tel: 077-757400), and **Inland Pacific Air** (Tel: 077-753866). **Pure Pleasure Tours** (Tel: 077-213555) has a three-day eco-tour from Townsville to Cairns spending good periods in the Wet Tropics World Heritage area. **Townsville & N.Q Motor Cycle Tours** (Tel: 25-3274) has several short excursions for those who enjoy the wind in their hair, while **Aussi Adventure Motorcycle Tours** (Tel: 78-3922) has one-, two-, three-, and seven-day up-market trips on two wheels.

Whitsundays/Mackay

SBS Tours (Tel: 079-573330) in Mackay has a weekday city tour, and three full-day tours covering Cape Hillsborough, Eungella National Park, and Greenmount/Homebush. **Reeforest Adventure Tours** (Tel: 079-554100) has bush safaris to Eungella National Park that include billy tea, damper, and a barbecue lunch. **Coastal Explorer Tours** (Tel: 079-562287) has tours to Sarina, Cape Hillsborough, and Goonyella Mine. **Mackay City Cabs** (Tel: 079-514999) has some taxi tours.

In the Whitsundays, there is an **Airlie Action Pack** (Tel: 079-466550) that combines a skydive, an assault craft ride, a scuba dive, a bungy jump, and a survival skills test in Skirmish.

Mission Beach

Whitewater rafting on the Tully River is a popular tour from Mission Beach. Two companies offer trips. **Mission Beach Rainforest Treks** (Tel: 070-687152) has morning, night, full-day, and three-day treks through the rain forest. **River Rat Wildlife Cruises** (Tel: 070-687250) takes you along the Hull River for crabbing, crocodile spotting, fishing, and mangrove viewing. Dawn and dusk horseback rides are offered by **Equitreks** (Tel: 070-687501). **Hinchinbrook Adventures** (Tel: 070-668270) operates day walks and longer treks from Cardwell.

8. The Reef and Islands

The Central Reef Region offers excellent viewing opportunities to enjoy the Great Barrier Reef to the full. Here are some of the options.

Day Trips

This is the way most visitors experience the reef, and most come away thrilled with the experience. When the weather is right, this can be a "memories for a lifetime experience," but for others seasickness, rain, or cloudy seas lead to disappointment. The Great Barrier Reef is not immediately adjacent to the shore, so appreciate this when making your plans. Pick your day, and take precautions against rough weather and sunburn. I have been fortunate, and my reef trips remain some of my outstanding life experiences.

Day trips to the reef operate from Mackay, Airlie Beach, Shute Harbour, Townsville, and Mission Beach, although not all run every day. Most use high-speed catamarans, but one Mission Beach operator has a conventional vessel. Some have large pontoons anchored at the reef, with glass-bottomed boats or semi-submersibles for coral viewing. All offer snorkeling equipment, and most offer the chance to scuba dive. Kelso Reef off Townsville offers excellent coral, while Beaver Cay off Mission Beach is the closest area to the mainland, so travel time is shortest.

Here are the major operators:

Fantasea Cruises (Tel: 079-465111) operates from Abel Point Marina, Airlie Beach, to its Reefworld pontoon.

Friendship Cruises (Tel: 070-687262) departs Clump Point, daily, for Beaver Cay.

Pure Pleasure Cruises (Tel: 077-213555), Sir Leslie Thiess Drive, Townsville, runs daily to Magnetic Island and Kelso Reef.

Quickcat (Tel: 070-687289) leaves Clump Point Jetty at Mission Beach, daily, for Dunk Island and Beaver Cay.

Roylen Cruises (Tel: 079-553066) departs from Mackay Harbour to Credlin Reef.

Whitsunday Connections (Tel: 079-466900) departs from Shute Harbour for Hardy Reef, six days a week.

If traveling by water is not your thing, a 30-minute flight from Mackay Airport by seaplane allows you to land in Bushy Lagoon adjacent to Bushy Island, where you can walk in shallow water among the coral gardens.

Longer Cruises

Coral Princess Cruises (Tel: 077-211673) in Townsville and **Roylen Cruises** (Tel: 079-553066) in Mackay both specialize in extended Great

Barrier Reef cruising. *Coral Princess* departs Townsville for a four-day trip to the islands and reef while traveling between Townsville and Cairns. The purpose-built vessel has excellent accommodations, good meals and facilities, and it introduces you to eco-tourism at its best.

The Roylen ships operate five-day cruises through the Cumberland and Whitsunday islands then to the Great Barrier Reef and return to Mackay. Uninhabited and resort islands are visited, and the cruise is relaxed and friendly. International tourists make up a sizeable proportion of passengers on both these excellent cruises.

Sun Mining (Tel: 71-5411) has a five-day sailing trip from Townsville to Dunk Island.

Bareboat Sailing

The Whitsunday area has become the bareboat capital of Australia due to the ideal weather conditions and interesting waters. There are several companies offering a range of vessels. They advertise that little experience is needed to skipper the boats, and you are shown the ropes by an expert before you head off yourself. Here are some of the operators:

Australian Bareboat Charters—Shute Harbour (Tel: 1-800-075000)
Blue Water Sailing—Airlie Beach (Tel: 018-185729)
Coral Sea Boat Hire—Shute Harbour (Tel: 018-182584)
Cumberland Charter Yachts—Airlie Beach (Tel: 1-800-075101)
Whitsunday Charter Fleet—Airlie Beach (Tel: 1-800-639520)
Whitsunday Cruising Catamarans—Airlie Beach (Tel: 1-800-060016)
Whitsunday Rent a Yacht—Shute Harbour (Tel: 1-800-075111)

THE ISLANDS

There are undoubtedly more developed islands along this section of coast than along any other in Australia. Almost all, however, are mainland-type islands rather than coral cays. This means that many of them are large, mountainous, and rugged. In many cases the islands are national parks with the resorts occupying just a small section. I will cover the islands in a general south to north direction.

Newry Island

This is one of the islands in the Newry Group, just a few kilometers offshore from Seaforth. The **Newry Island Resort** (Tel: 079-590214) is very low-key, and it has some self-contained cabins, some with bathrooms but no kitchen, and some with shared facilities. These cost from A$20 per person per night. There are also some camping sites, and a small restaurant and bar. The resort boat will pick up guests from Victor Creek near Seaforth, for a small charge. This boat also operates fishing and sightseeing trips on occasion, and there are waterski facilities. The beaches are not great, but fishing is popular. There are a few walking tracks through the national park, and you will see koalas along them. Camping is possible at national park sites on adjacent **Rabbit** and **Outer Newry Islands,** for those with a permit from P.O. Box 623, Mackay 4740.

Brampton Island

This is a forested, mountainous island surrounded by several sandy beaches and coral reefs. Most of the island is a national park, and there is a large resort on one corner, complete with air strip. The Qantas Airways-operated **Brampton Island Resort** (Tel: 079-514499) has 92 units that come with airconditioning, refrigerator, TV, IDD telephone, radio, tea/coffee-making facilities, in-house movies, and balcony or verandah. Although the island was first developed in 1933, nothing remains from those days. The bone-shaking mini-railway that operates from the wharf to the resort is about the oldest construction. That dates from 1962.

The resort is considered mid-range and appeals to couples and families. Some young singles will find it slow. There is, however, plenty to do if you want to be active rather than relaxed. There is swimming (in the ocean or in a fresh water or a saltwater pool), sailing, sailboarding, surfskiing, tube riding, and waterskiing. On land there are beach walks, a six-hole pitch and putt golf course, tennis, billiards, archery, table tennis, beach volleyball, touch football, cricket, or bushwalking. Trails lead to beaches on the other side of the island and to the top of Brampton Peak. Facilities include a restaurant, cafe, bar, shop, bank agency, Kid's Club, and gymnasium. Night activities can range from dancing through floor shows, talent quests and theme nights, to a disco.

You reach the island via a 15-minute Sunstate flight from Mackay (about A$70 one way) or by a 50-minute trip by Roylen catamaran (about A$40 round trip). Room costs on the island are around A$250 per couple per night, but there are some package rates available for longer stays. (Book with the resort at Brampton Island, Queensland 4740 or Fax: 6179-514097.) There are basic camping facilities—toilets, fireplaces, and tables—on **Goldsmith** and **South Repulse Islands,** farther north.

Lindeman Island

This is the southernmost of the Whitsunday Islands with any resort development. The Whitsunday group was named by Captain Cook when he sailed through the area in 1770, but Linderman itself was not named until 1868. The Nicholson family leased the island in 1923 and later opened a resort, the first on any of the islands. They operated it until 1979 when it was

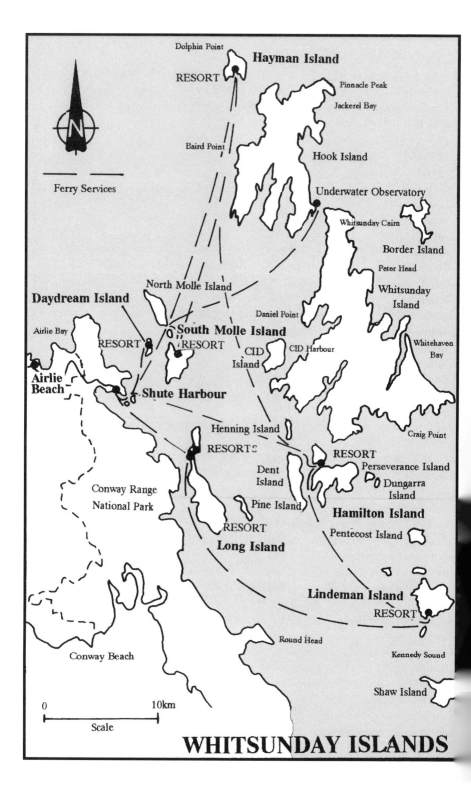

WHITSUNDAY ISLANDS

sold. Since then, there have been several owners. The island, except for the resort, is a national park. There are seven beaches, a 210-meter peak, some forest, areas of grassland, and a national park campsite at Plantation Beach.

Since 1992 the resort has been operated by the **Club Med** organization (Tel: 079-469333). It is a typical development of this company—relaxed, oriented towards the young at heart, activity-generated. The resort was completely rebuilt in 1988, so facilities are modern and extensive. Rooms are airconditioned and have refrigerators, TV, telephone, tea/coffee-making facilities, balconies or verandahs, and good views. The daily activity sheet can include golf, tennis, archery, beach volleyball, aerobics, table tennis, basketball, bushwalking, badminton, and the use of catamarans, paddle boats, and windsurfers. There are two swimming pools, buffet meals, a lunch barbecue, a la carte dining, nightly shows, and a nightclub that operates into the early hours.

Access is by light plane from **Whitsunday Air Strip** (Tel: 079-469933), by light plane from **Mackay** (Tel: 079-423161), or on Saturday and Sunday by **Roylens Cruises** from Mackay (Tel: 079-553066). The resort operates on a fully inclusive tariff covering transfers, accommodations, meals, and activities. Day visits are possible, and there are one- and two-night packages as well as longer stay options. A two-night package starts at around A$350 per person. (Book by Fax: 6179-469776.)

Hamilton Island

Hamilton is a hilly, medium-size Whitsunday island with reasonable beaches, a peak which reaches 230 meters, and by far the most development of any island in this area. The whole development has been labeled "controversial," from its 20-story accommodations towers, its artificial marina, and its hill-leveling international airport, to its remarkable early deals with the Queensland government. Some love it, others hate it. The package was created in the 1980s by a Gold Coast entrepreneur, Keith Williams, but it went into receivership in 1992 and has been struggling ever since. In 1994, Holiday Inn took over management of the resort, and it now trades as a Crowne Plaza Resort.

The resort offers more mid- and up-market accommodations choice than any other island. There are hotel rooms, Polynesian bures, self-contained units, one- and two-bedroom apartments, and luxury penthouses. All rooms have airconditioning, ceiling fans, refrigerator, TV, iron and ironing board, hair dryer, direct-dial telephones, and balcony or patio. There are nine restaurants, eight bars, a post office, bank, medical center, taxi service, Kid's Club, a church that specializes in Japanese wedding blessings, and 24 shops and boutiques. Many of the services on the island, particularly those at the

Marina Village, are operated independently of the resort, and these also cater to day-trippers, boaties, permanent residents, and so forth.

Activities abound, but some are expensive even by island standards. There are eight swimming pools, six tennis courts, two squash courts, a gymnasium, jetskiing, waterskiing, paraflying, skydiving, volleyball, catamarans, sailboards, scuba diving, golf driving range, mini-golf, clay target shooting, game fishing, a fauna park, and bushwalking. A variety of short boat and sailing trips, dive trips, and Great Barrier Reef trips depart from the island. There are boat connections to several other islands.

Hamilton Island airport has Ansett Australia jet connections to Brisbane, Sydney, and Cairns. There are also commuter flights to Mackay (around A$90), and Whitsunday. **Fantasea Cruises** (Tel: 079-465111) operates a large catamaran twice daily from Shute Harbour (A$32 round trip). Resort accommodations start at around A$200 per couple per night. Meals and most activities are extra. (Book with the resort at Hamilton Island, Queensland 4803 or Fax: 6179-468888).

Long Island

This island is aptly named, being 11 kilometers long but only around one kilometer wide. It is the closest resort island to the mainland and was once a popular anchorage for ships traveling along the coast. Lumber was logged on the island about 100 years ago, but there is still quite a bit of timber left. There are signposted walks that take you through some of the national park. Beaches on the west side of the island are not bad, but the eastern shore is mainly rocky. The island has three resorts, and two of these are low-key traditional island style.

The most southerly is the recently reopened **Paradise Bay** (Tel: 079-469777). There are eight renovated cabins with private bathrooms and verandahs, and a large gazebo where guests gather for drinks and meals. There are no TVs, radios, airconditioners, swimming pools, or tennis courts. Guests are taken on full-day guided boat, snorkeling, and bushwalking tours of beaches, reefs, rain forests, and surrounding islands. All meals and transfers from Shute Harbour are included in the A$160 room rate. (Book at P.O. Box 842, Airlie Beach 4802 or Fax: 6179-469777.)

Palm Bay Hideaway Resort (Tel: 079-469233) first opened in the 1930s, but it was destroyed by a cyclone in the mid-1970s. The resort has since been restored, but it has retained its peaceful and unhurried environment for those looking for a simple informal holiday. There are no bands, shopping centers, cars, or discos here, simply six bures, eight cabins, a bar and dining hall, spa, swimming pool, and small shop. Units do not have airconditioning, TV, radio, clocks, or telephone, but they do have comfortable beds, a bathroom, a refrigerator, ceiling fans, cooking facilities, and a verandah with a hammock. Linen is replaced after three nights for guests to remake their own room. Catamarans, snorkeling gear, volleyball, windsurfing, paddle skis, hand lines for fishing, card and board games, and a library are provided free to guests. Motorized sports and cruises are available. Room rates are from A$200 per couple per night. A catamaran transfer is provided four times daily from Shute Harbour (A$35 round trip). (Book through P.M.B. Mackay, Queensland 4740 or Fax: 6179-469233.)

Whitsundays Long Island Resort (Tel: 079-469400) is the third resort. This was also originally developed in the 1930s, but it was redeveloped in the 1980s and has had several owners since then. Currently it is operated by the Club Crocodile group who have a popular resort near Airlie Beach on the mainland. This is much more an activities resort and is more up-market than the other two on the island. The 160 rooms are airconditioned, are serviced daily, and have ceiling fan, bathroom, TV, radio, IDD telephone, refrigerator, tea/coffee-making facilities, in-house movies, and balconies. There are two pools, several restaurants and bars, a gymnasium, a nightclub, evening entertainment, a spa, a sauna, floodlit tennis courts, a shop, and a full range of water sports. Room rates start at around A$150 per night. (Book with the resort at P.M.B. 26, Mackay, Queensland 4740 or Fax: 6179-469555.) Boat transfers are possible from either Shute Harbour or Hamilton Island.

South Molle Island

This is the largest of the Molle Group, but it rates in the small category of Whitsunday islands. The island is hilly, and there are some fair beaches at high tide. Much of the vegetation was destroyed before the island became a national park, but there are some nice trees around the resort. The **South Molle Island Resort** (Tel: 079-469433) is one of the older ones in the Whitsundays, and it has never been completely rebuilt at any stage so it lacks some of the visual appeal of other islands. It tries to make up for this by providing a wide range of activities, three meals a day, and nighttime entertainment, in a reasonably priced all-inclusive package.

There are six different types of rooms, but all are comfortable, unpretentious motel-style. Rooms are airconditioned and have ceiling fan, TV, iron, refrigerator, tea/coffee-making facilities, and radio. Some have carpet, and there are various bed combinations. There are four bars, coffee shop, an a la carte restaurant, a milk bar, and scheduled barbecue meals. Banking, shopping, and medical facilities are available. Full water sports facilities as well as nine-hole golf course, day/night tennis, a pool, a spa, a sauna, a gymnasium, squash, archery, volleyball, and parasailing are provided. Daily rates are from around A$150 per person inclusive of meals, but various package deals are available that can lower this cost. Transfers are from Shute Harbour or Hamilton Island. (Book at P.M.B. 21, Mackay 4741 or Fax: 6179-469580.)

Daydream Island

This is one of the smallest of the Whitsunday islands, at about one kilometer long and a few hundred meters wide. It is surprisingly hilly, and there is some good natural vegetation as well as lush landscaping around the resort. **The Daydream Island Travelodge Resort** (Tel: 079-488488) is the closest island resort to Shute Harbour, and it is one of my favorites. The original resort was developed in the 1930s but was demolished in the 1950s. A new Daydream opened in the 1960s and developed a reputation for racy holidays, but this, along with several other resorts, was demolished in the 1970s by a cyclone. A totally new resort at a different location on the island was opened in 1990, and it has proved to be extremely popular. There are good reasons.

The island claims to offer value because so many activities are free to guests. Many of the activities are at the Beach Club, which is at the opposite end of the island from the main resort. There are scuba-diving excursions, glass-bottom boat trips, windsurfing, paddle skis, catamarans, water polo, fish feeding, live music, pools, tennis, indoor bowls, and shopping. Other facilities include a gymnasium, a sauna, a spa, aerobics classes, beach volleyball, and a Kid's Club. Palm-fringed Sunlover's Beach at the back of the resort is a good place for a swim or to relax in the sun.

The 300 rooms are in a three-level complex that provides excellent sea or garden views. The rooms are large, although fairly conventional, and they are extremely well equipped. Rates are from around A$180 a night, but there are cheaper package and stand-by rates. There are several restaurant choices in the resort, and cafe lunch options at the Beach Club. Live entertainment is provided most evenings, and a disco is available. I like it because there is plenty to do, but it also can be free and easy. (Book with the resort on P.M.B. 22, Mackay 4740 or Fax: 6179-488499.)

Hook Island

This is the second largest Whitsunday island and one of the most interesting. There are some good beaches, some of the best diving in the Whitsunday region, popular deep-water anchorages for yachts, caves with some fairly poor Aboriginal paintings, an underwater observatory, and a low-key resort.

The **Hook Island Wilderness Lodge** (Tel: 018-775142) operates mainly on a per-person basis, and you share a room with up to seven others when it is busy. There are 12 units with external bathrooms and toilets, a restaurant, a bar, a small shop, a pool, a dive shop, paddle skis, and snorkeling gear. Rates are around A$20 per person a night. You can get a cabin for two for A$50. Camping is permitted adjacent to the resort with use of the resort facilities, a kitchen, and barbecue for around A$12 a night. The resort location is impressive, there is a range of wildlife close by including some large goannas, and it has found favor with backpackers and budget-conscious families. The underwater observatory is interesting, but there are better ways to see coral and sea life elsewhere.

Hayman Island

This is the most northerly of the Whitsunday islands and has been the site for resort development since 1935. In the early days it was a fishing resort catering to the enthusiast and the famous. In 1950, aviation mogul Reg Ansett opened the luxurious Royal Hayman Hotel. This was progressively developed until the 1980s when it was closed to make way for the present resort. A$260 million was plowed into Hayman, and it reopened in the late 1980s as "one of the best and most exclusive resorts in the world."

Hayman (Tel: 079-469100) is undoubtedly a great resort, but these days it is not so exclusive—families are now being encouraged rather than children being prohibited as previously. That doesn't mean that service standards, facilities, or prices have dropped, it just means that 400 beds in the exclusive category are difficult to fill in the Whitsundays. The resort is better for it. Realize, however, that Hayman is unique among the Whitsunday island resorts, and you pay accordingly. Room rates are from around A$400 to over A$1,000 a night. Six restaurants offer a great choice of cuisine, but several will be over A$100 a meal, for two. Most of the extensive sporting and entertainment facilities work on the user-pays principle.

The architecture, the landscaping, and the facilities are most impressive. All rooms have the usual resort facilities plus video players, bathrobes, safes, and so forth. The resort never feels crowded due to the sprawling layout and the multitude of facilities. As the Hayman advertisements say, "With its grace, style, and superb service, Hayman is the best of all possible worlds. On an island." There are luxury boats operating between the Hamilton Island air strip and Hayman, and you can also be picked up from Shute Harbour. Amphibious planes run from the Whitsundays air strip. (Book at Hayman Island, Whitsundays, Queensland 4801 or Fax: 6179-469410.)

Other Whitsunday Islands

Camping is permitted on many of the islands, but facilities and water are limited. Two of the better sites are at Cockatoo Beach on North Molle Island, and at Dugong Beach on the west side of Whitsunday Island. Famous Whitehaven Beach on Whitsunday Island has a camping area on the southern end of the beach, but there is no water supply. For further information and camping permits contact the ranger, Whitsunday District Office, Queensland Department of Environment and Heritage, Shute Harbour Road, Airlie Beach 4802.

Magnetic Island

This large granite island close to Townsville, with 40 kilometers of coastline, and mountains to 500 meters, was named by Captain Cook when he believed the magnetic compass on his ship was being affected by the land mass. Today over half the island is national park, while the other areas support a permanent population of around 2,500. Inland from a score of secluded bays, the national park landscape is very rugged with large granite boulders and rock faces among vegetation ranging from open forest to rain forest. There are more than 20 kilometers of well-maintained, sign-posted walking trails through the park. Many are comfortable one-to-two-hour treks.

The island has become one of the most popular along the coast for families and backpackers because it is relatively cheap, it is easy to get to, and there are many things to do. There are four towns complete with shops, restaurants, and accommodations places linked by a paved road, and a rough dusty road follows the west coast to West Point. **Rental mini-cars** (Tel: 78-5377), **motorscooters** (Tel: 78-5222), and **bicycles** (Tel: 78-5411) are available, and there is a **bus service** (Tel: 78-5130) and **taxi** (Tel: 78-5946) to all centers. The **Magnetic Island Car Ferry** (Tel: 72-5422) operates three times daily from South Townsville to Nelly Bay, while fast **catamaran ferries** operate about every hour from the Wonderland and Breakwater terminals in Townsville (Tel: 72-7122) to **Picnic Bay** on the island. This is the main shopping center, and many visitors decide to stay here. **Nelly Bay,** the next town, is over a headland. This is the largest residential area and the site of the **Shark World** (Tel: 78-5777), a hospital, a school, and the proposed Magnetic Quays marina.

Acadia is the next center. This fronts Geoffrey Bay with its reef walk and car ferry landing ramp, and attractive Alma Bay with its lifesaving club. There are shops and restaurants, and the **Arcadia Hotel Resort** provides facilities and entertainment for locals and visitors. The road then continues through the national park to **Horseshoe Bay** where there is an excellent beach, rental water sports equipment, a bird sanctuary, a **horse ranch** (Tel: 78-5109), and **koala park** (Tel: 78-5260). You also pass a turnoff to **Radical Bay,** and walking tracks to **The Forts.** Elsewhere on the island there are good bushwalks to various lookouts and other points of interest. You will see opossums, koalas, rock wallabies, bush curlews, sulphur-crested cockatoos, and rainbow lorikeets. No wonder it is so popular!

Accommodations range from resorts such as **Latitude 19** (Tel:

077-785200) at Nelly Bay, through holiday apartments such as **Magnetic Retreat** (Tel: 077-785357, Fax: 6177-781089) at Arcadia, to budget centers such as **Geoff's Place** (Tel: 077-785577) at Horseshoe Bay. Daily rates start at around A$60 double, A$70 a unit, and A$10 each person per night, respectively. The resorts have airconditioned rooms, restaurants, bars, swimming pools, sporting facilities, and entertainment. The holiday apartments have fans, kitchens, living areas, barbecues, and many have pools.

Here are some other choices: **Palm View Chalets** (Tel: 077-785596, Fax: 6177-785256) has modern self-contained, airconditioned units at Sooning Street, Nelly Bay, from A$75. The **Island Leisure Resort** (Tel: 077-785511, Fax: 6177-785042) in Nelly Bay, has large, fanned, self-contained units with sleeping facilities for two adults and three children within a complex containing a pool, spa, tennis court, recreation room, kiosk, tour desk, laundry, barbecue, library, gymnasium, and massage room. Daily rates are A$89 double. **Tropical Palms Inn** (Tel: 077-785076, Fax: 6177-785897) has 12 airconditioned, limited-kitchen units at Picnic Bay. The complex has a pool, barbecues, laundry, landscaped gardens, and vehicle rental. Daily unit rates are from A$60. The **Beachcomber Apartments** (Tel: 077-785333, Fax: 6177-785347), at Marine Parade, Arcadia, offers modern airconditioned, two-bedroom self-contained units from A$65 a day.

The problem with Magnetic Island accommodations is that there is so much choice. It is impossible to list all the alternatives. Despite this, at times you will find that the island is full, so it is best to arrange something for the first night before you arrive. The **Picnic Bay Hotel** (Tel: 077-785166) has motel-style rooms, gardens, a pool, and laundry. Room rates are from A$45. The **Arcadia Hotel Resort** (Tel: 077-785177, Fax: 6177-785939) is on a great site overlooking Geoffrey Bay. The rooms and facilities are good, and it is understandably popular with room rates from A$65. **Hideaway Budget Resort** (Tel: 077-785110) at Picnic Bay has renovated twin rooms with fans and wash basins for A$30. It is friendly, and there is a pool and barbecue. **Magnetic Island Tropical Resort** (Tel: 077-785955, Fax: 6177-785601) at Nelly Bay has spacious, self-contained A-frame units sleeping up to six people, a bar, bistro, pool, spa, kitchen, and laundry facilities. This started as a budget property, but has since gone up-market a bit to A$50 a night. It's quiet and away from the beach. **Marshall's Bed & Breakfast** (Tel: 077-785112) is at 3 Endeavour Road, Arcadia, for those who enjoy staying with a family. Rates are around A$45 a double. **Nautilus House** (Tel: 077-785802) is a guest house in the old-Queensland style at the relatively isolated West Point. Bed and breakfast is also available.

To complement all these accommodations, there are many eateries. Up-market places include **Gatsby's** at the Arcadia Resort Hotel; **Cotters on the Beach** (Tel: 78-5786) for seafood, steaks, or chicken dinners in a relaxed indoor-outdoor setting at Horseshoe Bay; **La Trattoria** (Tel: 78-5757) for provincial Mediterranean cuisine on the hill overlooking the beach at Alma Bay; and the fun-filled **Mexican Munchies** (Tel: 78-5658) at Warboys Street, Nelly Bay. Several of the resorts have bistros, and you will find **Banisters** (Tel: 78-5700) has good seafood at Arcadia; the **Chinese Restaurant** (Tel: 78-5706) in the Picnic Bay Arcade does all the favorites; **Alla Capri** (Tel: 78-5448) has pasta, pizza, and steaks, and an attractive atmosphere at Hayles Avenue at Arcadia; while **Blue Waters** (Tel: 78-5645) around the corner provides seafood, steaks, and salads in the Australian way. Snacks, take-outs, coffee, cakes, and so forth are available from many outlets.

Entertainment comes in the form of nightclubs at the Picnic Bay and Arcadia Resort hotels, poker machines at the Magnetic Island Golf Club, toad races, bingo, lawn bowls, and film nights on Friday and Saturday and a blues club Sunday afternoons at the Sports and Recreation Club. The **Magnetic Island Country Golf Club** (Tel: 78-5188) welcomes visitors to its nine-hole course and clubhouse at Picnic Bay. Rental clubs are available. There is a public swimming pool at Nelly Bay open every day. Shopping covers all requirements with the **Arcadia Pottery Gallery** (Tel: 78-5600), **Island Fever** (Tel: 78-5811) for tropical island leisure wear, and **Art Gallery** (Tel: 58-1170) at Nelly Bay especially recommended. There are markets in Arcadia on the last Saturday in the month and in Horseshoe Bay on the second Saturday.

Pleasure Divers (Tel: 78-5788) has PADI dive courses, reef dives, and gear rental. The large Polynesian catamaran *Worripa,* has day trips from Horseshoe Bay which include boomnetting, fishing, snorkeling, and a barbecue for around A$50. **Magnetic Island Harley Tours** (Tel: 018-757238) operate from the end of the Picnic Bay jetty. **Pure Pleasure Cruises** call at Picnic Bay to pick up passengers on the day trip from Townsville to Kelso Reef.

Great Palm Island

This is the largest island in the Palm Group to the north of Townsville. Great Palm Island, together with another seven or eight smaller islands, is a self-governing Aboriginal local authority. At present, you must obtain prior approval from the council before you can go there. Captain Cook landed here in 1770 and reported seeing Aborigines. In the 1910s, an Aboriginal mission was established here, and a leper colony was built on nearby Fantome Island. The community on Palm Island now numbers around 1,500. There are several daily flights from Townsville to the Palm Island air strip, and there is a regular sea barge service. The town has a good range of services including a school, a hospital, shops, and sporting clubs. On occasion, the island has expressed interest in tourism, but nothing has yet developed.

Orpheus Island

This is part of the Palm Group, but it is not part of the Aboriginal council area. The island is a national park, but there is a James Cook University research station. There is also a small privately owned resort. There are many sheltered bays with excellent fringing reef that can be explored by snorkeling or diving. The island is long and narrow and is mostly dry woodland with some rain forest in the gullies. The native animals are mostly nocturnal, but you can sometimes see echidna, bandicoots, and snakes.

The research station specializes in raising clams, and many of these are transported to Pacific island reefs where their numbers have been depleted. You should telephone 077-777336 to inquire about visiting the station, which is about two kilometers from the resort. Camping is permitted at Pioneer Bay north of the research station, and near Yank's Jetty at the south of the island. Both sites have toilets and picnic facilities but no permanent water. A permit is required from Queensland Department of Environment and Heritage offices in Townsville or Ingham.

The **Orpheus Island Resort** (Tel: 077-777377) is small, low-key, and expensive. The maximum number of guests is restricted to around 70, but often there are many less. The present development originates from the early 1980s, and everything is modern, restrained, but sophisticated. Rooms deliberately do not have TV or telephones, but they are well equipped and spacious. Above the main resort are six Italian-designed two-bedroom villas, which are a real touch of luxury. Meals are included in the tariff, and the resort prides itself on its food. Coffee, tea, fruit juice, and ice water are always available. Facilities include a tennis court, a swimming pool, catamarans, windsurfers, a dive shop, and dinghies, and there is an afternoon snorkeling trip. Apart from that, guests relax, read, talk, and escape from the outside world. Normal access is by amphibious plane from Townsville (A$130 one way) or you can get a water taxi from Dungeness near Lucinda. Daily room rates start at around $450 for one or A$700 for two. The villas are around A$1,000 for two. (Book at P.M.B. 15, Townsville, Queensland 4810 or Fax: 6177-777533.)

Hinchinbrook Island

This spectacular island is by far the largest off the north Queensland coast, and it is Australia's largest island national park. It has rugged **Mt. Bowen** (1,142 meters) as its highest point, and it is separated from the mainland by the deep, narrow, mangrove-fringed **Hinchinbrook Channel.** Vegetation ranges from lush rain forest, through scrub and heaths, to mangrove forests, while the plentiful wildlife provides unrivalled opportunities for the keen naturalist. At various times mosquitoes, sand flies, and march flies can be a problem to walkers and campers, so take insect repellent and wear suitable clothing.

The island has several man-made features. At the far northern tip there is a nice, low-key resort. Elsewhere, there are three camping areas with toilets and tables, and two of these have permanent water. A boardwalk along the bank of an inlet provides a fascinating path through the dense tangle of air-breathing mangrove roots. Several marked trails link various features of the island. The most spectacular is the 32-kilometer **Thorsborne Trail** along the east coast. It is not a graded or hardened track, but is managed on the "minimal impact bushwalking" and "no-trace camping" ethic, with permits limited to a maximum of 40 people at any one time. This very popular walk takes three to four days to complete and is recommended for fit and experienced bushwalkers only. An excellent brochure is produced by the Queensland Department of Environment and Heritage. Trail and camping permits are available from offices in Townsville, Ingham, and Cardwell.

The **Hinchinbrook Island Resort** (Tel: 070-668585) has a lovely location at Cape Richards. The original resort was developed in the 1970s and was attractively extended and refurbished in 1990. The aim of the developers has been to create a secluded environment which fits into the site while providing a good level of sophistication. Most visitors agree that this has been achieved. The newer "tree houses," which are linked with timber boardwalks, are particularly appealing. All units are well equipped, but there are no TVs, airconditioners, or telephones. The attractive restaurant, bar, and pool area is separate. Daily rates start at around A$250 for a single and A$400 for a double, including meals. At the time of this writing, the resort was not operating for some reason. (Contact is P.O. Box 3, Cardwell, Queensland 4816 or Fax: 6170-668742.) Access to the resort is from Cardwell by daily boat or from Townsville by float plane.

Trips for fishing or sightseeing, and transfers for walkers and campers are available from **Hinchinbrook Adventures** (Tel: 070-668270) at Cardwell, or from Dungeness. Water holidays are available through **Hinchinbrook Rent a Yacht** (Tel: 070-668007, Fax: 6170-668003) at Cardwell, or **Cardwell Love Boats** (Tel: 077-763466, Fax: 6177-763406) in Ingham.

Goold Island

This is 4.5 kilometers north of Cape Richards and 17 kilometers from Cardwell. Eucalypti woodland is the main vegetation on this granite island, but there is some rain forest in the gullies. Turtles, dugong, and flocks of noisy sulphur-crested cockatoos can often be seen. A camping area has pit toilets, tables, and fireplaces, but water is usually not available from August to December. The island is a national park, so a camping permit is required. Tiny **Garden Island**, just to the south, has no camping restrictions, but there is no water. The **Brook Islands** to the east are densely vegetated national parks which are important breeding grounds for Torresian imperial pigeons and black-naped terns. The islands have good reef and are a popular snorkeling location, but camping is not permitted.

Bedarra Island

This rain-forested island is five kilometers off Hull Heads, and is shown on some maps as Richards Island. It is privately owned and has two small, delightful, exclusive resorts operated by Qantas Airways. One has been closed for some time waiting on economic conditions to improve. No daytrippers are allowed, and children under 15 are not permitted on the island. Access is by boat from nearby Dunk Island where there is an airport.

The two resorts on the island are totally separate, but they are marketed together, have similar facilities, and cost the same. They have slightly different atmospheres, but are both delightful, and I would be very happy at either. I stayed for one night at the **Bedarra Bay Resort** (Tel: 070-688233) a few years ago, and the experience is still fresh in my mind. It was the most enjoyable island experience that I have had anywhere. **Bedarra Hideaway,** which has had several "royal visits," is the other resort. Both have 16 large, individual architect-designed cottages, restaurants, pools, spas, a beach, water sports facilities, tennis, and peace. They are joined by a 45-minute-long, mountainous rain forest trail.

The resorts operate on the all-inclusive principle, and they mean it. If you wish to use one of the power boats to visit a private beach, that's included. So you would like a picnic lunch of lobster and French champagne to take with you? That's just fine. The bars at the resort don't have barmen because the liquor is all included. There is a menu for meals, and I found it more than adequate, but if you speak to the chef ahead of time he will prepare you something of your own choice. Guests are referred to only by their first names, so you can remain somewhat anonymous if you wish. It is all very sophisticated. Daily rates are around A$540 per person for the first few nights, then they reduce a little. (Book on Bedarra Resort, Bedarra Island via Townsville, Queensland 4810 or Fax: 6170-688215.)

Dunk Island

This is the largest island in the Family group. It is 75 percent rain-forested national park, and there are 13 kilometers of walking trails, so you can visit beaches, forest, and hilltops and see the prolific bird life and brilliant blue Ulysses butterflies that inhabit the island. There is a large resort owned by Qantas Airways, a well-established camping area with toilets, tables, fireplaces, and water supply, and day-tripper facilities. There are several daily aircraft from both Townsville and Cairns (around A$100 one way), water taxis from Mission Beach (around A$20 round trip), and boat connections from Clump Point. Many consider it one of the most attractive of the northern islands, and it is certainly the best known due partly to the writings of E. J. Banfield, who lived here with his wife for 26 years from 1897. Banfield wrote a regular column in the *Townsville Daily Bulletin* newspaper during this period, and he also published *The Confessions of a Beachcomber* and other books.

The **Dunk Island Resort** (Tel: 070-688199) has the capacity to house over 400 guests, but it generally manages to avoid a crowded feel. The accommodation has been built with little imagination, but fortunately, much of it is hidden behind lush landscaping which is encouraged by regular tropical rain. This rain can be a problem for guests in the January to March period. There are various levels of accommodations with the Bayview Villas and the Beachfront Units being the best situated, newest, and most expensive. All rooms have airconditioning, fans, TV, in-house movies, telephone, refrigerator, tea/coffee-making facilities, irons, and verandahs or patios. Guests can take a meal package in the main Beachcomber Restaurant or use the a la carte Rainforest Brasserie. There is nightly entertainment and often a late night disco.

Dunk isn't a rage-till-you-drop resort, but there is a wide range of activities. There are two swimming pools, a squash and tennis court, a small golf course with novel night facilities, archery, horseback riding, clay-target shooting, tandem skydiving, indoor bowls, volleyball, scuba diving, water-skiing, parasailing, catamarans, paddle skis, power boats for rent, and cricket matches. Children are catered to with the Kids Korna, and there is a daily visit to the small dairy farm for milking. The island also sports an artist's colony, and guests are welcome to visit there on Tuesday and Friday mornings to learn about activities and to purchase works. The resort has a shop, a bank agency, and conference facilities. Daily room and activities rates start at around A$200 single, A$330 double. (Book at Dunk Island Resort via Townsville, Queensland 4810 or Fax: 6170-688528.)

9. Sports

Townsville is the sports capital of north Queensland. The city supports several teams in national competitions, and there are excellent facilities for sports participation. You will find that elsewhere in the region there are many options, and you will be welcomed no matter where you go. Here are a few suggestions.

Basketball

The Townsville Suns play in the National Basketball League. Home games are played at the **Townsville Breakwater Entertainment Centre** (Tel:

077-714222) in the April-September period. The Townsville Heat (men) and Townsville Sunbirds (women) play at the **Murray Sports Complex** (Tel: 077-783400) in the CBA competition. A Burdekin team and a Mackay team play in the same competition.

Rugby League

Twenty-five thousand fans pack Townsville's **Stockland Stadium** (Tel: 077-730777) to support the North Queensland Cowboys in the national competition. Games are usually held Saturday evenings in the April-September period.

Hockey

The **Townsville Hockey Centre** (Tel: 077-784810) is the home of the North Queensland Barras who play in the National Hockey League.

Golf

Townsville has the 27-hole **Townsville Golf Club** (Tel: 077-790133), the 18-hole **Willows Golf Tourist and Sports Resort** (Tel: 077-734352), the 18-hole **Rowes Bay Golf Club** (Tel: 077-741288), and the **Lavarack Golf Club** (Tel: 077-254959). There are also clubs at **Ayr** (Tel: 077-831296), **Home Hill** (Tel: 077-821632), **Bowen** (Tel: 077-851206), **Whitsundays** (Tel: 079-467882), **Proserpine** (Tel: 079-451337), **Laguna Quays** (Tel: 079-477777), **Mackay** (Tel: 079-421521), **Balgal Beach** (Tel: 077-707355), **Ingham** (Tel: 077-765600), **Cardwell** (Tel: 070-668680) and **Tully** (Tel: 070-681236).

Diving

There are better facilities for reef diving here than just about anywhere else in the world. Scores of operators offer dive courses, resort dives, dive trips, and extended dive excursions. The **Mike Ball Dive Expeditions** headquarters in Townsville (Tel: 077-723022) is claimed to be Australia's most advanced diver training facility. The S.S. *Yongala* wreck dive off Townsville is often referred to as the best in the country. The 90-meter-long ship, which went down in 1911 during a cyclone, lies in 30 meters of water. It has since attracted a large range of spectacular marine life including gropers, manta rays, sea snakes, turtles, sharks, and huge schools of fish.

For courses and/or dive trips contact the following:

Barrier Reef Diving Services—Whitsundays (Tel: 079-466204)
Bluewater Scuba Diving—Bluewater (Tel: 018-779267)
Friendship Cruises—Mission Beach (Tel: 070-687262)
Mackay Adventure Divers—Mackay (Tel: 079-511472)
Mike Ball Dive Expeditions—Townsville (Tel: 077-723022)

Mission Beach Dive School—Mission Beach (Tel: 070-688288)
Oceania Dive—Whitsundays (Tel: 079-466032)
Pro Dive Townsville—(Tel: 077-211760)
Pro Dive Whitsunday—(Tel: 079-466508)
Reef Enterprises—(Tel: 1-800-621133)
Reef Magic Charters—(Tel: 016-782286)
Sun City Watersports—Townsville (Tel: 077-716527)
The Dive Bell—Townsville (Tel: 077-211155)

Sailing

The Whitsundays is the sailing capital of Queensland. There are numerous opportunities to day trip or take an extended sailing cruise through this area. Some of the options are:

Apollo Maxi—(Tel: 079-466922)
Apollo 111 Charters—(Tel: 079-469334)
Coral Trekker—(Tel: 079-467197)
Destination Whitsundays—(Tel: 1-800-644563)
Gretel—(Tel: 079-467529)
Mollo Catamaran—(Tel: 018-776032)
Trinity Trimaran—(Tel: 079-466255)
White Swan—(Tel: 079-466133)

Horse and Dog Racing

Horse races are conducted Saturdays at **Cluden Racecourse** (Tel: 077-782933) in Townsville, and at **Ooralea Racecourse** (Tel: 079-521009) in Mackay, There are also race clubs at Ayr, Home Hill, Bowen, Proserpine, and Ingham.

Greyhound races are held Thursday evenings at the **Townsville Showground** (Tel: 077-721742) on Ingham Road, and the **Mackay Showground** (Tel: 079-573916) on Milton Street.

Fishing

Fishing is available to everyone. No licenses are required for amateur fishing in Queensland, but fishing is not permitted in some zones of the Great Barrier Reef Marine Park. Reef fishing trips operate from many centers. Some are day trips, others overnight. Game fishing enthusiasts can take a boat from Townsville and try the bountiful waters of Bowling Green Bay, now regarded as one of the best light-tackle fishing grounds in the world. The Sheraton Game Fishing Classic in Townsville, and the Dunk Island Bill Fishing Tournament are two annual events that bring competitors from a wide area. Fishing information is available from the following:

Action Sport Fishing—(Tel: 077-796370)
Aussie Barra Charters—(Tel: 018-988229)
Elizabeth E Cruises—(Tel: 079-574281)
M. V. Moruya Whitsunday—(Tel: 079-467127)
Power Play Charters—(Tel: 077-872666)
U-Beaut Barra Charters—(Tel: 015-635066)
Wyllaway Cruises—(Tel: 079-522033)

Other Sports

Information on a wide range of other sports is best obtained from the local telephone book, the local newspapers, or from **Townsville Enterprise** (Tel: 077-713061), **Tourism Mackay** (Tel: 079-522677), or **Whitsunday Visitors and Promotions Bureau** (Tel: 079-466673).

Some of the sports with local facilities are: archery, athletics, Australian rules football, badminton, baseball, bicycle racing, bocce, boxing, bridge, car racing, cricket, croquet, darts, gliding, gymnastics, judo, karate, lifesaving, model remote control sports, motorcycle racing, netball, racing pigeons, rowing, rugby union, shooting, soccer, softball, speedway, squash, table tennis, tennis, waterskiing, and volleyball.

10. Shopping

There are extensive shopping facilities in Townsville and Mackay but little to buy that is not available elsewhere in Australia. **Townsville** shopping is centered on several regional shopping centers where national chain stores and local outlets provide all the needs of the region's population. The **Flinders Mall** shopping area in the city center is just a shadow of its former glory but there is still enough here for most visitors. **Mackay** central city has remained more of a center, while several shopping malls have also appeared.

Because of the distances between towns in this region, **Proserpine, Whitsunday, Bowen, Home Hill, Ayr, Ingham,** and **Tully,** all have good local shopping centers supported by the locals. Visitors will find they have sufficient range for their needs. The Sunday morning **Cotters Market,** held each week in Townsville's Flinders Mall, is North Queensland's largest arts and craft market and there are many interesting items. Free parking is available in the Ogden Street multi-story car park. Some of the smaller centers also have markets.

11. Entertainment and Nightlife

Townsville has excellent facilities. The **Breakwater Entertainment Centre** (Tel: 71-4000), **Civic Theatre** (Tel: 72-2677), and **Sound Shell** (Tel: 72-5099) offer everything from international artists and shows to local performers, theater, and dance. Several North Queensland musicians are near the top of their field in country, folk, rock, classical, and jazz. **Dance North** is the only professional dance company in Northern Australia. **Theatre Up North** is a professional theater company. The **Mackay Entertainment Centre** (Tel: 57-2255) and the **Burdekin Theatre** (Tel: 83-3455) in Ayr have regular performances. The **Proserpine Cultural Centre** (Tel: 45-2312) and the **Ingham Theatre** also have performances.

Hotel lounges and other venues have single performers or groups with rock, blues, jazz, bush sounds, or country music. Numerous discos throb to the beat of the latest dance beat until late. Both high rollers and first timers revel in the fun and excitement of Townsville's friendly **Sheraton Breakwater Casino.** It operates until the early morning hours seven days a week. Some dress rules apply, but they are quite reasonable, and there is no admission charge. Visitors are welcome to look or play.

These are some of the current favorite music venues for the young at heart.

Townsville

> **Bullwinkles**—108 Flinders St. East (Tel: 715647)
> **Langs Tavern**—129 Flinders St. East (Tel: 715727)
> **Playpen Nightclub**—719 Flinders St. (Tel: 211200)
> **Quarterdeck on the Marina**—Sheraton Hotel (Tel: 222333)
> **The Bank**—169 Flinders St. East (Tel: 716148)

Mackay

> **Australian Hotel**—Victoria & Wood St. (Tel: 572220)
> **Blue Moose Night Club**—148 Victoria St. (Tel: 575626)
> **Legends Nite Club**—99 Victoria St. (Tel: 573965)
> **Paradise Nights**—85 Victoria St. (Tel: 514365)
> **Stargazers**—176 Victoria St. (Tel: 572811)

Airlie Beach

> **Club Crocodile**—Shute Harbour Road (Tel: 467155)
> **Hotel Airlie Beach**—The Espanade (Tel: 466233)
> **KC's Chargrill**—Shute Harbour Road (Tel: 466320)

12. The Townsville and Central Reef Contact List

Townsville

> Ambulance—Townsville Communications Centre (Tel: 254899)
> Bus Service Information—(Tel: 131230)
> Churches—Anglican, 155 Denham St. (Tel: 714175)

—Catholic, 41 Mooney St. (Tel: 255888)
—Church of Jesus Christ (Tel: 251681)
—Uniting, 73 Wills St. (Tel: 712584)
Dental Services—Cambridge St. (Tel: 270229)
Emergency Calls—Ambulance, Fire, Police (Tel: 000)
Fire Service—Morey St. (Tel: 712111)
Hospital—Townsville General, Eyre St. (Tel: 819211)
Immigration—143 Walker St. (Tel: 726811)
Lifeline—24-hour counseling service (Tel: 131114)
Mayor's Office—103 Walker St. (Tel: 220200)
Medical—Aitkenvale 24-hour, 301 Ross River (Tel: 757444)
Museums—Maritime, 42 Palmer St. (Tel: 215251)
—National Trust (Tel: 725195)
—Townsville, 81 Sturt St. (Tel: 725725)
—Tropical Queensland, Flinders St. (Tel: 211662)
Police—Stanley Street, City (Tel: 818511)
Post Office—252 Flinders Mall (Tel: 716133)
Qantas Airways—320 Flinders Mall, domestic (Tel: 131313)
international (Tel: 008177767)
RACQ Breakdown Service—motor vehicles (Tel: 212360)
Rail Services—502 Flinders St. (Tel: 728211)
Rotary International—(Tel: 716721)
Taxi—11 Yeatman St. (Tel: 721555)
Telephone Calls—international operator (Tel: 0101)
Townsville Enterprise—The Strand (Tel: 713061)

Mackay

Ambulance—15 Brisbane St. (Tel: 578099)
Bus Terminal—11 Milton St. (Tel: 513088)
Churches—Anglican, Holy Trinity (Tel: 573341)
—Catholic, St. Mary's, Juliet St. (Tel: 574807)
—Uniting, 21 MacAlister St. (Tel: 573557)
Dental—Clinic, Bridge Road (Tel: 515444)
Fire—Sydney St. (Tel: 572244)
Hospital—Bridge Road (Tel: 512677)
Medical—29 Brisbane Street (Tel: 511311)
Police—Brisbane Street (Tel: 69444)
Post Office—69 Sydney Street (Tel: 577333)
Qantas—105 Victoria Street (Tel: 574999)
Rail Services—(Tel: 1-800-177693)
Taxi—Victoria Street (Tel: 1-800-815559)
Tourist Information—Nebo Road (Tel: 522677)

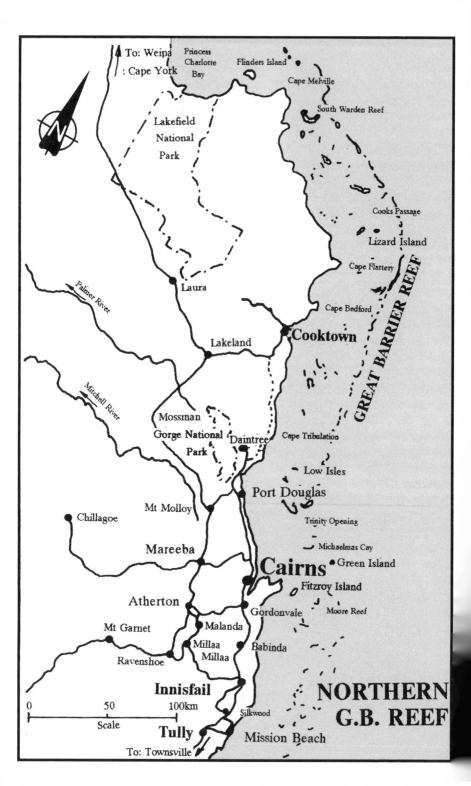

8

Cairns and the Northern Great Barrier Reef

1. The General Picture

Picture a place with lush, tropical greenery, hot days and warm nights, dense rain-forested mountains, blue sea, soft green islands, stunning reef, wilderness, and outback. That is the way Far North Queensland wants to be seen by the world. Increasingly, the world is watching, and people from many countries are taking the chance to visit.

Cairns is the major city in this region. It is growing rapidly, largely due to a booming tourism industry. The central area of the city is small, cosmopolitan, and compact. New buildings stand side by side with the architecture of the past. There is a focus towards the sea with the marina and wharfs almost an extension of the city's wide tree-lined streets.

Throughout the region, the air is clean, traffic is light, and the lifestyle is seductive. Many locals only planned to visit for a short while but have found it impossible to move away. When the swimming pool can be used for most of the year, and the house verandahs and patios become the most used living area, life almost becomes one long holiday. It helps, too, when you can often find a lonely stretch of beach, a private picnic spot, or a rain forest walk close to home.

The tourist boom has meant a growth in places to eat, rooms to stay, shops to explore, venues for sport, and outlets for nighttime fun. It has, of course, also meant more people on the streets, rising prices, some shops where English is a second language, and a feeling among some locals that this is no longer their city. For visitors, Cairns can present a problem. At times it almost seems that there are more tourists than locals. While some Japanese and Chinese appreciate the opportunity to shop, eat, and stay in places run by their countryfolk, others are asking, "Is this the real Australia?" It is something that Cairns will have to decide on in the near future.

While Cairns is on the coast, a major disappointment to many people is that there are no beaches here. If you need a beach, you will have to stay on the **Marlin Coast** north of the city, at lovely **Port Douglas** about 70 kilometers to the north, or at **Cape Tribulation** 140 kilometers from the city. Fortunately, some of these beaches are great, and still surprisingly deserted at most times.

Parts of the northern reef are the closest sections of Great Barrier Reef to the coast, and some of the more northerly reefs are still almost untouched. Hundreds of day-trippers head out from Cairns and Port Douglas, but many serious divers take three-, four-, and five-day excursions into areas farther from civilization. They are rewarded by some of the best diving in the world.

Cooktown stands on the site of Australia's first British settlement, when Captain Cook and his crew lived here for 48 days while they repaired their ship *Endeavour*. The town was not officially founded for another 100 years until the gold rushes of the 1870s, and today it is a small settlement serving the surrounding community and acting as a base for visitors who are interested in history, fishing, cruising, or exploring the wilderness to the north and west. This wilderness, which sits beside the Great Barrier Reef from Cooktown to the Torres Strait, is a lure for adventure seekers, botanists, geologists, and those looking for the ultimate escape. It culminates in Thursday Island, off the northern tip of mainland Australia, where you can see the Torres Strait culture and lifestyle that has been inherited from its South Pacific neighbors.

2. Getting There

Cairns International Airport is one of the fastest-growing and most important airports in Australia. It has become the northern gateway to Australia with numerous airlines flying in from many countries. Cairns is a long way from the southern centers in Australia, so air travel is also the preferred mode of domestic transport for many people. **Qantas Airways** has established a major organizational base here that operates services connecting Cairns with Honolulu, Japan (Sapporo, Tokyo, Osaka, Fukuoka), Taipei, Hong Kong, Bangkok, Auckland, and Singapore. Domestically, there are direct Qantas services to Alice Springs, Ayers Rock, Brisbane,

Darwin, Dunk Island, Gold Coast, Gove, Lizard Island, Melbourne, Sydney, Thursday Island, and Townsville.

Innisfail and Cairns are on the North Coast rail line from Brisbane, and are served by the **Queenslander** and **Sunlander** passenger trains. These centers are also served by **long-distance buses** from Brisbane.

Several tour companies offer one-way bus tours from Brisbane with accommodations, sightseeing, and some meals included.

Australians have been driving to Cairns from southern centers for many years, but now there is a growing number of international visitors doing the same. It is 1,700 kilometers from Brisbane to Cairns but the **Bruce Highway** has recently been upgraded, accommodations are readily available, and there are numerous attractions on the way.

3. Local Transportation

All of the major centers have 24-hour **taxi services,** and because distances within centers are small, fares generally are quite reasonable. In the Cairns region, however, some of the northern beaches are a surprising distance from the city, so fares here rapidly rise.

Local bus services are available in many centers, but, except in Cairns, frequencies can be poor, particularly outside business hours. There is a bus service from Cairns airport to many city hotels, and several other hotels in Cairns, on the Marlin Coast, and at Port Douglas have their own courtesy transportation.

Commuter air services link Cairns with Lizard Island and Dunk Island. There are **ferry services** from Cairns to Green Island and Fitzroy Island.

Rental cars are readily available in Cairns, Port Douglas, and some other centers. The choice is between the national operators and local outfits. Some of the locals have older and cheaper vehicles, which can be okay to use in the immediate area. Some operators also have four-wheel-drive vehicles, sports models, and recreational vehicles for those who want something different. Here are some of the operators:

Cairns

Avis—135 Lake Street (Tel: 51-5911)
Brits Australia (campervans)—411 Sheridan St. (Tel: 1-800-331454)
Budget—153 Lake Street (Tel: 51-9222)
Cairns Rent-a-Car—137 Lake Street (Tel: 51-6077)
Hertz—Sheridan & Shields Street (Tel: 53-6701)
Koalas Camper Rentals—403 Sheridan Street (Tel: 53-6740)
Leisure Wheels—196 Sheridan Street (Tel: 51-5656)

National—143 Abbott Street (Tel: 51-4600)
Network—145 Lake Street (Tel: 31-6632)
Thrifty—40 Aplin Street (Tel: 51-8099)

Port Douglas

Allcar Rental—21 Warner Street (Tel: 99-4123)
Avis—13 Warner Street (Tel: 99-4331)
Network—41 Macrosssan Street (Tel: 99-5111)

4. The Accommodations Scene

The Cairns accommodations scene is one of the most varied in Queensland. Port Douglas, although only small, also has good variety. Other areas have fewer properties in the up-market segment, but generally you can find reasonable accommodations in the area as far north as Cooktown. In this section I will only cover accommodations in Cairns, the Marlin Coast, and Port Douglas. For accommodations at other mainland centers, see the relevant part of Section 6 within this chapter. For island accommodations, see Section 8 within this chapter. The following is only a selection of what is available.

Cairns

The city has more accommodations than all other Queensland centers except Brisbane and the Gold Coast. The up-market accommodations are excellent but expensive, and this trend continues through to the mid-market category. Budget accommodations are in line with most other centers due to the intense competition in Cairns. The expensive category is above A$160 a night in this region.

EXPENSIVE ACCOMMODATIONS

The **Reef Hotel Casino** (Tel: 30-8888), which opened early in 1996, now sets new standards here. The 128-suite hotel is part of the new casino complex, and it reeks elegance and quality. All the suites have lounge areas, spa baths, garden balconies, and butler service. The top two floors of 39 suites house the Australis Club, which includes a presidential suite, two junior suites, and 12 themed suites. These floors have private access, butler and valet services, a hospitality area for evening cocktails and breakfast, and limousine transfers to and from the airport.

The Anthias Restaurant has Asian and European influences in its decor and cuisine. The Pacific Flavours Brasserie is more casual. Undoubtedly the most striking feature is the huge glass-domed conservatory where there is a living rain forest. A reverie featuring singing, dancing, aerobatics, and spectacular lighting plays here each night for the candlelit diners. For variety, guests can wine, dine, and dance the night away among the rooftops and alleys of a stylized New York at the 1936 Nightclub. (Book at 35 Wharf Street, Cairns, or Fax: 6170-308788.)

The **Cairns Hilton** (Tel: 52-1599), 264 rooms, was the first of the major hotels with a waterfront location. It has been very successful and is a fine property. I must confess, however, that I feel it could be better. The architecture is a little cold for my taste, and some of the public facilities seem to just lack that final personal touch. I'm really being picky here, but at A\$230 a room, I think I can be. The rooms are very well presented and have all the usual facilities. There are restaurants, bars, an attractive large pool, and other public areas. Guests are a mix of business and holiday clients. (Book with the hotel at Wharf Street, Cairns 4870 or Fax: 6170-521370.)

The **Cairns International Hotel** (Tel: 31-1300), 321 rooms, is close by. It is a highrise property with a spectacular grand lobby, spacious rooms, and three pools set in a large garden area. Some guest rooms have water views (although the hotel is not on the waterfront), some have views over Cairns city. Kingsfords Restaurant has fine dining, Cafe Coco is more informal, while Daintree's overlooks the pool. There are several bars. Room rates are around A\$200 a night. (Book with the hotel at 17 Abbott Street, Cairns 4870 or Fax: 6170-311801.)

The **Pacific International Cairns** (Tel: 51-7888), 180 rooms, is the oldest and smallest of the modern international-style hotels. It should have been overshadowed by its more recent competition, but it says much for the hotel that it is not. Many regulars to the city still stay here, and its reputation is intact. It is close to the waterfront, the new casino, and the central city, so its future seems assured. The hotel has a pool, a spa, a business center, restaurants, bars, and noticeable friendly service. Room rates are around A\$190 a night. (Book at Spence Street and The Esplanade, Cairns 4870 or Fax: 6170-311445.)

The **Radisson Plaza Hotel** (Tel: 31-1411) is a low-rise property with a waterfront location, built over the Pier Marketplace shopping complex. The lobby contains some spectacular recreated rain forest which you will either love or hate. The rooms are large and well appointed, and many have great water views. Facilities include a pool, an open deck, several restaurants and bars, and there are the shops and marina to explore. I prefer low-rise buildings but admit that they have the problem of long corridors, and that certainly applies here. In summary, though, I like this hotel. Room rates are from A\$220. (Book at Pierpoint Road, Cairns 4870 or Fax: 6170-313226.)

The **Holiday Inn** (Tel: 31-3757), 235 rooms, is a very nice property with perhaps a little less class than the previous hotels. Some people may even feel more comfortable here. The rooms are standard up-market style, some are non-smoking, and some others have facilities for the disabled. Other features are a landscaped atrium, large sun deck, pool, spa, guest laundry, business center, restaurant, and two bars. Room rates are from A$180. (Book at Florence Street and The Esplanade, Cairns 4870 or Fax: 6170-314130.)

In many ways, the nearby **Tradewinds Hotel** (Tel: 52-2111), 250 rooms, is similar. Everything about this hotel will suit most people prepared to pay the A$180 a night price tag. It's just that there is nothing particularly outstanding on which to comment. Many rooms have water views, the large pool area is attractive, and the three restaurants and four bars draw guests in for nourishment and entertainment. (Book at 137 The Esplanade, Cairns 4870 or Fax: 6170-518649.)

The final two properties are different in that they provide self-contained apartments. **181 The Esplanade** (Tel: 52-6888) is a highrise condominium with 37 two-bedroom, two-bathroom units complete with full kitchen and laundry facilities. The complex has a pool, spa, sauna, barbecue, and covered parking. It is about 1.5 kilometers from the city center. The **Il Palazzo** (Tel: 1-800-813222) offers similar elegant one-bedroom units at a location close to the city center. The complex has a rooftop gazebo and pool, a brasserie, and room service. Room rates are A$175. (Book at 62 Abbott Street, Cairns 4870.)

MEDIUM-PRICE ACCOMMODATIONS

The **Matson Plaza Hotel** (Tel: 31-2211), 242 hotel rooms and 106 self-contained apartments, really covers both this category and the expensive category. This property has all the facilities of a major hotel, including two restaurants, two bars, three pools, a health and fitness center, and tennis courts, but in my mind it lacks something in style. A one-room apartment in the suite complex starts at A$130, a hotel room is A$170, a one-bedroom suite is A$190, and a two-bedroom apartment is A$275 with a minimum of three nights. (Book at The Esplanade and Kerwin Street, Cairns 4870 or Fax: 6170-312704.)

Tuna Towers (Tel: 51-4688) is a comfortable property with motel units, studio units, and suites with limited cooking facilities. You can relax in the cocktail bar, have a drink beside the pool, or dine in Sails Restaurant. Rates start at around A$105. (Book at 145 The Esplanade, Cairns 4870 or Fax: 6170-518129.)

The **Cairns Colonial Club Resort** (Tel: 53-5111), 264 motel units and 82 self-contained units, at 18 Cannon Street, Manunda, Cairns, is an amazing success story. The resort was built on some swampland in an unlikely part of suburban Cairns, but it was marketed brilliantly and has been a success from the start. Now, after several enlargements, it has developed its own environment and is very attractive. There are three pools, two restaurants, a poolside cafe, room service, a gym, a tennis court, in-room video rental, and live entertainment. Rates are from A$100.

Reef Gateway Apartments (Tel: 52-1411), has 24 airconditioned two-bedroom units with full kitchens and laundries, about one kilometer from the central city. Facilities include pool, spa, barbecue, and tour desk. The units are serviced weekly but may be booked nightly at A$100. (Book at 239 Lake Street, Cairns or Fax: 6170-516108.)

Aawon Holiday Units (Tel: 54-1722) has airconditioned one-bedroom ground-level units at Westcourt, about three kilometers from central Cairns. Major shopping centers are close by, but these units are more suitable for couples or families with transportation. Rates are from A$60. (Book at 288 McCoombe Street, Westcourt, Cairns or Fax: 6170-542734.)

There are quite a number of motels along the Bruce Highway and Sheridan Street that fall into this category. They adjust rates depending on occupancy, so you are likely to get the best deal outside the July-October and school holiday periods. Drive these areas and make your own choice.

BUDGET ACCOMMODATIONS

Everything below A$50 falls into this category in Cairns. The **Pacific Coast Budget Accommodation** (Tel: 51-1264) at 100 Sheridan Street, is a bed and breakfast place in a traditional Queenslander building about two minutes from the city center. It has a pool, restaurant, tour desk, laundry, and off-street parking. Airconditioned rooms are available for those who want them. Singles are from A$29 and doubles from A$39. **Uptop Downunder Holiday Lodge** (Tel: 51-3636) at 164 Spence Street, is about a 10-minute walk from the center of town. There is a real family atmosphere here, a large pool, and airconditioned rooms are available. Room-only rate is from A$25, and bed and breakfast from A$30.

Coles Villa & Caravan Park (Tel: 53-7133) at 28 Pease Street, is farther out again, but a city bus stops outside the complex. The park has four hectares of tropical gardens with fully self-contained villas and cabins, budget cabins, and a camping ground. Facilities include a swimming pool, games room, laundry, and mini-mart. **Treetops** (Tel: 55-1048) at 7 Tanner Street, Stratford, has a rain forest location on the edge of Cairns. The motel-style airconditioned units can sleep up to six people. Half of them have a kitchenette, and all have refrigerator, TV, fan, radio, in-suite bathroom, and telephone. Multi-share prices start at A$15 per night. Facilities include a swimming pool, restaurant, barbecue, laundry, and tour information desk.

Backpackers who wish to stay close to the action tend to head for the Esplanade. There are many places along here, including **YHA On the Esplanade** (Tel: 31-1919) at Number 93 from A$14 a night; **Bellview** (Tel:

31-4377) with dorms and budget motel rooms at Number 85; **International Hostel** (Tel: 31-1545) at Number 67; and **Rosie's** (Tel: 51-0235) at Number 155. Others prefer to be a bit removed from hundreds of other like-minded people and will prefer other parts of the city. You could try **Captain Cook Backpackers Hostel and Motel** (Tel: 51-6811) at 204 Sheridan Street, with a multi-share bed in a room with four costing from A$12, including an evening meal; **U2 Backpackers Hostel** (Tel: 31-4077) with pool, barbecue, kitchen, and laundry at 77 McLeod Street; or the small **Dreamtime Cairns** (Tel: 31-6753) with doubles, three- and four-share rooms, pool, spa, barbecue, and kitchen at 4 Terminus Street.

Marlin Coast

While in some ways this area is an extension of Cairns, it really is a genuine accommodations alternative. If you want beaches but are not much into nighttime raging, this is probably the region for you. Many visitors come here straight from Cairns airport and never see the city before they leave.

EXPENSIVE ACCOMMODATIONS

The **Allamanda** (Tel: 55-3000) at Palm Cove somehow manages to combine the comforts of home with the luxury of a resort. The site is absolute beachfront, and the two- and three-bedroom luxury self-contained suites have flair and style. There are lush gardens, three pools, a spa, a games room, a shop, a barbecue, in-house movies, and a tour desk. Rates are from around A$220 a night. (Book at 1 Veivers Road, Palm Cove 4879 or Fax: 6170-553090.)

Reef House (Tel: 59-1818) is also at Palm Cove. I well remember the original small resort which was the first luxury accommodations in the Cairns region about 30 years ago. Since then, the complex has grown and changed, but the philosophy remains. There are now 70 rooms and suites, three pools, a fine restaurant, a poolside cafe, and quiet charm. Rates are from around A$180. (Book at 99 Williams Esplanade, Palm Cove 4879 or Fax: 6170-591295.)

Kewarra Beach Resort (Tel: 57-6666) at Kewarra Beach, a few kilometers south of Palm Cove, is a place I have heard many guests go into raptures about. While it is very nice, it never quite has that effect on me, so I am not sure what I am missing. There are 60 lodges and bungalows, a restaurant, bars, a pool, tennis, croquet, and sailing at the absolute beachfront site. Room rates are around A$200 a night. (Book by Fax: 6170-577525.)

MEDIUM-PRICE ACCOMMODATIONS

The **Ramada Great Barrier Reef Resort** (Tel: 55-3999), 184 rooms, has an Esplanade site at Palm Cove. The hotel hides behind tall melaleuca trees and a huge free-form swimming pool. There are tennis courts, a playground, restaurants, and bars, and the beach is just across the road. Room rates are from A$140. (Book at Veivers Road, Palm Cove 4879 or Fax: 6170-553902.)

The **Novotel Palm Cove Resort** (Tel: 59-1234), 341 rooms and apartments, is the largest resort in the area. It has 10 swimming pools; a resort golf course; a sports center with tennis, squash, and training pool; and a dive shop, all set among 40 hectares of gardens. Unfortunately, it is not on the beach. There are two restaurants, three bars, a nightclub, and a gym. Room rates are from A$130.

There are many self-contained apartments close to the beach at several centers. **Marlin Waters** (Tel: 55-3933) at 131 Williams Esplanade, Palm Cove, has 21 airconditioned units at around A$90 a night, across from the beach. Facilities include a swimming pool, spa, barbecue, and tour desk. The **Reef Retreat** (Tel: 59-1744) at 10 Harpa Street, Palm Cove, has one- and two-bedroom apartments, suites, and villas from A$75 a night, a short distance from the beach. Facilities here include pool, spa, barbecue, laundry, and tour desk. **Coral Sands** (Tel: 57-8800) at Vasey Esplanade, Trinity Beach, has one-, two-, and three-bedroom modern, up-market, beachfront apartments, each with two bathrooms. There are two barbecue areas, a large pool, and a restaurant. Rates start at A$120. **Yorkeys Beach Bures** (Tel: 55-7755) are closer to Cairns at Sim's Esplanade, Yorkeys Knob. The open-style bures are self-contained, and the resort has a pool, barbecue, and lounge bar amid palms and native bushland. Rates are from A$70 a unit.

BUDGET ACCOMMODATIONS

The choice is very limited. **Palm Cove Retreat** (Tel: 55-3630) on the mountain side of the Cook Highway opposite the Palm Cove turnoff is one place to try. Dorm beds are from A$10 a night. The **Ellis Beach Resort** (Tel: 55-3538) is on the beach about five kilometers north of Palm Cove. There are cabins with in-suites, three holiday units, caravan sites, and camping sites with a pool and restaurant.

Port Douglas

Fifteen years ago, Port Douglas was a small holiday village with a few motels and vacation apartments. Now it is an international holiday center with some of the best accommodations in Far North Queensland.

EXPENSIVE ACCOMMODATIONS

The **Sheraton Mirage Resort** (Tel: 99-5888) is probably my favorite Queensland mainland property. No expense was spared to create this fully integrated complex with its luxury accommodations, huge swimmable saltwater lagoons, restaurants, bars, golf course, tennis, gym, country club, and retail shopping center. Everything is grand and classy, but I have never found a feeling of snobbishness, despite the high cost of everything. If you can afford it, you will love this place. Room rates are from around A$400. (Book at Davidson Street, Port Douglas 4871 or Fax: 6170-985885.)

Beaches (Tel: 99-4150) on the Esplanade within walking distance of the center of Port Douglas is a modern luxury apartment block. All apartments and suites are airconditioned and have master bedroom in-suite spa, gourmet kitchen, second bathroom, large balcony, and laundry. Facilities include a pool, a spa, barbecues, a coffee shop, and covered parking. Units for two start at A$225 in the holiday season and A$170 in the off season. (Book by Fax: 6170-995206.)

MEDIUM-PRICE ACCOMMODATIONS

The **Radisson Royal Palms Resort** (Tel: 99-5577), 315 rooms, is a large property without beach frontage. There is a large pool and plenty of activities including floodlit tennis courts, pitch 'n' putt golf, volleyball, aerobics, a gymnasium, nightly live entertainment, bicycle rides, movie and games nights, and a children's club. Room rates are from around A$150. (Book at Port Douglas Road, Port Douglas 4871 or Fax: 6170-995559.)

Reef Terraces Resort (Tel: 99-3333) is an attractive nearby property with two-story, airconditioned, two-bedroom self-contained townhouses. If you don't want to cook, there is a bistro and bar. Facilities are a pool and two spas. Rates are from A$135. (Book at Port Douglas Road, Port Douglas 4871 or Fax: 6170-993385.)

Port Douglas Terrace (Tel: 99-5397) on the Esplanade within walking distance of the center of Port Douglas is a popular apartment block with a range of one- and two-bedroom units. All are airconditioned and well equipped. Features of the complex are a pool, tennis court, barbecue, and tour desk. In the tourist season, garden apartments for two people start at A$120 a night. (Book by Fax: 6170-995206.) Similar but somewhat more expensive units are found at **The White House** (Tel: 99-5600) nearby at 19 Garrick Street (Fax: 6170-995006), and slightly cheaper units farther from the beach are at **The Mango Tree** (Tel: 99-5677) at 91 Davidson Street.

BUDGET ACCOMMODATIONS

Coconut Grove Motel (Tel: 99-5124) at 58 Macrossan Street in the heart of Port Douglas has some fanned units that just squeeze into this category. The units are quite acceptable, and other facilities include two pools and a restaurant. Rates start at A$50. The **Port O'Call Lodge** (Tel: 99-5422) on Port Street has motel rooms, and dorm-style rooms with in-suites. There are pool and restaurant facilities in this quiet setting. Rates are from A$50 for units and A$15 for a dorm bed. The **Pandanus Van Park** (Tel: 99-5944) on Davidson Street has cabins from A$45 a night for two. Two pools, barbecues, a store, bike rental, and tour desk are available.

5. Dining and Restaurants

Cairns and Port Douglas restaurants are discussed here. See Section 6 of this chapter for dining options in other mainland areas, and Section 8 for island information.

Cairns

The major hotels offer excellent dining choices. The **Red Emperor,** a speciality Cantonese restaurant at The Reef Hotel Casino, has great food at reasonable prices. **The Conservatory** at the same hotel offers a fixed-price meal and exciting reverie while diners sit at candlelit tables set among trees, pools, waterfalls, and shimmering lights, all under a huge glass dome with the stars above. The **Captains Table** at the Radisson Plaza Hotel, and **Kingsfords** at the Cairns International, are two elegant restaurants serving international cuisine. The **Waterfront Restaurant** at the Pacific International specializes in hot stone steak and excellent seafood.

Outside the hotels, the correct choice depends on the cuisine you fancy. Seafood is very big in Cairns. **Barnacle Bill's Seafood Inn** (Tel: 51-2241) at 65 The Esplanade, and **Tawny's** (Tel: 51-1722) at the Marlin Wharf are two long-time favorites that are very popular. **Cafe Seafood** (Tel: 51-1122) at 252 Sheridan Street tries to maintain restaurant quality while offering cafe prices. At all these places you will find that the barramundi (a prized local fish), the prawns, and the mudcrabs (particularly in the warmer months) are all excellent.

The **Red Ochre Grill** (Tel: 51-0100) at 43 Shields Street has some great creative, native cuisine using traditional Aboriginal foods, including kangaroo, emu, quandong, yabbies, and lilli pilli. There is a formal dining area, a casual cafe, and alfresco-style dining. **Dundee's** (Tel: 51-0399) at Aplin and Sheridan Streets is another place with exotic Australian cuisine, and there is a nice informal atmosphere.

There are probably more Japanese restaurants in Cairns than anywhere else in Queensland. Most cater to the Japanese tour groups that visit here, and some are excellent. Perhaps the better ones are the relaxed **Kamome** (Tel: 51-4318) at 45 Grafton Street where there is a range of grills and provincial cooking and a nice sushi bar; **Cherry Blossom** (Tel: 52-1050) at Spence and Lake Streets featuring a sushi bar, teppanyaki bar, and a la carte menu; and the up-market **Yamagen** (Tel: 31-6688) next to the Cairns International Hotel at 40 Abbott Street.

Other ethnic cuisines are also readily available. There are many Chinese options with **Harbourview** (Tel: 31-1346) in the Pier Marketplace being more traditional, and **Taste of China** (Tel: 31-3668) at 36 Abbott Street featuring contemporary Chinese cuisine. **George's Greek Taverna** (Tel: 41-1500) at Aplin and Grafton Streets is the place to go for innovative Greek and seafood cuisine. **Pa'd'Oro** (Tel: 51-2198) at 51 Grafton Street has a cafe that is open seven days all day and a restaurant that is open for dinner, both with Italian specialities. **Damari's** (Tel: 31-2155) at 171 Lake Street is another Italian eatery with affordable dining and friendly hospitality. The **Taj** (Tel: 51-2228) at Spence and Sheridan Streets is the oldest and perhaps the most authentic Indian restaurant in the region.

Among my other favorites are the **Memphis Rock Cafe** (Tel: 51-3063), a themed restaurant of the 1960s with a heap of rock 'n' roll memorabilia at the Pier Marketplace; **Kipling's** (Tel: 31-1886), a classy coffee shop and restaurant in Orchid Plaza, 79 Abbott Street, with some brilliantly presented dishes; and **Hog's Breath Cafe** (Tel: 31-7711), at 64 Spence Street, for the best steak in town.

A few other suggestions are the evening dinner cruise on the *Tropic Sunbird* departing Trinity Wharf at 7 P.M. Thursday to Sunday; the **Kunjal Cabaret Restaurant** (Tel: 31-2755), which serves dinner then offers two shows featuring Aboriginal dance, didgeridoo, song, and comedy at 33 Spence Street; and the dinner show under the stars at **Battsy's** (Tel: 015-159631) in the Tradewinds Esplanade hotel, where there is dinner followed by the Gulbari Wata Aboriginal dancers every Tuesday, Thursday, and Saturday evenings.

Port Douglas

There is much debate about which is the best restaurant in Port Douglas, and I have decided not to nominate one. It really depends on what you are looking for. I have never been disappointed with a meal at **Sassi's Island Point** (Tel: 99-5323). The seafood and the European cuisine are excellent, while the location and atmosphere are outstanding. Almost all restaurant critics rave about **Nautilus** (Tel: 99-5330). I had my first meal here 27 years ago, and I have been back many times because of its lovely location, innovative food, and the whole dining experience. A few years ago, however, I had one of the worst and most grossly overpriced meals I have had anywhere here, so I am wary about recommending it. **Danny's** (Tel: 99-5535), a seafood place on the waterfront, has been around for quite some time and continues to please.

Someone did a count of Port Douglas restaurants and decided that there were more than 40. I haven't eaten at anything like this number, but of those that I have sampled, I can recommend **Macrossans**, a silver service restaurant at the Sheraton Mirage for a great dining experience; **Palms** at the Radisson with its nightly buffets; **Taste of Thailand** (Tel: 99-4384) in Pandanus Plaza, Macrossan Street, for affordable authentic Thai cuisine; the casual and often noisy **Tide Tavern Steakhouse** (Tel: 99-4199) at the Marina Mirage; and the fun-style **Mango Jam Cafe** (Tel: 99-4611) at 24 Macrossan Street, where there are wood-fired pizzas, exotic cocktails, and late-night music.

6. Sightseeing

The Northern Reef region stretches along the coast from Mission Beach to Cape York, a distance of some 1,000 kilometers. Much of the area is wilderness, Aboriginal reserve, or national park. Of all this vast area it is only an area 150 kilometers north and south of Cairns that most people visit. I have arranged this sightseeing section by starting in Cairns, then traveling south to near Mission Beach, then going north up the coast. The islands are covered separately in Section 8 of this chapter.

CAIRNS

City Place is a good introduction to Cairns. Two streets have been truncated, and the resulting area has been turned into a pedestrian area. There are always people here, waiting for buses, shopping, sightseeing, or just wandering around. It is a good place to see what is happening. I like Cairns, but I must admit that there is not much to do in the central city. If you are not into shopping, other options are limited. In fact, many visitors are disappointed with the city, but this doesn't necessarily spoil their vacation experience because the surrounding area has plenty to offer.

The waterfront area has some interest. The **Esplanade** at the end of Shields Street has lawn, palm trees, seats, and a walking path. When the tide is out you may see a range of birdlife on the extensive mudflats. The **Pier Marketplace** is worth visiting. There are many shops and restaurants, and some interesting weekend markets. Along the waterfront, you see some of the game fishing boats, private craft, and commercial vessels that are a big part of Cairns. Reef and island cruise boats leave from areas just south of here. The **casino,** which opened in 1996, has brought a new focus to this area.

Edge Hill, a suburb a few kilometers north, is home to several places of interest. The **Flecker Park Botanic Gardens** has giant trees and tropical plant life which can be seen from meandering paths. There is a path that leads to **Centenary Lakes** where there are barbecue and picnic facilities, and another that treks through jungle-clad hills behind the gardens. Out off the airport road, there are boardwalks that go through several different types of

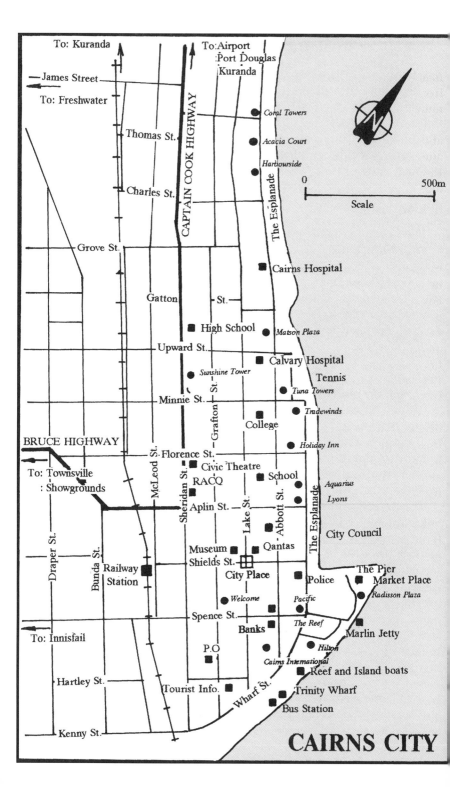

CAIRNS CITY

mangrove forest. The **Royal Flying Doctor Base** (Tel: 53-5687) is not far from the gardens. You can see a video and a demonstration of early communications, then wander through the museum.

Farther afield, **Crystal Cascades** is a popular swimming and picnic area about 22 kilometers from the city via **Redlynch.** The cascades are reached after a two-kilometer walk along Crystal Creek. **Lake Placid,** on the Barron River, is another place for swimming, and there is also kayaking, fish feeding, and a kiosk. I recommend the short spectacular drive from here along the Barron River to the hydro-power station where free tours are conducted each afternoon.

GO SOUTH

The Bruce Highway takes you through the uninteresting southern suburbs, before opening onto sugar fields. The **Pyramid** at **Gordenvale** is a big landmark. The small sugar town, which has gained almost a dormitory suburb status, is off to the left. A highway leads to the right, through hundreds of turns, to the Atherton Tablelands. There are good swimming, fishing, and picnicking spots on the way. The ranges crowd in on the west, while fields of green sugar cane stretch to the east. The **Bellenden Ker National Park** is rugged, and parts are unexplored, but there are some walking tracks. **Eubenangee Wetlands** is a center for birdwatchers.

Babinda has a sugar mill beside the highway, and there is a thriving Aboriginal craft co-operative in town. The **Boulders** is a delightful stretch of river a few kilometers from town. **Bramston Beach** has self-contained and motel-style units with a restaurant, bars, a pool, a tennis court, and par-3 golf at the **Plantation Village Resort** (Tel: 67-4133) on an old coconut plantation. You will find there are many delightful parks, waterfalls, and walking trails among the World Heritage-listed wet tropics in this whole region.

Innisfail is a prosperous town on the Johnstone River, supporting the surrounding sugar region. The influence of early settlers from Italy, other parts of Europe, and China show in its buildings, culture, and lifestyle. There is a well-maintained joss house here, and the early Chinese settlers introduced new fruits, which are the basis for today's export orchards. Nearby **Etty Bay,** is a classic tropical beach fringed by rain forest. Another highway leads inland to the Atherton Tableland from Innisfail, and about 15 kilometers along this road you can visit **Nerada Tea**—Australia's major tea plantation. Innisfail has hotel and motel accommodations, some interesting restaurants, a little nightlife, and a multicultural feel that is quite stimulating.

South Johnstone is a delightful small town, 11 kilometers southwest, with an "old-world" atmosphere which is quite unique. It is worth some time here just taking it in. The **sugar mill** has tours during the June-November crushing season. About 8 kilometers farther south at **Mena Creek,** you can visit the ruins of a Spanish castle set in tropical gardens and rain forest. Back on the coast, **Kurrimine Beach** has an offshore reef, and some accommodations.

GO WEST OF CAIRNS

Some of the most attractive areas of Far North Queensland are away from the coast, and while this book does not generally cover inland areas, in this region the interior can't be ignored. The first attraction is the village of **Kuranda,** set amid rain forest high on the edge of the Atherton Tableland. This has enticed visitors since its rail link with Cairns opened over a century ago.

The train still winds daily up the mountains over bridged ravines, through tunnels, and past the Barron Gorge waterfalls, to Australia's most photogenic railway station. My suggestion is to travel one-way by train and the other way on the new **Skyrail** (Tel: 31-2977), a 7.5-kilometer cableway above World Heritage rain forest. You travel in six-person gondolas, make two descents to see the forest floor, and learn about the amazing diversity of plants and animals in a wet tropics rain forest.

Within the village, everything is within walking distance. Visit the terraced stalls at the **arts and crafts markets** (Tel: 93-8772) on Wednesday, Thursday, Friday, and Sunday; watch the outstanding professional **Tjapukai Dance Theater** (Tel: 93-7544) perform twice daily in their own airconditioned theater; wander through rain forest and 2,000 butterflies at the **Australian Butterfly Sanctuary** (Tel: 93-7575); come face to face with some of the animals of the rain forest at the **Kuranda Wildlife Noctarium** (Tel: 93-7334); and explore the main pedestrian strip between the railway station and the markets to mix with a host of "arty" people who choose to live in the rain forest. Take lunch at such places as **Frogs Restaurant** (Tel: 93-7405) or **Kuranda Trading Post** (Tel: 93-7166), and buy some local crafts and produce. If you plan to stay, **Kuranda Rainforest Resort** (Tel: 93-7555) has 30 two-bedroom pole cabins and 40 standard units, a restaurant, bar, tennis court, gymnasium, laundry, pool, spa, and tour desk.

The actual **Atherton Tablelands** is another 60 kilometers southwest. This attractive plateau is 600 to 1,000 meters above sea level, so temperatures are cooler, and everything thrives on the rich red volcanic soil. Primitive ferns and giant kauri trees grow much as they did millions of years ago. A huge strangler fig has aerial roots hanging 15 meters to the ground. There are national parks, volcanic crater lakes, mountains, and waterfalls. Swim at **Lake Eachum** and **Lake Barrine**; bushwalk at **Euramo, Mt. Hypipamee,** and **Wongabel State Forest**; birdwatch at **Broomfield Swamp**; swim, canoe, ski, sail, or drive around **Lake Tinaroo**; go ballooning at dawn; or pick your own strawberries.

Cattle and deer graze on the green pastures and rolling hills, and farms grow tea, coffee, nuts, corn, vegetables, and flowers for local and export markets. The towns have classic old hotel, motel, guest house, bed and breakfast, and caravan park accommodations, and there are restaurants, weekend markets, galleries, historic buildings, and arts and craft shops. Each town has its special attractions: **Mareeba**'s annual rodeo; **Tolga**'s homestead park and woodcraft gallery; **Atherton**'s Crystal Caves, art gallery, Chinese joss house, and steam train; **Yungaburra**'s village square, heritage walk, and clock museum; **Millaa Millaa**'s waterfall circuit; **Malanda**'s natural history museum; **Herberton**'s historic village; **Ravenshoe**'s train, timber crafts, and waterfalls.

GO NORTH

The **Captain Cook Highway** goes north from Cairns along the coast to Mossman. You pass the right hand turnoffs to a string of beaches—Machan's, Holloway's, Yorkey's Knob, Trinity, Clifton, and Palm Cove. To the left, there is the lower terminal of the **Skyrail Rainforest Cableway**; the fascinating **Tjapukai Aboriginal Cultural Park** with its famous dance troupe; **Paradise Palms Golf Course** (Tel: 59-1166), which is one of the best public courses in the country; **A. J. Hackett Bungy Jumping** (Tel: 31-1119), where you launch yourself into freefall from a high tower with a length of rubber tied to your ankles; and **Wild World** (Tel: 55-3669), where there are native animals and an Aboriginal cultural show.

Palm Cove is the pick of these northern beaches. The white sand is fringed with giant paperbark trees, there is a stinger-resistant enclosure, accommodations options are large, shopping and restaurant facilities are good, and there is a jetty for fishing and for boat trips to the reef. **Ellis Beach** is the first place where the road actually travels on the coast, but from here on it is quite spectacular. **Hartley's Creek Crocodile Farm** (Tel: 55-3576) is 12 kilometers farther north, and just beyond is the wonderful view from **Rex Lookout.** Some magnificent coastal scenery follows until you pass **Oak Beach.** The turnoff to Port Douglas is well marked, then you just follow the palm trees.

Port Douglas was once a sleepy, secret paradise for a handful of lucky permanent residents. Now it has changed. The world has discovered the beauty of Port Douglas, and with the discovery has come luxury resorts, up-market shops, tourist attractions...and people. The port has changed, but the outstanding beauty remains. Now you just have to share it! **Four Mile Beach** is picture perfect—white hard sand and clear water, backed by tropical vegetation, and used by few people. **Marina Mirage** has cruise boats, charter vessels, shoppers, sightseers, restaurants, shops, and entertainment. Adventurer Ben Cropp will show you relics from the *Pandora* and Cook's

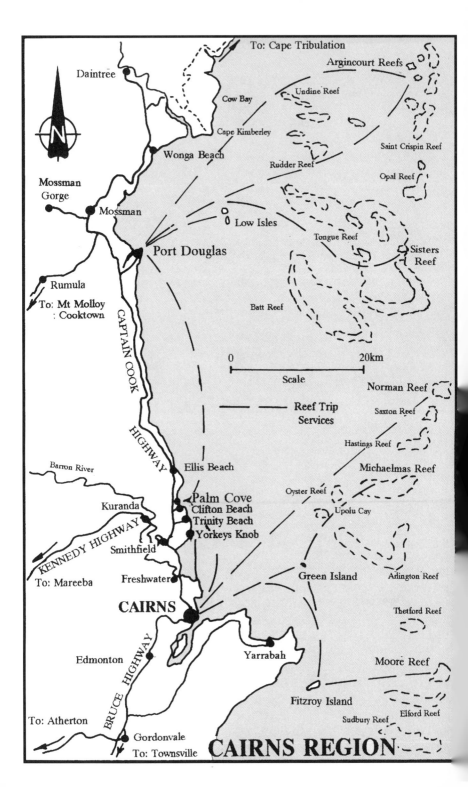

Endeavour at the **shipwreck museum,** while continuous films show Ben's adventures over the years. The huge **Sheraton Mirage Resort** will be an eye-opener to most. Non-guests are welcome in the lobby, shops, and restaurants, but are restricted from the pool and accommodations areas. At **Rainforest Habitat** (Tel: 99-3235) you will find birds, butterflies, kangaroos, koalas, and crocodiles in surroundings close to those found in nature. Inside, the free-moving rain forest wildlife has adapted to the naturally evolving habitat.

Mossman is 20 kilometers north of Port Douglas. The sugar mill dominates the town, and a tram track goes through the main street. You can ride the "Bally Hooley" steam train through the cane fields to Port Douglas during the crushing season. To the west of town, **Mossman Gorge** is a beautiful area of rain forest, rock pools, rapids, and peace. There are walking trails to various points, and natural flora and fauna of the rain forest. This is also the site of one of Queensland's most exclusive wilderness lodges—**Silky Oaks Lodge** (Tel: 98-1666). There are luxury airconditioned treehouse chalets, a gourmet restaurant, bar and lounge, pool, tennis court, guided rain forest walks, kayaking, mountain bikes, and courtesy bus to Mossman and Port Douglas. Rates are around A$350 a night.

Eighteen hundred and twenty kilometers of paved road from Brisbane ends at **Daintree,** an old timbercutters' town. Today Daintree is more into welcoming tourists and providing them with tours, food, provisions, and a glimpse at a way of life that is fast disappearing. Some few kilometers downriver, the **Daintree Ferry** provides access to the popular **Cape Tribulation** region. The ferry operates from around 6 A.M. until midnight each day, whenever there are vehicles wanting to cross. Several sightseeing tours on the Daintree River operate from this point, and there is a store for provisions and information. Try **Daintree Rainforest River Trains** (Tel: 90-7676).

North of the ferry, you travel on a gravel road through lowland and tropical rain forest. The road is passable to conventional vehicles except after heavy rain, but many rental companies will not let you use their vehicles here. There are some excellent coastal views, and several tourist attractions adjacent to the road. You can take side roads to **Cape Kimberley,** and **Cow Bay,** and stop at the botanical boardwalk and at some of the resorts hidden away in the rain forest. The beaches here are not the best in the world, but the combination of clean water, good sand, rain-forested hills coming right to the shore, and few people, make this a remarkable area. Fortunately, both the forests and the water are protected by World Heritage listings.

The area has a growing list of accommodations options. **Coconut Beach Rainforest Resort** (Tel: 1-800-816525) at Cape Tribulation, has up-market accommodations, two restaurants and bars, two swimming pools, a shop, and its own beach. Rates are around A$180 for bed and breakfast. The nearby **Ferntree Rainforest Resort** (Tel: 98-0000), and the **Daintree Wilderness Lodge** (Tel: 98-9105) at Alexandra Bay, are similar style properties. All make good use of their rain forest locations. Somewhat down-market from here is **Club Daintree** (Tel: 90-7500) with 10 cabins and a camping area at Cape Kimberley Beach; **PK's Jungle Village** (Tel: 98-0040) at Myall Beach, with single, double, share rooms, camping facilities, restaurant, and bar; and the YHA-operated **Crocodylus Village** (Tel: 98-9166) at Cow Bay, where dormitory beds are A$15 a night and in-suite huts are A$45 a double.

Experienced four-wheel drivers may wish to take the track north from here to the **Bloomfield River** then on to Cooktown; however, this is not recommended for anyone during the wet season. Conventional vehicles have to use the inland route to Cooktown. This involves returning to Mossman then taking the paved road to **Mt. Molley** and on to **Mt. Carbine.** This is now dry country, with ant hills and eucalyptus replacing the lush coastal rain forest. The country north of here becomes more lonely, and the blacktop is replaced by gravel after 80 kilometers. It's about 90 kilometers from here to where the coastal road from Cape Tribulation rejoins this road. Cooktown is 30 kilometers ahead.

Captain Cook and his naturalist Joseph Banks had plenty of time to look around this area as they waited for their boat to be repaired after it struck the Great Barrier Reef around 225 years ago. That is still the pace of Cooktown today. It is a place to visit for atmosphere not frantic sightseeing. There are some things to see, but just walking the main street and sitting in a local pub are the best ways to appreciate that this is a frontier town, different from just about anywhere else in Far North Queensland. The Shire of Cooktown covers an area almost the size of England, but it contains a mere 5,000 people. The whole shire has less than 100 kilometers of paved road yet the streets of Cooktown are wide enough for a population of half a million. This is country where "big" is normal.

Cooktown is big on history. Two hundred and twenty-five years of it is encapsulated in the **James Cook Historical Museum.** There is a cannon and the original anchor from Cook's ship the *Endeavour,* a reconstruction of a Chinese joss house from the days when Cooktown was the second largest town in Queensland, and much more. You can walk to **Grassy Hill** where Cook charted his passage north through the reefs of the Coral Sea. The botanical gardens which were established in 1880 have been recently restored. The cemetery chronicles the last 125 years of settlement, and features a Chinese shrine which was constructed because of the tens of thousands of Chinese who were in the area during the 1870s gold rush.

The main street of Cooktown is where most of everything else happens. At one end of Charlotte Street there is the wharf where fishing boats, pleasure craft, and the occasional passenger cruise ship mix. Back towards town

is the **Cook Memorial,** the **waterfront park,** and the **Cook Shire office.**
There are several hotels, the historic Westpac Bank building, shops, and several restaurants in the center of town. The **Sovereign Hotel** (Tel: 69-5400) is the up-market place to stay. The old building has been graciously renovated, extended, and improved. There are motel units, resort-style units, self-contained suites, a pool, a restaurant, and a bar. Rates start at around A$65.
Cooktown Alamanda Inn (Tel: 69-5203) is a cheaper property (around A$45 a night) with motel units, barbecue, laundry, and some meals available.
Cooktown Backpackers (Tel: 69-5166) has beds from A$15.

CAPE YORK

It has become a popular challenge to some Australians to drive from Cairns to the tip of Cape York. I discourage international visitors from doing this, however, because this is pioneering country and unless you fully understand the weather, road, and living conditions, it is potentially dangerous. If you want to see this fascinating area, take one of the organized tours.

From Cairns, the road to Lakeland through Mareeba and Mount Molloy is of reasonable standard. At **Lakeland,** you leave the Cooktown road and head northwest. It is 800 kilometers of four-wheel-drive track from here to Cape York. The road can be fair in the May to November period, but is often impassable during the rest of the year. This is very isolated country, and you need to be self-sufficient to enjoy the experience. There are few road signs, fuel is unobtainable for a length of 400 kilometers on the main track, no medical facilities exist, and there are few comforts. The good news is that despite these difficulties, it is becoming easier to travel to Australia's most northerly point.

Laura is the first settlement north of Lakefield. There is a hotel, store, airstrip, school, public toilet block, and a few houses. It's a forgettable place, but the **Lakefield National Park** to the north, and the **Quinkan Reserve** to the south are outstanding. The Quinkan Reserve houses several excellent Aboriginal rock painting sites. The paintings may cover a period of 13,000 years, and at one or two sites they are well displayed and explained. Lakefield National Park is a large area of mainly wetlands, which is home to crocodiles, birds, and animals. There is some opportunity for bushwalking, fishing, birdwatching, and photography. A camping permit can be obtained from any of the three ranger stations within the park.

Musgrave Telegraph Station and Roadhouse is an historic fortified building that opened in 1886 and was one of many telegraph stations on the cape providing a communications link. It now serves as a roadhouse providing fuel, meals, telephones, camping, and limited accommodations. From here, it is 110 kilometers to the small township of **Coen.** The discovery of gold in the 1870s brought a flood of prospectors, but the boom was short lived

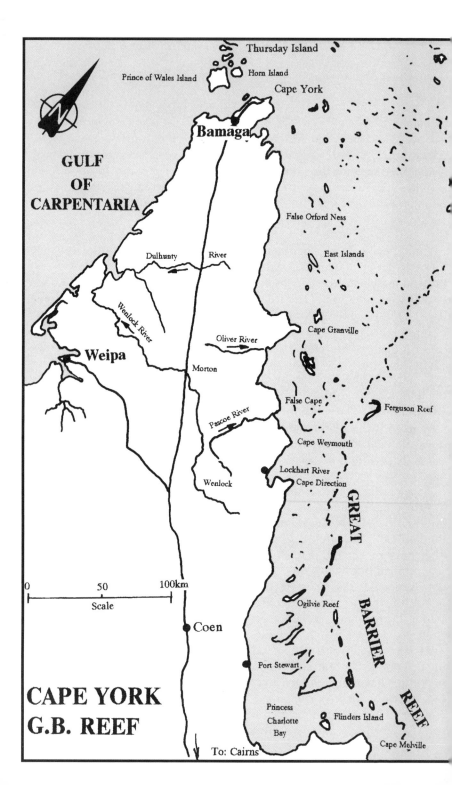

and today the town serves as a center for surrounding cattle ranches. There are two stores, a hotel, a post office, a police station, a vehicle repair shop, a campground, and some accommodations. This is the last place for food supplies for 450 kilometers.

The next point of interest is the **Archer River.** Twenty kilometers north of here, a track to the right leads to **Lockhart River Aboriginal Reserve, Iron Range National Park, Chili Beach,** and **Portland Roads.** There is some spectacular country in this area, and there are two campgrounds. Another 25 kilometers farther along the main track, a track to the left goes 140 kilometers to the bauxite mining town of **Weipa.** This is a full-fledged town with shopping center, bank, hotel, swimming pool, cinema, and sporting facilities. Visitors are welcome at the golf club and the lawn bowling club. The **Albatross Hotel Motel** (Tel: 69-7314) has 51 self-contained units, motel units, and bungalow units, and a restaurant, a bistro, and bars.

The **Wenlock River** is the first major river crossing that has to be negotiated. On the north bank, **Morton Station** has a telephone and a campground. From here it is 215 kilometers to the **Jardine River ferry.** You are now on **Injinoo Aboriginal land,** and you need a permit to enter and to camp. The community has constructed a road house on the south bank of the river, and the adjacent ferry operates seven days a week. The Injinoo community has some stores, and fuelling, banking, food, and mechanical repair facilities.

Bamaga is the largest community on the northern cape. This, and nearby **Seisia,** were established in the late 1940s when people were moved from Saibai Island in the Torres Strait. Bamaga has a shopping center with a supermarket, bank, post office, bakery, and facilities for ice, cooking gas, fuel, and mechanical repairs. Seisia has an excellent foreshore camping area, a kiosk, and a vehicle service center. The **Seisia Island Dancers** regularly perform traditional island dancing during the tourist season from June to October. The area has some of the most pristine fishing grounds you could imagine, and there are some organized trips. You will also find small settlements with some visitor facilities at **New Mapoon** and **Umagico.** The surrounding area has a number of World War II relics.

It's 30 kilometers from Bamaga to the **"Top."** The road leads to the **Pajinka Wilderness Lodge** (Tel: 69-1444), which is owned and operated by the Injinka Aboriginal community. The accommodations and facilities are of a high standard, and it is a very attractive place. Rates are from around A$230 a night. There is an adjacent campground with a kiosk that stocks food, drinks, alcohol, and souvenirs. It is a short walk through the rain forest and across rocks to the most northerly point of mainland Australia.

In this same area, you can visit **Punsand Bay Private Reserve** where there is a small safari-style permanent camp with excellent fishing, a kiosk, and a ferry service to Thursday Island. Another attraction is the site of **Somerset,** a government residency built in 1863. It was hoped that a town could be created that would eventually rival Singapore in importance. Captain John Jardine took up his position as Government Resident Captain in 1864, but the plan was a failure and both Jardine and his wife died and were buried here. There is not much left of the old settlement, but a few relics remain. The graves are about 100 meters away from the main site.

7. Guided Tours

There are more water tours, and perhaps more land-based tour operators, in Cairns than anywhere else in Queensland. If you want it, Cairns can almost guarantee that you can get it. Here is a selection of the land tours that are available. Most have pick-up services from Cairns, the Marlin Coast, and Port Douglas. Tours to the reef and the islands are covered in the next section of this chapter.

The **Cairns Explorer** (Tel: 55-1240) is a good way to see some of the attractions in and around Cairns city. You buy a day-use ticket and can get on and off the bus at any of the nine stops on its circular route. The route takes in some of the major suburban shopping centers, Freshwater, the mangrove boardwalk, the botanic gardens, and the Royal Flying Doctor base. It departs hourly from the Transit Mall, Lake Street. The **Terri-Too** (Tel: 31-4007) offers calm-water half-day tours of Cairns Inlet and the Everglades.

The highly regarded **Kuranda Rail trip** can be done as a round-trip rail tour, it can be combined with the Skyrail, or it may be included in a one-day bus trip to the Atherton Tablelands. Several operators offer alternatives. Try **Down Under Tours** (Tel: 008-079119) or **Tropic Wings** (Tel: 35-3555).

These two operators, and several others, offer one-day trips to Port Douglas, Daintree River, Cape Tribulation, and Atherton Tablelands. **Wait-a-While Rainforest Wildlife Tours** (Tel: 33-1153) has daily day/night wildlife tours in small groups. **Suncoast Safaris** (Tel: 55-2999) has morning and afternoon/night four-wheel-drive adventure tours on the Atherton Tablelands, and a one-day four-wheel-drive tour to Cape Tribulation. **Wet Tropics Safaris** (Tel: 32-2860) gives an in-depth rain forest experience on its daily trip to Cape Tribulation. **Queensland Adventure Safaris** (Tel: 50-0678) has a two-day four-wheel-drive trip to Palmer River, Cooktown, Cape Tribulation, and Daintree River.

A host of small operators run four-wheel-drive tours from Cairns to Cape York. **Billy Tea Bush Safaris** (Tel: 32-0077) has a five-day tour to Cooktown, Laura, and Lakefield National Park and return, and a 14-day return safari to

Cape York visiting Cooktown, Weipa, Lakefield, and rock art sites. **OZ Tours** (Tel: 1-800-079006) has Cairns-Cape York-Thursday Island combined land and sea safaris, and land and air safaris for those with less time. Something similar is offered by **Wild Track** (Tel: 55-2247).

Other interesting possibilities include **Pure Pleasure Tours** (Tel: 1-800-079797) with two-day, three-day, and five-day packages to the Atherton Tablelands, Charters Towers, and Townsville; a flying day tour in an old DC3 aircraft to Cooktown via the tropical rain forests and returning via the reef with **DC3 Australia** (Tel: 35-9900); and the chance to visit some of the world's most remote cattle properties with **Cape York Air Services** (Tel: 35-9399) on one of its scheduled aerial mail runs.

Rafting is another form of "touring" from Cairns. The **Raft'N'Rainforest Company** (Tel: 1-800-079039) has half-day trips on the Barron River, full-day tours to the Tully River, a half-day river drift on the Mulgrave River for a calm-water rafting experience, and two- and five-day whitewater heli-rafting camping adventures on the North Johnstone River for those wanting a real adventure. **Raging Thunder** (Tel: 31-1466) also has a variety of options.

Champagne Balloon Flights (Tel: 67-7444) offers tours from Cairns which include a 30- or 60-minute balloon flight over the Atherton Tablelands. **Jayrow Helicopters** (Tel: 31-4214) has flights to the reef and other locations in Far North Queensland. **Cairns Helitours** (Tel: 35-9243) has Cairns city and Kuranda tours. **Aussie Airways** (Tel: 53-3980) has one-day air tours to Lizard Island, and to Cooktown, and two- or three-day air safaris to Cape York and Thursday Island.

8. The Reef and Islands

The Northern Reef offers excellent viewing possibilities. Here are some of the options.

Day Trips

This is the way most visitors experience the reef. While these trips are very popular, some people return disappointed because of rough seas, rain or dull conditions, or cloudy skies. The answer to this is simple: you need to pick the right day, take precautions against seasickness and sunburn, and appreciate that this is untamed nature which cannot be totally controlled. You will then probably have the time of your life. Several operators have tours from Cairns and Port Douglas.

Great Adventures (Tel: 51-0455) has several options available each day from Cairns. The lowest-priced tour is a full-day trip to Fitzroy, including fast catamaran transfers, lunch, guided island tour, and the use of snorkeling equipment. A similar tour operates to Green Island, and this also includes a glass-bottom boat ride and a visit to the underwater observatory. You can combine the two islands for just a little extra cost. There are also trips that combine Fitzroy Island with the Great Barrier Reef at Moore Reef, and Green Island with Norman Reef. There is a daily direct trip to Norman Reef, but I feel the stop at Green Island is better.

Quicksilver Connections (Tel: 99-5500) is the major operator from Port Douglas, and it also has bus and catamaran connections from Cairns and Palm Cove. Some people believe this is the best operation on the reef. The 30-meter sailing catamaran *Wavedancer* makes a daily tour from Port Douglas to Low Isles. You receive morning and afternoon tea, a smorgasbord lunch, glass-bottom boat coral viewing, guided snorkeling tour, guided beach walk, and a reef presentation from a marine biologist. There is a daily trip to Argincourt Reef with underwater observatory coral viewing, a semi-submersible ride, and the extra-cost option of a helicopter flight or scuba dive.

Other operators at Cairns include **Sunlover Cruises** (Tel: 31-1055) who operate Fitzroy Island, Moore Reef and Fitzroy Island, and Arlington Reef trips; **Reef Jet Cruises** (Tel: 31-5559) who offer half-day and full-day trips to Green Island; **Compass Reef Trips** (Tel: 35-4354) who have low-priced reef trips to Hastings Reef and Michaelmas Reef; **Big Cat** (Tel: 51-0444) who runs a Green Island cruise tour; **Ocean Spirit Cruises** (Tel: 31-2920) who operate a large sailing catamaran to either Michaelmas Cay or Upolu Cay; **Coral Sea Line** (Tel: 31-3513) who have a heritage tall ship going each day to Upolu Cay; and **Don Cowie's Down Under** (Tel: 31-1588) who visits two different reef locations each day.

There are also tours to other places. **Frankland Islands Cruise and Dive** (Tel: 31-6300) has a day tour from Cairns to the Frankland Islands, a small island group south of Cairns. You travel by bus to Deeral Landing on the Mulgrave River, take a cruise with morning tea along the forest-lined river where you may see crocodiles and giant river herons, then enjoy the 35-minute sea crossing to the islands and reefs of the Franklands. Lunch is provided on one of the islands, there is a reef presentation and guided snorkeling tour, and the opportunity for diving. Normanby Island is a national park with guests restricted to 50 per day, so it has remained in a natural state.

Dunk Island Cruises (Tel: 68-7211) has a bus from Cairns to Mission Beach, then a Dunk and Bedarra Island cruise. **Quick Cat** (Tel: 68-7289) has a bus to Mission Beach then a cruise to Dunk Island and Beaver Cay. **Sail Away** (Tel: 99-5599) goes from Port Douglas to Low Isles and includes boomnetting, lunch, and glass-bottom boat coral viewing. **Taipan Lady** (Tel: 98-0040) operates from Cape Tribulation beach to either Mackay Cay or Undine Cay. **Aquaflight Airways** (Tel: 31-4307) has seaplane tours to Green Island, Hastings Reef, or Sudbury Cay.

Longer Cruises

Captain Cook Cruises (Tel: 31-4433) has three-night and four-night round-trip cruises from Cairns. The airconditioned mini-liner comes complete with cabins and staterooms, restaurant, lounge and piano bar, swimming pool, sauna, spa, sun deck, nightly entertainment, shop, library, glass-bottom boat, and snorkeling equipment. Tours go to Cooktown, Lizard Island, and Ribbon Reef, or Fitzroy, Dunk and Hinchinbrook Islands, and Hedley Reef.

Coral Princess (Tel: 31-1041) has weekly one-way cruises to Townsville. You visit the Outer Great Barrier Reef, overnight on board at Dunk Island Resort one night, cruise the Hinchinbrook Channel, and visit the Palm Group of islands en route to Townsville. The **Kangaroo Explorer** (Tel: 55-8188) offers tours from Cairns to Thursday Island. Some trips are four-day one way, others are seven-day round trip, while others are seven-day one way. **El-Torito** (Tel: 1-800-810634) has a six-day Torres Strait adventure from Thursday Island which takes you to Possession Island where Captain Cook proclaimed British sovereignty for the east coast of Australia, then on to Cape York, Albany Island, Warraber Island, and Naghir Island.

There are also a few shorter tours. **New Image Cruises** (Tel: 33-2664) offer a two-day sailing cruise to various reefs off Cairns. There is also a three-day sailing cruise to Moore and Sudbury Reefs and the Frankland and Fitzroy Islands.

Charter Vessels

A variety of boats are available for charter. **Ocean Spirit Cruises** (Tel: 31-2920) offers the *Ocean Gallant* for day, overnight, and weekly charter. There are three double cabins and crew quarters. **VIP Yacht Vacation International** (Tel: 31-4355) has luxury craft available for six to twelve guests. **Lizard Island Charters** (Tel: 98-5425) at Port Douglas has the luxury *Laura-J* available for charter for six to eight people at around A$4,200 a day.

THE ISLANDS

Although there are not as many developed islands in this region as in the Central Reef region, some are very popular with staying guests, campers, and day visitors. Here are the significant ones.

Frankland Islands

These are relatively untouched continental-type national park islands and reefs with high conservation and recreational values. Their position close to the mainland, safe anchorages, and camping facilities make this area a good location for nature-based recreational activities. The day-trip operator from Deeral Landing on the Mulgrave River is permitted to take a maximum of 50 guests to **Normanby** Island. This island has good sandy beaches and some fine snorkeling opportunities. A barbecue is provided for day visitors.

Campers with permits from the Department of Environment and Heritage in Cairns can be dropped off at **Russell Island,** but there are no facilities, so you must go fully equipped.

Fitzroy Island

This is one of the largest islands off the Far North Queensland coast and was named by Captain Cook in 1770. It is 26 kilometers from Cairns but only six kilometers off the coast. The continental-type island rises to 266 meters, has some coral beaches, and there is good snorkeling and diving close by. In the 1870s, the island was a quarantine station for Chinese immigrants heading for the gold fields, and later there was a beche-de-mer (a Chinese delicacy) industry here.

A resort was established on the northwest side of the island in the 1970s. The **Fitzroy Island Resort** (Tel: 51-9588) is now operated by the Great Adventures company, a major tourist operator in Cairns. There are villas (around A$250 a night with breakfast and dinner included), beach bungalows (around A$25 a bed or A$100 a room), and camp sites (around A$12 a site). The villas are reasonable two-bedroom units with bathroom. The bungalows are bunk rooms for four people with shared showers and toilets, and there is a kitchen and dining area for meals. The camp site has barbecues and cold showers. There is a mini-market for supplies, a kiosk for snacks and light meals, a lunchtime grill, a restaurant, and a bar.

This island does not have as many organized activities as many of the islands. There is a swimming pool which can also be used by day-trippers; catamarans, windsurfers, and canoes for rent; and some island walks. **Great Adventures** (Tel: 51-0455), and **Sunlover Cruises** (Tel: 31-1055) both have island transfers and packages available each day.

Green Island

This small island is a coral cay about 27 kilometers from Cairns. The island was named by Captain Cook and was made a national park in the 1930s. It has the longest history of tourism of any island on the Great Barrier Reef; tourism started in the 1890s. The island is small, and you can walk around it in about 15 minutes. There is dense rain forest in the interior, and there are good beaches and clear water on all sides. The major disappointment is with the coral: it has been badly damaged by visitors, the crown-of-thorns starfish, and pollution from the old resort.

Green Island is a hugely popular day-trip destination from Cairns, with over 200,000 people visiting each year. Some come for the day, others visit for a few hours as part of a reef trip. A few stay longer. The **Green Island**

Resort (Tel: 51-4644) was completely rebuilt in the early 1990s at a cost of around A$50 million for a maximum of 92 guests, and now it is one of the more up-market resorts on any of the islands. Rates are around A$700 a double, including meals and use of most equipment. The accommodation is stylish, but it has been restrained so that it fits into the setting extremely well. (Book at Green Island Resort, via Cairns, Queensland 4870 or Fax: 6170-521511). The service and facilities are of an equally high quality. There is a separate day-visitor area with a swimming pool, bar, shop, and several eateries. Snorkeling and diving gear is available for rent, and there are regular organized guided snorkeling tours.

The island also has two other attractions. Both are showing their age, but **Marineland Melanesia** (Tel: 51-4032) is probably worth visiting. This is a combination museum, aquarium, zoo, and art gallery. There are crocodiles, fish, turtles, coral, memorabilia from the days of sailing ships, and items of primitive oceanic art. The other feature is the **underwater observatory** at the end of the pier. If you have seen coral elsewhere, or have taken a glass-bottom boat or semi-submersible ride, I would give this a miss.

Michaelmas Cay

This barely qualifies as an island because it is presently nothing more than a small sandy cay with some low grassy vegetation. It is possible, however, that over time it will become something similar to Green Island. The cay is formed from coral sand that results from the breakdown of corals and shells. It is important as a breeding site for terns and noddies, and at the peak of the summer season more than 30,000 birds can be found here. Several day-trip operators from Cairns come here, and some land on the cay. Visitors are restricted to one area of beach and are not allowed on the vegetated area at all. The seabirds are extremely sensitive to disturbance, so visitors are requested to avoid sudden movements, and avoid touching any birds or eggs. There is some good snorkeling and diving on the adjacent reef.

Low Isles

This was named by Captain Cook, and it is a popular day-trip destination from Port Douglas. **Low Island** is a lovely coral cay similar to Green Island, while nearby **Woody Island** is many times larger but is covered with mangroves. Low Island has a well-kept lighthouse which dates from the 1870s. Several companies run day trips here, which include snorkeling, swimming, and exploring the island. These are justifiably popular.

Lizard Island

This is a large continental-type island about 240 kilometers north of Cairns. It is about 27 kilometers off the coast and about 18 kilometers from the outer edge of the Great Barrier Reef. The island is hot and dry, and the natural vegetation is grass and small scrub. The main attraction on the island is the beaches; probably the best on any Barrier Reef island. The water is clear, and there are some excellent reefs in the area, so diving and snorkeling are very popular. The island has a research station and an up-market resort.

It is known that Aboriginal tribes have visited the island over a prolonged period. The first recorded white visitors were Captain Cook and Dr. Joseph Banks in 1770. The region around here was to prove to be a major problem for Cook. After sailing more than halfway around the world, Cook managed to put his ship the *Endeavour* up on a coral reef some 150 kilometers south of Lizard Island. By jettisoning an anchor and some cannons, Cook got the ship off the reef, then he limped up the Endeavour River to the site of present-day Cooktown. After spending nearly two months here while he patched the boat, Cook headed north again. It became obvious to all on board that there was a major reef along the coast, so Cook decided to climb **Cook's Look** on Lizard Island to see if he could find a way out to open water. His climb paid off and he was able to successfully sail through **Cook's Passage.** Meanwhile, the island was named by Joseph Banks because of the many large lizards that he and Cook saw on the island.

The **Lizard Island Resort** (Tel: 60-3991) is operated by Qantas Airways. It is modern, comfortable, up-market, and exclusive, but is not stylish in the way of Bedarra Island or Hayman Island. The rooms are no architectural dream, but they have airconditioning, ceiling fans, refrigerator, tea/coffee-making facilities, IDD telephones, and bathrobes. You come here to escape the pressures of the outside world or to do some serious fishing or diving. Facilities include a swimming pool, a floodlit tennis court, wind surfers, catamarans, paddle skis, glass-bottom boats, and dinghies. Meals are provided as part of the inclusive tariff. There is a buffet-style breakfast, and a small a la carte lunch and dinner menu. The emphasis is on quality with a good choice of fresh seafood. The nightly rate is around A$440 per person, but some cheaper packages are available at certain times of the year.

Lizard Island is well known for its diving and fishing, and these are major attractions for guests. September to December is the heavy-tackle fishing season, and at this time the resort is always busy. There are often many boats using the **Marlin Center,** and the bar here is a good place to catch up with the latest fishing news. Boats can be chartered from the resort for game or light-tackle fishing. Diving around the island can be very good, and the outer Great Barrier Reef is only about 18 kilometers away. **Bank's Bank,** just north of Lizard Island, has excellent coral formations and a big variety of fish. **North Direction Island,** to the south, has excellent coral for both divers and snorkelers off its northern side. One of the most popular dive locations is **The Cod Hole** at **Cormorant Pass,** due east of Lizard Island. Boats from Cairns come here regularly, and the two-meter-long potato cod have become very familiar with people. Divers can swim with the fish while they eagerly take the food handouts, and snorkelers can usually get a good view because the water is clear, and the depth only around eight meters.

There is a **research station** (Tel: 60-3977) on the island which investigates matters concerning the marine and birdlife of the region. Tours of the station are offered twice a week, and there is sometimes the opportunity for visiting researchers or university students to stay here. The other option for staying on the island is camping. You must obtain a permit from the Department of Environment and Heritage in Cairns and be self-sufficient with food and fire fuel. A camp site on **Watson's Bay** has toilets, barbecues, tables, and a water pump. Getting to the island is easy, but expensive. **Sunstate Airlines** (Qantas) has daily trips from Cairns (about A$150 one way). There are no ferries, but some of the cruise vessels out of Cairns call in on a regular basis.

From Lizard Island to Cape York

There are several island groups in this region, but none of them have any significant tourist activity. Lizard Island is at the northern end of the tourist stretch of reef, and it becomes very difficult to explore farther afield. Most of the northern islands do not have good boat anchorages, and there are no facilities on any of them. Most are windswept and not particularly attractive. There are some of historic interest, however.

The **Howick Islands** about 50 kilometers north of Lizard Island are continental-type islands. **Howick Island** has several hills and a large mangrove flat. Nearby **Watson Island** saw the end of a tragedy that started on Lizard Island around 115 years ago. Robert Watson and his wife, Mary, built a small stone cottage on Lizard Island in 1881 while they collected beche-de-mer. In late September, Mrs. Watson was left on the island with her baby and two Chinese servants while her husband and some others searched for new fishing grounds. Shortly afterwards, a group of Aborigines arrived on the island and killed one of the Chinese men. Two days later they attacked and speared the other Chinese servant, so Mrs. Watson decided to try and escape the island with her baby and the wounded man. They paddled away in an iron tank that was used in processing the beche-de-mer. Despite seeing several boats, they were unable to attract attention to themselves, and they all eventually died of thirst. Their bodies were later found, still in their iron tank, on what is now called Watson Island.

The **Flinders Group** is northwest of Cape Melville. This area is popular with prawn trawlers. One hundred kilometers farther north, **Morris Islet** is a small sandy cay with some low vegetation, on a huge reef. This type of island is rare along this stretch of coast: many of the reef islands and reef flats are covered by mangroves.

Bligh's Passage was used by Captain Bligh in 1789 to find his way towards shore, through the reef. Bligh had suffered a mutiny in Tonga on his ship the *Bounty* and had been set adrift in a seven-meter open boat with the remaining faithful crew. In a remarkable feat of seamanship, Bligh eventually managed to sail the boat 6,000 kilometers to safety on Timor in what is now Indonesia. Bligh sailed through this passage, accurately charting his progress all the way, and landed on **Restoration Island,** which he named. He and his party spent some time here recuperating before proceeding further.

Captain James Cook also found a passage through the reef near here. After finding a way out to sea near Lizard Island, Cook headed north but found that he was being constantly driven back towards the reef. After several close calls he decided to again head towards the coast and try to travel north inside the reef. He made his way through narrow **Providential Channel** and then stayed inside the reef for the rest of the journey north.

A further passage north of here also has some significance. Captain Edwards in the *Pandora* had been sent to the south Pacific to capture the *Bounty* mutineers and take them back to England for punishment. He had rounded up some of them and was heading home when his ship foundered as it was trying to pass through the reef. Edwards, some of the crew, and most of the mutineers survived the wreck, and they eventually followed Bligh's map to Timor. The wreck of the *Pandora* was rediscovered in 1979, and some significant items were recovered by a Queensland government expedition in 1995. At the time of this writing it had not been decided if these would be displayed in Brisbane or Townsville.

Possession Island is just to the west of the tip of Cape York. This is where Captain Cook took possession of all of the east coast of Australia for the British government. There is a monument on the island to this event.

Thursday Island

This is the administration center for the Torres Strait region. The island is a small continental-type island, 40 kilometers off the tip of Cape York. Before white settlement, it appears that this island was uninhabited because it lacked any water. The settlement that had been established by the Queensland government at Somerset near Cape York proved to be a problem, so in 1877 it was decided to shift it to Thursday Island. With the opening of the Suez Canal and the development of Singapore and the Dutch East Indies, the northern route around the Australian coast had become much more important. The reef, however, was still proving to be a problem, so Thursday Island became an important point for pilots who guided ships through the reef waters.

By the 1890s, there was a major pearling industry in the Torres Strait, and the population of Thursday Island was around 2,000. It was a very cosmopolitan place with a mixture of Torres Strait Islanders, Europeans, Aborigines, Asians, Melanesians, and Micronesians. At times it was also a very lively place with things occasionally getting out of hand. The pearl industry struggled on until after World War II, but it is no longer significant. The pilot service, however, remains today.

Thursday Island is not a resort island, but there are accommodations, restaurants, a post office, a bank, shops, and other facilities. The **Jardine Motel** (Tel: 69-1555) is the most up-market accommodation. This has 32 air-conditioned units at around A$160 a night, and there is a pool, restaurant, and bar. The **Federal Hotel** (Tel: 69-1569) has some airconditioned motel-style rooms for around A$90 a night, and some hotel rooms for around A$65 a double. The **Torres Hotel** (Tel: 69-1141) has cheaper hotel rooms. Each of these places has a restaurant that is open to the public, and there are some other places in town with light meals and take-out food.

There is not a great deal of interest on Thursday Island but a visit to the cemetery shows some history and culture in the form of elaborate graves of Japanese pearl divers and some Torres Strait Islanders. A fort was built on Green Hill in 1891, and some rusting guns remain today. It never saw any action even during World War II because the Japanese seemed to ignore Thursday Island. The **Court House** is the oldest building on the island, dating from 1876. The **Catholic Sacred Heart Church** remains unchanged since its construction in 1885. The **Quetta Memorial Church** is worth visiting. It was opened in 1893 as a memorial to the *Quetta* which sank near Thursday Island with the loss of 130 lives. There is a memorial window and a number of relics from the ship including the bell, a porthole, and a light.

Getting to Thursday Island is relatively easy. There is an airport on adjacent **Horn Island,** and there are **Sunstate** (Qantas) services direct from Cairns or via Weipa or Bamaga. The *Kangaroo Explorer* has a regular shipping service from Cairns. There are frequent ferry services from Bamaga on Cape York.

9. Sports

Cairns has good sporting facilities, and some other centers have some facilities.

There are excellent golf courses. The **Paradise Palms** (Tel: 59-1166) course in Cairns, and the **Mirage Resort** course in Port Douglas are both world class. By Australian standards, the green fees are high. The **Cairns Golf Club** (Tel: 54-1208), the **Innisfail Club** (Tel: 61-2223), the **Half Moon Bay Country Golf Club** (Tel: 55-7182) at Yorkeys Knob, the **Novotel Palm Cove** (Tel: 59-1117), the **El Arish Country Club** (Tel: 68-5140) near Mission

Beach, the **Gordonvale Golf Club** (Tel: 56-3999), and the **Mossman Golf Club** (Tel: 98-1570) on Newell Beach Road, all welcome visitors.

Diving

Cairns rivals Townsville as a diving center, and because there are more tourists here, the number of operators is larger. There are some good dive sites within 35 kilometers of Cairns and Port Douglas, and these are accessible on day trips. Two- or three-day cruises are also available to places such as **Flynn Reef** and **Saxton Reef.** The **Ribbon Reefs** near Lizard Island are considered one of the better locations on the reef for divers, with **The Cod Hole** the most renowned and popular spot.

Most of the regular day-trip operators such as Great Adventures, Quicksilver, and Sunlover have facilities for divers, and there are many specialist operators. Some of these are:

Adventure Connection Australia—Port Douglas (Tel: 99-5788)
Cairns Dive Centre—Cairns (Tel: 51-0294)
Cape Tribulation Dive Service—Cairns (Tel: 31-1588)
Deep Sea Divers Den—Cairns (Tel: 31-2223)
Down Under Aquatics—Cairns (Tel: 31-1288)
Great Barrier Reef Diving Centre—Cairns (Tel: 31-2599)
Haba Dive—Port Douglas (Tel: 99-5254)
Mike Ball Dive Expeditions—Cairns (Tel: 31-5484)
Nimrod Dive Adventures—Cairns (Tel: 31-5566)
Port Douglas Dive Centre—Port Douglas (Tel: 99-5327)
Pro Dive Cairns—Cairns (Tel: 31-5255)
Rum Runner Cruises—Cairns (Tel: 32-1699)
Taka 11 Dive Adventures—Cairns (Tel: 51-8722)
Tusa Dive Connection—Cairns (Tel: 31-1248)

Fishing

Reef fishing trips operate from several centers. Some are day trips and some overnight. Four options are available: calm water fishing for barramundi, mangrove jack, queenfish and so forth; bottom fishing on the reef for coral trout, red emperor, sweetlip, or a dozen other species; light tackle game fishing for marlin, sailfish, spanish mackerel, and tuna; and black marlin big game fishing. The black marlin season is from September to December, while the other fishing types are available all year. These are some of the operators:

All Tackle Sportsfishing—Cairns (Tel: 53-3599)
Australian Sportfishing Charters—Cairns (Tel: 58-1726)

Bramston Beach Fishing Charters—Bramston Beach (Tel: 67-4186)
Cairns Reef Charter Services—Cairns (Tel: 31-4444)
Catcha Crab—Cairns (Tel: 32-1992)
Charter Boat Centre—Trinity Beach (Tel: 57-7475)
Dreamtime Fishing—Cairns (Tel: 015-159663)
Estuary Charters—Cairns (Tel: 36-2260)
Fishing the Tropics—Trinity Beach (Tel: 34-2668)
Marine Tech—Cairns (Tel: 51-2939)
Marlin Coast Charter Services—Cairns (Tel: 018-774410)
M.V. Aquacat—Cairns (Tel: 018-770187)
Outer Barrier Reef Charter—Port Douglas (Tel: 99-5506)

10. Shopping

There are good shopping facilities in Cairns and reasonable facilities in Port Douglas and Innisfail. Other centers have limited facilities. Cairns central business district has no large department stores, and shopping is geared towards the needs of visitors. Most of the locals use regional shopping centers for their needs. **Lake Street** and **Abbott Street** have reasonable streetfront and arcade shopping, and the **Pier Marketplace** has a collection of shops with a different style from most areas of Cairns. Both areas trade seven days a week. The weekend Mud Markets at the **Pier,** and the Wednesday, Thursday, Friday, and Sunday markets at **Kuranda** are popular attractions.

Cairns has a good range of art shops and galleries selling everything from Aboriginal art to modern prints. Try the following:

Done Art and Design—Village Lane, Lake St. (Tel: 31-5592)
Editions Gallery—Village Lane, Lake St. (Tel: 31-2052)
Helen Wiltshire Gallery—12 Lake St. (Tel: 31-7699)
The Original Dreamtime Gallery—34 Lake St. (Tel: 51-3222)
The Pier Gallery—Pier Marketplace (Tel: 51-6533)

11. Entertainment and Nightlife

Cairns has quite a good nightlife with an emphasis on activities for the young. The **Civic Theatre** at Florence and Lake Streets has regular live entertainment and performing art for a wider audience. Several pubs, taverns, and nightclubs have live bands, and **Johnos Blues Bar** (Tel: 31-5008) has a big reputation.

Some of the current favorite gathering places are:

Karaoke 101—43 The Esplanade (Tel: 31-3136)
Playpen Nightclub—Lake and Hartley Streets (Tel: 51-8211)
Reno Club—Lake Street (Tel: 52-1480)
The End of the World—Abbott and Aplin Streets (Tel: 31-3944)
The Nest—82 Mcleod Street (Tel: 51-8181)
Troppo's Non Stop Rock—Spence and Lake Streets (Tel: 31-2530)

12. The Cairns and Northern Reef Contact List

Cairns

Ambulance—Anderson Street (Tel: 51-1511)
Bus Service Information—Beach Bus (Tel: 57-7411)
     —Cairns Trans, 36 Buchan (Tel: 35-2600)
Churches—Anglican, St. John's, Lake & Minnie Sts. (Tel: 51-8055)
     —Catholic, 183 Abbott Street (Tel: 51-2838)
     —Uniting, 327 Brown Street (Tel: 51-2513)
Dental Services—Wallamurra M. C., 191 Abbott (Tel: 018-770500)
Emergency Calls—Ambulance, Fire, Police (Tel: 000)
Fire Service—36 Shields Street (Tel: 52-8762)
Hospital—Cairns Base Hospital, Esplanade (Tel: 50-6333)
     —Calvary Hospital, 1 Upward St. (private) (Tel: 52-5200)
Lifeline—24-hour counseling service (Tel: 51-4300)
Mayor's Office—151 Abbott Street (Tel: 50-2402)
Medical—Shields St. Medical Center, 29 Shields (Tel: 31-3717)
Police—5 Sheridan Street (Tel: 30-7000)
Post Office—13 Grafton Street (Tel: 51-4200)
Qantas Airways—Lake & Shields Sts., Domestic (Tel: 13-1313)
     International (Tel: 1-800-226449)
RACQ—112 Sheridan St., 24-hour service (Tel: 51-6543)
Rail Services—McLeod Street (Tel: 13-2232)
Taxi—333 Sheridan Street (Tel: 51-5333)
Telephone Calls—international operator (Tel: 0101)
Tourist Information—Far North Qld. P. Bureau (Tel: 51-3588)

Index

OUTBACK AUSTRALIA
AT COST
3rd Edition

By Malcolm Gordon

Bring this guide along with you and you'll be sure to escape the wonders of the Outback alive. It is the most comprehensive guide to one of tourism's last frontiers. Rugged and scenic, this wonderland holds many surprises and adventures for its visitors from Ayers Rock to Kakadu National Park to the Bungle Bungles.

Covering more than 150 settlements, from lonely roadhouses to major cities like Darwin and Alice Springs, *Outback Australia At Cost* will guide you from point to point with information on history, local hazards, natural wonders, dining, and accommodations. The book also discusses touring suggestions, road conditions, climate, landscape, and geology. Detailed maps are included to aid visitors' orientation in even the remotest parts of the Outback.

Whether you prefer bush camping or silver service dinners, you can locate your preference in this book. Consider it essential reading for even the most experienced Outback traveler.

496 pp. 4³/₄ x 7³/₈
Maps
ISBN: 1-86315-046-3 $19.95 pb

THE AUSTRALIA BED AND BREAKFAST BOOK

Compiled by J. and J. Thomas

Attractive B & B establishments—along with a sprinkling of farms and private hotels—make any visit Down Under memorable. This updated guide lists prices, available facilities, addresses, directions, telephone numbers for making reservations, and a short description of each guesthouse and its owners. Some entries also offer information on transportation services, local or homestay dining, and nearby attractions.

336 pp. 5½ x 8½ Illus. Maps Index 8th ed.
ISBN: 1-56554-259-2 $15.95 pb

THE NEW ZEALAND BED AND BREAKFAST BOOK

Compiled by J. and J. Thomas

"An excellent directory."
Frommer's New Zealand on $40 a Day

"I can't begin to tell you how valuable your book was . . . Thank you for playing such a big part in making our visit such a memorable one." **Bed and Breakfast Bulletin**

Similar in format to its Australian counterpart, this comprehensive guide presents descriptions of more than 400 inviting private homes and hotels and their services. Along with maps and illustrations, this book includes names, addresses, prices, telephone numbers, and specific accommodations available, as well as lists of nearby towns and directions.

688 pp. 5½ x 8½ Illus. Maps Index 7th ed.
ISBN: 1-56554-260-6 $17.95 pb

THE MAVERICK GUIDE TO NEW ZEALAND
10th Edition

By Robert W. Bone
Edited by Susan Buckland

"A lively and informative guide to travel in New Zealand. . . . This is the best guide to New Zealand ever seen by this New Zealander."
Library Journal

"Even someone who has been to New Zealand before should find information here." **Great Expeditions**

"Besides the usual guidebook tips, Bone gives an insider's view of places . . ." **The Times-Picayune**

Revised and updated, *The Maverick Guide to New Zealand* contains accurate and detailed information on every aspect of this explorer's wonderland, including a glossary of indigenous terms the traveler is likely to encounter.

An entire chapter entitled "Who Are the New Zealanders?" presents the highlights of New Zealand history and profiles of the people.

Current price information for attractions, restaurants, and hotels is included, as well as ideas for unconventional activities such as safari tours with Maori guides, unsurpassed whitewater rafting, and bungee-cord jumping.

368 pp. 5½ x 8½
Maps Index
ISBN: 1-56554-140-5 $15.95 pb

THE MAVERICK GUIDE TO AUSTRALIA
11th Edition

By Robert W. Bone
Edited by Kevin Voltz

"[This] is an excellent, comprehensive guide, invaluable to the traveler." **Australia Bulletin**
Australian Embassy
Washington, D.C.

A fully updated version, the eleventh edition portrays Australia as an alluring, yet accessible, vacation destination. Travelers with a penchant for the extraordinary will find valuable information on the "do's"—and just as important, the "don'ts"—of an Australian vacation. With twelve complete chapters and twenty-eight useful maps, this enjoyable guide offers recommendations on every travel aspect, from sight-seeing and recreation to dining and transportation.

This guide has been recognized as one of the best books to carry along on excursions down under for more than fifteen years.

A lengthy chapter entitled "Who Are the Australians?" provides a wonderful background on the native antipodeans, including a glossary of "Strine" expressions a visitor is likely to hear.

416 pp. 5½ x 8½
Maps Index
ISBN: 1-56554-151-0 $15.95 pb

First-Place Winner
1993 Hawaii Visitors Bureau
Travel Journalism Award

THE MAVERICK GUIDE TO HAWAII: 19th Edition

By Robert W. Bone
Edited by Carol Greenhouse

"One of the most complete guides to these paradisiacal islands in the Pacific . . . An invaluable handbook."
Washington Times

"The best guide to Hawaii, and one of the best travel guides I've ever read, is The Maverick Guide to Hawaii.*"*
Chicago Sun-Times

For more than fifteen years this comprehensive book has guided travelers to remote and familiar points on the Hawaiian Islands. Updated annually, it offers the most current information on prices, accommodations, hours, must-sees, and must-avoids. The lively, informative text includes background chapters on each island's history, the people, the language, and how to get the most enjoyment out of a Hawaiian vacation.

With a full complement of landscapes, from beaches to mountains to flowered fields, the islands await you with unlimited outdoor activities. From centers of shopping to the hottest night spots on the beach, you can get the opportunity to see how the Hawaiians live indoors, as well.

448 pp. 5½ x 8½
Maps Appendix Index
ISBN: 1-56554-060-3 $15.95 pb

MAVERICK GUIDE TO BALI AND JAVA
2nd Edition

By Don Turner

"Turner, a frequent visitor to the islands of Bali and Java for the past 15 years, reveals the adventure and mystery of their cultures and provides readers with practical information on sights . . . transportation, hotels, dining and entertainment."

The Shoestring Traveler

"I found Turner's guide a handy companion and usually right on the money with its easy-to-find information."

Michael Wetzel
The Decatur Daily

These Indonesian islands offer the traveler a scenic panorama of plantation-covered plains, lush forests, rugged mountains, sandy beaches, bountiful coral reefs, and live volcanoes. This exquisite and appealing landscape is mixed with the colorful, friendly Balinese and Javinese people.

In this updated edition, Turner guides you through these two exotic islands, whose history dates back 35,000 years. He describes the weather, geography, flora and fauna, local food, and useful phrases. He covers the cities, towns, and resorts of each country, listing the finest as well as budget-priced accommodations and restaurants.

Turner also explains the intricacies of Indonesian society to ensure a carefree and culturally enriched vacation experience.

This guidebook includes maps and distance tables.

312 pp. 5½ x 8½
Photos Maps Index
ISBN: 1-56554-052-2 $14.95 pb

MAVERICK GUIDE TO VIETNAM, LAOS, AND CAMBODIA
3rd Edition

By Len Rutledge

In this updated third edition, veteran travel writer Len Rutledge introduces the most adventurous travelers to the lost secrets of Vietnam, Laos, and Cambodia. Four decades of conflict have created an aura of mystery around these gems of the South China Sea. As part of the changing world order, these countries are opening their doors to Western tourists and business people.

Visitors can now experience the brilliant achievements of the Khmer, the Cham, and the Vietnamese civilizations. Tourists will be dazzled by the brilliant green rice paddies, the white beaches, the rugged mountains, fertile valleys, and the modern growing cities that house ancient temples and ruins as well.

With color photos and more than forty maps, this guide offers directions, practical travel advice, and everything else a visitor would need to know in order to visit the region.

392 pp. 5½ x 8½
Color photos Maps Index
ISBN: 1-56554-126-X $17.95 pb

OTHER PELICAN BOOKS ON AUSTRALIA AND NEW ZEALAND

THE KOALA BOOK
By Ann Sharp with The Australian Koala Foundation
The koala's story is presented with 160 photographs and accompanying text to educate the public about the koala's predicament, while celebrating its presence.
160 pp. 8½ x 11 Color photos Map
ISBN: 1-56554-160-X $29.95

A PERSONAL KIWI-YANKEE DICTIONARY
By Louis S. Leland, Jr.
Illustrated by Bruce B. Nye
Designed to amuse as well as enlighten, this entertaining lexicon will enable any visitor to New Zealand to prepare for the linguistic culture shock that is sure to come.
120 pp. 4¼ x 7 Illus
ISBN: 0-88289-414-5 $6.95 pb

NEW ZEALAND BY MOTORHOME
By David Shore and Patty Campbell
In New Zealand, where endless recreational opportunities and friendly people abound, traveling by motorhome is an ideal way to go. This husband-and-wife team tells travelers how to acquire, maneuver, and enjoy a motorhome.
208 pp. 5¼ x 8½ Illus. Photos Maps Charts Index
ISBN: 0-88289-716-0 $14.95 pb

AT COST TRAVEL GUIDE SERIES

Lightweight, portable, and packed with information on each area's climate, geography, history and culture, population, entry regulations, currency, and more. How to get there, travel within the country, attractions, tours, accommodations, restaurants, shopping, and entertainment also covered. Pelican is exclusive U.S. distributor of this series.

SYDNEY AT COST

By the Editorial Staff of Little Hills Press

This guide takes you all over this exciting city and includes day trips to Blue Mountains and Central Coast.

256 pp. 4³/₄ x 7½ 16 Maps
ISBN: 1-86315-031-5 $14.95 pb

NEW ZEALAND AT COST

By Fay Smith

Auckland, Wellington, Christchurch, Hamilton, and Dunedin are featured, plus over 300 other locations.

352 pp. 5¹/₈ x 7½ Photos Maps
ISBN: 1-86315-054-4 $16.95 pb

SOUTH PACIFIC AT COST

By Joan Beard

Includes the smaller Pacific islands, such as Cook Islands, Fiji, Tahiti, Tonga, and Western and American Samoa.

256 pp. 5¹/₈ x 7½
Photos Maps 2nd ed.
ISBN: 1-86315-103-6 $16.95 pb

Smaller versions of the At Cost Guides, these Pocket Guidebooks are easy to carry:

THE MELBOURNE POCKET GUIDEBOOK

By the Editorial Staff of Little Hills Press

This fascinating city is described in detail here.

64 pp. 4³/₈ x 7¹/₈ Maps
ISBN: 1-86315-033-1 $3.95 pb

THE SYDNEY POCKET GUIDEBOOK

By the Editorial Staff of Little Hills Press

This is the guide to get you around Australia's leading city.

128 pp. 5¹/₈ x 7½ Photos Maps
ISBN: 1-6315-082-X $9.95 pb